RECOVERING ARMENIA

RECOVERING ARMENIA

The Limits of Belonging in Post-Genocide Turkey

LERNA EKMEKÇIOĞLU

Stanford University Press
Stanford, California

Stanford University Press
Stanford, California

©2016 by the Board of Trustees of the Leland Stanford Junior University. All rights reserved.

No part of this book may be reproduced or transmitted in any form or by any means, electronic or mechanical, including photocopying and recording, or in any information storage or retrieval system without the prior written permission of Stanford University Press.

Printed in the United States of America on acid-free, archival-quality paper

Library of Congress Cataloging-in-Publication Data

Ekmekçioglu, Lerna, 1979- author.
  Recovering Armenia : the limits of belonging in post-genocide Turkey / Lerna Ekmekçioglu.
     pages cm
  Includes bibliographical references and index.
  ISBN 978-0-8047-9610-1 (cloth : alk. paper) -- ISBN 978-0-8047-9706-1 (pbk. : alk. paper) -- ISBN 978-0-8047-9719-1 (ebook)
  1. Armenians--Turkey--History--20th century. 2. Armenians--Turkey--Ethnic identity--History--20th century. 3. Feminism--Turkey--History--20th century. I. Title.
  DR435.A7E35 2015
  956.6'202--dc23
                              2015029817

Typeset by Bruce Lundquist in 10.25/15 Adobe Caslon Pro

For my mother, Röne,
Who
Made
Everything
Possible
&
For my daughters, Zepure and Zulal,
for every minute that they had to share me with this book.

You are all part of it.

CONTENTS

	List of Illustrations	ix
	Preface	xi
	Afterlife of Armenians in Post-Genocide Turkey: An Introduction	1
1	The Rebirth of a Nation	21
2	Can Feminists Revive a Nation?	53
3	An Exodus and Its Aftermath	81
4	A Tamed Minority	101
5	Can Armenian Feminism Survive the New Turkey?	131
	When History Became Destiny: A Conclusion	159
	Notes	165
	Index	207

LIST OF ILLUSTRATIONS

Figure 1. Hayganush Mark and Vahan Toshigian in 1920	xviii
Figure 2. Map of Armenia and Turkey	3
Figure 3. Armenian Children Defending Their Fatherland	20
Figure 4. Haydar Pasha Refugee Station	25
Figure 5. *Hay Gin*'s Pretty Baby Contest	31
Figure 6. Orphans at the Armenian Red Cross Dispensary in Pera	36
Figure 7. Armenian Red Cross Scutari Branch Shelter	37
Figure 8. Armenian Red Cross Şişli Branch Hospital	39
Figure 9. A Marriage from the Kalfayan Orphanage	44
Figure 10. The Little Army Against Disease	48
Figure 11. Hayganush Mark as a Suffragette	52
Figure 12. Writers for *Hay Gin*	61
Figure 13. Hayganush Mark in 1910	63
Figure 14. Cover Page of *Hay Gin*	65
Figure 15. Takuhi Kalantar and Her Harvest of Students	73
Figure 16. Bishop Kevork Aslanian and His Grandchildren	80
Figure 17. Cover Page of the Armenian National Hospital's Almanac	100

Figure 18. The Republic of Turkey Is Immortal   115
Figure 19. Atatürk Dancing with His Adopted Daughter   119
Figure 20. Hayganush Mark and Keriman Halis, Miss Universe 1932   130
Figure 21. Champagne   141
Figure 22. Duration of Love   142
Figure 23. Toward Feminism   142
Figure 24. Hayganush Mark in Her Office, 1924   144
Figure 25. Hayganush Mark in Her Office, 1925   145
Figure 26. Hayganush Mark in 1954   156
Figure 27. Tombstone of Hayganush Mark and Vahan Toshigian   158

PREFACE

As I am finishing this book in early 2015, all kinds of organizations, Armenian and non-Armenian alike, have been laying plans to commemorate the centenary of the Armenian genocide with special programs, memorials, and conferences. Inevitably, many of these commemorative events will raise the issue of denial. The Republic of Turkey has refused to acknowledge its role in bringing about a decisive end to Ottoman Armenians' collective presence in their native lands. The Turkish state's official rejection of the term "genocide" with regards to the Ottoman government's "wartime deportations" has long been the focus of Armenian politics, especially among diaspora communities worldwide, communities that came to existence largely as a result of forcible dispersal from their homeland. As the offspring of 1915 come together to honor their dead and invite the world to do the same, they prioritize the long-sought demand for justice and accountability.

Of the Armenian communities worldwide, one does not commemorate the centenary like the rest. Turkish Armenians stick out in this respect too as they do in almost every other aspect of their lives. Unlike other Armenians, they live under an unapologetic Turkish state that has viewed their continued presence in the new Turkey as a problem, even though at present only about sixty thousand Armenians live in a Turkey of nearly 75 million.

That their history has evaded scholars and community members alike is another peculiar point about Turkish Armenians. Unlike other major diaspora communities such as American Armenians, French Armenians, or Lebanese Armenians, whose pasts have been objects of scholarly scrutiny, Armenians of Turkish citizenship have escaped the attention of scholars for a long time. The most important reason for this is the Turkish state's uneasy relationship with its past. Histories of minority communities, not just Armenians, are usually written by insiders first and then later taken up by others. It would not be easy for Turkish Armenians to produce such "insider historians" given the continued discrimination their community faces in Turkey. For instance, students in Armenian minority schools are not allowed to learn Armenian history. Legally, students in Turkish schools (public, private, minority) can only learn history from textbooks prepared centrally by the Ministry of Education. These textbooks represent the state's perspective. By "Turkish history" such books mean "the history of Turks," a perspective shared by most historians of Turkey to this day, both inside Turkey and outside. "Turks" in this usage excludes non-Muslim, non-Turkish peoples of Turkey. Minorities appear in these books largely as traitors ever ready to stab their host state in the back. Moreover, in minority schools the subject of history can only be taught by ethnically Turkish citizens who do not belong to any minority group. Compounded with the continued tension between the Turkish state and Armenians worldwide, including the state of Armenia with which Turkey has no diplomatic relations, this fraught situation has deprived Turkish Armenians of a history of their own.

This book, a history of Armenians in post-genocide Turkey, then, has multiple aims. At this moment of commemoration and remembrance, it hopes to move the global conversation about the Armenian genocide to victims who survived not just the genocide but also the new Turkey, the reluctant host of remaining Armenians. It also aims to write Armenians into Turkish history, Turkish Armenians into Armenian history, and women and feminists into both. The book is my way of paying tribute to the resilience this community has shown in the face of multiple challenges over the past century. I offer this history as a modest corrective.

༄

In 2002, I left my hometown for the United States to study the history of Armenian feminism in the Ottoman Empire and Turkey. I had to work in near-complete darkness for the history of Armenians in Turkey in the aftermath of the 1915 Armenian genocide had not been studied before. It was for political and historical reasons that the ways survivors endeavored to make a life for themselves in a land ruled by unapologetic perpetrators escaped the radar of various historiographies. Even the basic narrative of the transformation that post-genocide Armenians had gone through as the Ottoman Empire evolved into the Republic of Turkey was missing. This emptiness forced me to excavate the "big picture" from scratch, a time-consuming, labor-intensive endeavor that surprisingly proved to be quite feasible simply because, although there was a dearth of secondary sources, there was no shortage of primary sources. On the contrary, I soon recognized that there are multiple and equally legitimate sources for studying Armenians in post-genocide Turkey and multiple and equally legitimate ways of dealing with those sources. Given my initial curiosity and the lack of a formative framework in which to understand the Armenian communities in post-genocide Turkey, I have focused on Istanbul, where the majority of Armenians lived, and on elites and intellectuals who actively worked on inventing and re-inventing Armenianness where it remained most unwanted.

I arrived at New York University where additional challenges might have presented themselves: there was no specialist in Armenian history. But this ultimately turned out to be a boon, as I had the opportunity to benefit from conversations and collaborations with numerous non-specialists inside NYU as well as with specialists at other institutions. I am especially grateful to Vartan Matiossian and Hourig Attarian, now good friends, who responded to my endless queries about Armenian history, literature, and language. Vartan Matiossian found many of the primary sources mentioned in this book and guided me toward new ones; he is my Armenian studies mentor. Hourig Attarian supported this project both with her deep knowledge of anything Armenian but also with her attention to imagination, emotion, and the lived world of the scholar. I will remain grateful to both of them. I also thank Ara Sanjian, who similarly helped me navigate Armenian scholarship, responded to my queries, and helped me locate sources. It was thanks to him that I first accessed the full collection of *Hay Gin*, the heart of this book, at Beirut's Haigazian Library. Aram Arkun, Howard Eissenstat, Khachig Tölölyan, Fatma Müge Göçek, Gerard Libaridian, Taner Akçam, Keith Watenpaugh,

Rıfat Bali, Irvin Cemil Schick, Abraham D. Krikorian, Matthias Bjørnlund, Bedross Der Matossian, Yiğit Akın, Osman Köker, and Chaghig Chahinian shared their knowledge with me. I am equally grateful to my NYU advisers Leslie Peirce and Molly Nolan, as well as Elizabeth Frierson of the University of Cincinnati, for nurturing this project in so many ways. I first conceived of this book as a college student at Boğaziçi University's Sociology Department under the guidance of my excellent professors. I began working on it under the guidance of Ariel Salzmann, whose excellent scholarship continues to inspire me. My postdoctoral year at the University of Michigan's Armenian Studies Program gave me precious time to pause and think about the broader implications of my research.

I thank my colleagues at the Massachusetts Institute of Technology for providing the best academic home that I could hope for. Anne McCants and Craig Wilder, my two chairs at History, supported this book with relief from teaching. Christopher Capozzola has always asked the right questions and Elizabeth Wood, my faculty mentor, always knows what I need and guides me accordingly. Cristelle Baskins and Jeff Ravel have generously shared their time with me. Sana Aiyar answered endless questions regarding the technical side of publishing a book and Hiromu Nagahara and Christopher R. Leighton shared the joys of being "juniors" inside the MIT giant. I am also grateful to my two former chairs at the Women and Gender Studies program, Sally Haslanger and Emma Tang, for their continuous encouragement. Thanks also to our Associate Provost, Philip Khoury, who facilitated the endowment by the late Geneviève McMillan of a chair in the Department of History on "women in the developing world," the post I currently hold. History's administrative cadre, Mabel Chin Sorett, Margo Collett, and Chuck Manger, and Women and Gender Studies program manager Emily Neill, thank you for all the work you do to make our lives easier at work.

The book has greatly benefitted from the feedback that I received at a book manuscript workshop generously sponsored by the Department of History at MIT. I thank Ronald Suny, Fatma Müge Göçek, Betty Anderson, Molly Nolan, and Elizabeth Wood for all the suggestions that helped the book reach its near-final shape. Atina Grossmann's feedback was invaluable and helped the manuscript reach its final shape. My collaboration with the Stanford University Press went as smoothly as a first-time author could hope for. I thank Kate Wahl, Nora Spiegel, Emily Smith, and the excellent copy editor Richard Gunde for the labor they put in this project.

I thank librarians Anahit Astoyan of Madenataran (Mesrop Mashdots Institute of Ancient Manuscripts, Yerevan) and Helda Aynayüz of the Ormanyan Library of the Istanbul Armenian patriarchate for helping me locate sources. Like Helda and Anahit, Marc Mamigonian of NAASR (National Association for Armenian Studies and Research, Belmont, Massachusetts), Raymond Kévorkian and Boris Adjemian of the Armenian General Benevolent Union (AGBU) Nubar Library in Paris, and librarians at the Armenian National Library (Yerevan), the Yeghishe Charents Museum of Literature and Art (Yerevan), and the Haigazian Library (Beirut) were most helpful in finding and digitizing sources. I also appreciate the help that my research assistants, Sinan Çetin, Narek Dshkunyan, Aret Tatlıdil, and Tenzin Dongchung, offered throughout the years. I also thank my Istanbul contacts, Arsen Yarman and Murad Bebiroğlu, for helping me. I will always remember the late Yervant Gobelyan and the late Sarkis Seropian, both former contributors to the Turkish Armenian weekly *Agos*, as well as my high school principal, Silva Kuyumcuyan, who early on instilled in me a curiosity about Armenian history and the history of Armenian feminism.

Friends, some of them also colleagues, engaged with my work in multiple ways. Düriye Gökçebağ, Diane Baygin, Gonca Sönmez-Poole, Shane Minkin, Başak Tuğ, Abigail Jacobson, Selina Özuzun Doğan, Sarem K. Şeşetyan, Carole Woodall, Talinn Grigor, Johanna Vollhardt, Nora Nercessian, Jennifer Dixon, Özgen Felek, Elizabeth Thompson, Zeynep Kezer, Lale Can, Seda Altuğ, and Zeynep Kutluata, a big thank you. Thanks also to the Wong family of Montgomery St. and the Bilezikian family of the St. Stephens School for the multiple playdates during which they hosted my daughters and gave me some extra time to focus on this book. I thank Varteni Mosdichian for connecting me with elderly Bolsahays (Armenians of/from Istanbul) in the Boston area, joining me in my visits, and sharing with me her own family history. Similarly, Ara Toshigian, Vahan Toshigian's grandnephew, graciously agreed to an interview and responded to my various questions about the Toshigian-Mark couple. Nora Lessersohn did not let go of my "title problem" and eventually found the book title for me! Neda Bebiroğlu, her husband, Claude Abivien, and son, Sevan, are my Europe family. Thank you Neda for who you are and for the Belgian waffles. Melissa Bilal, my co-adventurer of the last two decades, lived with this book from the moment of its conception till its very end. I don't know how I will pay her back for all the intellectual, emotional, and physical investment that she put into this piece of work.

Whatever value this book has I owe to my mother, Röne Ekmekçioğlu, and my mother-in-law, Nazen Merdinoğlu, who embarked on planes, trains, buses, and cars, sometimes on very short notice, to help us with childcare and managing the household. They gave me what I needed most: time and peace of mind. Plus good, healthy, home cooking that comforted us. Their devotion is priceless. I thank my brother, Araks, for his loving presence and encouragement. My husband, Mardiros Merdinoğlu, shared the long journey with me in all possible ways, joining my enthusiasm with his intellectual curiosity and love of success. Our daughters, Zepure and Zulal, deserve a BIG round of applause for . . . everything. I hope they will one day understand the threads that connect this book with them.

My father, Murad Hagop Ekmekçioğlu, instilled in me a curiosity about the past and a strong sense of justice from very early on. I know that more than anyone else I am *his* daughter. Like my mother and brother, he too helped me locate sources in Turkey, put me in touch with the right people, and acted as an informal research assistant.

My grandparents are the invisible shadow behind this book. Meryem Evingülü Ekmekçioğlu (b. Adıyaman, 1932), Kevork Ekmekçioğlu (1930, Adıyaman–2010, Cologne), Garabed (Ohanyan) Yurtlu (1923, Mersin–1991, Mersin), Sofia Andonyadis Yurtlu (1927, Iskenderun–2011, Mersin) are descendants of survivors whose loving hands touched my head.

RECOVERING ARMENIA

Figure 1. Hayganush Mark and Vahan Toshigian in 1920. Yeghishe Charents Museum of Literature and Art (Hayganush Mark fond), Yerevan.

AFTERLIFE OF ARMENIANS IN POST-GENOCIDE TURKEY
An Introduction

Hayganush Mark lived the first half of her life as a subject of the Ottoman Empire belonging to the Armenian *millet* (ethnoreligious community). She spent the second half as a citizen of the Republic of Turkey and a member of the Armenian minority community. All without moving an inch. In 1882, when she was born to an illiterate mother and a blind father, Constantinople was the glorious capital of the empire.[1] In 1966, when she died as a once-famous editor, determined community activist, and the childless widow of the prominent journalist Vahan Toshigian, her *Bolis* (Constantinople) had long become Istanbul, a city bereft of its status as capital.[2]

Today, Hayganush Mark Toshigian is buried with her husband in the Intellectuals Section of the Şişli Armenian Cemetery, about a mile from their long-time home in Pangaltı. Their tombstone is titled *Hay Gin*, that is, Armenian Woman. To the uninitiated passerby it might seem as if "the Armenian Woman" was dead and buried here. Yet, as is inscribed on the epitaph, the title refers to a feminist fortnightly Mark edited from 1919 to 1933.[3] A short quotation from one of her editorials accompanies a picture of a youthful Hayganush. Only the last sixth of the stone is devoted to the husband, who, until his death in 1954, had published *Nor Or* (New Day), one of the most important dailies in the history of Turkish Armenians.

Mark's and Toshigian's life trajectory is representative of a generation of *Bolsahay* (Constantinopolitan Armenian) public figures who lived through the transformation from the Ottoman Empire to the Turkish Republic (Figure 1).[4] This book, the first in-depth study of post-genocide Armenians in Turkey, analyzes this generation's experiences and worldviews. How did Armenian elites' understanding, representation, and performance of their identity adapt to the changing political conditions around them?[5] By focusing on Armenian textual and visual materials produced in Istanbul from the immediate aftermath of World War I to a decade after the 1923 establishment of the Turkish Republic, the book tells the story of Armenians in post-genocide Turkey from the perspective of their spokespeople.[6]

This group did not constitute an ideological monolith. Some of them identified themselves as feminists and pursued a women's movement. Feminist Armenians had two goals: the betterment of their sex and the betterment of their *azk* (nation). Depending on the political context, these goals sometimes worked in unity and sometimes conflicted with each other. An analysis of how feminists' ideas about Armenianness converged with and diverged from those of their peers shows the limits within which Armenians committed to preserving their group identity had to operate in post-Ottoman Turkey. Since the World War and genocide straddled the shift from the empire to the republic and set into motion all that was to come, the story must start in 1914 when the Ottomans decided to enter what was until then a largely European war.

Great War, Great Crime

Aligning with Germany, the Ottomans entered World War I in order to put an end to the process of territorial disintegration. Beginning in the early nineteenth century, Ottoman Europe had been Balkanized into independent (Christian) states such as Greece, Serbia, Romania, and Bulgaria. Ottomans also lost territories in North Africa as the French and the British colonized Algeria, Tunisia, and Egypt. A decisive victory against the Great Powers, the Young Turk–controlled Ottoman government hoped, could reverse the breakup of the empire, allow for territorial expansion, and restore the Ottomans' long-lost international prestige. These grand goals bestowed legitimacy on various measures, the most radical being the near-complete decimation of a people in their native lands.

By 1914, Armenians were one of the last major Christian populations remaining under Ottoman control. Even though one could find Armenians in almost every Ottoman city, town, and village, they were mostly concentrated in what is today called eastern Anatolia, roughly the six Eastern Provinces (Doğu Vilayetleri) of the Ottoman Empire, which Armenians referred as the western part of their historical homeland (see Figure 2), that is, the western part of the geographic unit known as the Armenian Plateau.[7] This region comprised the critical borderland between the Ottoman Empire and Russia, the Ottomans' archenemy. On the other side of that border lived Armenians of the eastern part of the historical homeland who were Russian subjects. The Young Turks feared that Armenians from both sides of the border would exploit the crisis of the war and join forces to declare independence or merge with Russia. Exaggerating the importance of some cues of dissent as the early signs of a wholesale Armenian uprising, the Ottoman government decided to preempt any threat by deporting Armenians to the remote and uninhabitable corners of the empire. Under this "deportation" the Committee of Union and Progress (CUP), the ruling Young Turk faction, implemented policies aimed at eliminating Armenians as a meaningful demographic presence in any part of the empire. The war gave them the opportunity to finally solve

Figure 2. Map of Armenia and Turkey. Adapted from Robert Hewsen, *Armenia: A Historical Atlas* (Chicago: University of Chicago Press, 2000), 13.

"the Armenian Question" that had so bothered the empire since the 1880s. These "preventive" measures ranged from wholesale massacres to starvation, from long-term exposure to elements to abduction into Muslim households for forcible conversion to Islam. Together, these policies constituted the 1915 Armenian genocide.[8] According to most estimates, approximately one million Armenians, or about half of the community's prewar population, perished. The number of women and children absorbed into Muslim households and institutions remains unknown, but is conventionally estimated as about a hundred thousand.[9]

Bolsahays like Hayganush Mark and Vahan Toshigian experienced the war years quite differently from their compatriots in other parts of the empire. The capital was full of European and American residents, especially the diplomatic community. CUP shied away from ordering the mass deportation of Armenians there, probably because they did not want to attract undue attention.[10] But the Armenian leadership had to go. This started around midnight on April 24, 1915, and soon culminated in an event for which Armenians have many names, *Medz Yeghern*, Great Crime, being one of the most common.[11] The government ordered the arrest of about 250 notable Armenian figures on charges of engaging in separatism with the aim of gaining Armenian independence. These writers, journalists, musicians, clergymen, political party members, activists, members of the Ottoman parliament, and professionals such as doctors, lawyers, and pharmacists, were then dispatched to the Anatolian interior; 174 of them were executed.[12]

Vahan Toshigian evaded the tragedy ironically because he was already in prison, accused of a different crime and awaiting trial.[13] Hayganush Mark was not arrested likely because—as far as we know—she had not been openly involved in politics proper. Not that everyone arrested that month was a passionate revolutionary. But she was a woman. Her sex disqualified her and many of her colleagues from being perceived as politically dangerous. The capital was home to 120,000 Armenians.[14] Of all the prominent people arrested in this initial stage of the Armenian genocide, only two were women: Zabel Yesayan and Mari Beylerian, who had been so vocal in their political criticisms that even their sex wasn't going to be enough to save them.[15]

Like the rest of the intellectuals who were spared deportation, Mark and Toshigian spent three anxious years in wartime Constantinople. The government censored the newspapers and forbid Armenians' departure from or entry to the capital. While they knew that something unprecedented was unfolding in the provinces, Armenians in the capital would learn the scale of the devastation only after the war's end. During the war, and terrorized by the disappearance of their leading members, Armenians closed in on themselves and kept a low profile.[16] When the news of the establishment of an independent Armenia by Russian Armenians in Transcaucasia reached them in May 1918, Bolsahays felt thrilled but they refrained from openly celebrating.[17] The year 1918 was to bring even better news, news that they would celebrate without trepidation.

From Occupied Constantinople to Turkish Istanbul

In October 1918, the Ottoman government signed the Mudros Armistice with the British and accepted defeat. The next day, the CUP leadership escaped the country in humiliation. Within a few weeks, the Allies occupied parts of the Ottoman territory. Feeling vindicated, hundreds of Armenians rushed onto the streets to witness the Allied fleet of sixty warships sailing through the Bosphorus to commence the occupation of the capital.[18] As early as May 24, 1915, the Allies had warned the Ottoman government about the Armenian massacres and announced publicly that they would hold Ottoman government officials personally responsible for the "fresh crimes committed by Turkey against humanity and civilization."[19] After the war, Armenians believed the Allies would keep their promises, bring the perpetrators to justice, and remedy the wrongs of the war.

The remedy that they most wanted was the establishment of a free, united, Greater Armenia connecting the western and eastern parts of their historical homeland, a state of their own in which they could enjoy majority status, feel safe, and remain secure. The central goal for post-genocide Armenian politics, regardless of internal political and ideological divisions, was to expand the independent Republic of Armenia to include the western parts of ancestral lands that had been under Ottoman rule for more than four centuries. Together with their peers from other parts of the world, the Bolsahays' political, clerical, and intellectual leadership tried to win over the Great Powers to their cause. They formulated this Armenian cause (*Hay Tad*) as a right to national self-determination, the Wilsonian principle that dominated the postwar peace negotiations. They also defended their entitlement to these territories by appealing to the universal principle of justice: the victorious Allies had to punish the savages (i.e., Turks) and reward their victims (i.e., Armenians).

Armenian delegations lobbied the Western powers at the Paris Peace Conference and other conferences that were charged with deciding on postwar territorial divisions. Hayganush Mark and Vahan Toshigian, like their friends, colleagues, and even enemies in the Armenian community, devoted all their energy to the creation of a Greater Armenia. The majority of Armenian political and religious leaders, journalists, writers, relief workers, and intellectuals believed that the civilized Christian world, which had since the 1880s rushed to the Armenians' help with humanitarian aid whenever pogroms befell them, which had been so vocal about the suffering of this tiny, ancient Oriental Christian nation, would now bequeath Armenians the ultimate and the only permanent solution to their misery: their own state. A Promised Homeland.

They were mistaken. Historical developments unfolded such that in four short years those Allied warships left the Bosphorus without initiating even a fraction of the positive changes that Armenians had hoped for. On the contrary, the Armenians' welcoming and collaboration with the occupying forces, and the related separatism further jeopardized their already fragile existence among the Muslim majority. A new, post-Ottoman Turkey came into existence as a result of the Allies' indecisiveness and the military resistance Ottoman Muslims waged against foreign occupation and the partition of Anatolia. Mustafa Kemal (later, Atatürk) led this movement that culminated in the abolishment of the Ottoman sultanate and the 1923 declaration of the country as a republic with its capital in Ankara.

The Allies' evacuation of Constantinople sparked panic among Armenian residents who anticipated that Kemalists would retaliate against local Christians once they captured the city. Terror-stricken, most colleagues of Hayganush Mark and Vahan Toshigian fled the country. Much to the relief of those who chose to or had to stay, what they feared most did not materialize. The Kemalist entry to the city turned out to be a diplomatic affair rather than a violent encounter during which about two thousand Greeks and Armenians and their dependents were expelled for collaborating with the British.[20] But those who fled the country were never able to return home; Turkey denied them re-entry and confiscated their property. These Armenians thus joined thousands of dispossessed others scattered around the world as a result of the earlier genocide, trying to build new lives in various places from Buenos Aires to Boston, from Beirut to Bucharest.

Armenians who stayed behind knew all too well that the incoming Kemalist leadership accused them of treason. They also knew all too well that their Muslim neighbors would not want to share the new Turkey with leftover Armenians who had proven disloyal at a moment of acute national existential crisis. In the eyes of the Kemalists, the Armenians' behavior during the occupation years had indeed proven that the Young Turks had not deported the Armenians without good reason. That this logic rested on a distortion of chronology totally escaped them. Even though Ottoman Armenians had been politically active since the 1870s, and worked for various causes including reform in the Armenian-heavy Ottoman provinces, autonomy, and—for one political party—secession from the empire, after the 1908 Young Turk Revolution all Armenian political parties dropped their demand for separation and publically declared their commitment to remaining part of what they hoped was going to be an Ottoman homeland governed according to liberal, representative constitutionalism.[21] But even during the era before the 1908 Revolution it is difficult to say that a separatist agenda had spread among the Ottoman Armenian masses, most of whom remained peasants and artisans until the end. This would change with the Medz Yeghern. In the aftermath of the catastrophe, the survivor communities throughout the world, including in the Ottoman capital, massively supported Armenia's independence from the Turks who had just tried to annihilate them.

In the Turkish mainstream political imagination this chronology has since been distorted. Even though the putative mass Armenian "betrayal" happened *after* the Young Turks acted on their plan to eradicate Armenianness, Turkish nationalist narratives have used Armenians' "collaboration with the enemy" and secessionist agenda during the postwar occupation years as a justification for the 1915 "deportations," something that had happened *before* the occupation years. This way of thinking about Armenians as a fifth column continues to dominate Turkish popular national consciousness and is inscribed in Turkish national historiography taught in textbooks.

To give just one recent example, in 2014 the famous Turkish novelist Ayşe Kulin told a reporter on live TV (CNN Turk) that "Unlike what the Nazis did to the Jews, we did not butcher Armenians for nothing."[22] This is a summary of the official Turkish position since 1920: we killed Armenians, but with reason, and this does not amount to anything unprecedented or special, and is not genocide.

In 1923, Armenians who were committed to staying put in their homes had to adapt to the new circumstances and quickly. They had to fashion personal and communal strategies in order to survive the hostile environment without giving up their understanding of Armenianness. Fortunately for them, their half a millennium of experience as Ottoman *dhimmi*s (non-Muslims under Muslim rule) organized into a *millet*, a semi-autonomously administered non-Muslim community, equipped them with the necessary institutional, social, and mental repertoires to continue living—even thriving—in the new Turkey. Somewhat like Jews, another historically dispersed people, Armenians were accustomed to living as "second-class citizens," to use an anachronistic term. Since there was much continuity between the Islamic Ottoman Empire and the secular Turkish Republic, Armenians' boundary-making mechanisms and protective reflexes were largely transferrable from one context to the other.

Those repertoires that informed how Armenians responded to genocide and the subsequent "minoritization" followed a gendered blueprint: women and men were assigned different roles in the national project (however it may have been formulated) and therefore the consequences were different for male and female Armenians. At the most basic level, these inventories of worldview and habit relied on the Armenian family and the homespace for the continuation of that which was threatened with extinction in the Turkish public space. The two spaces were divided along gendered lines: women as mothers owned the homespace and men, as men, were to operate in the sphere of politics, exchange of ideas, and mixing with non-Armenians. The reproduction of that which made a person Armenian—church-going, language, endogamous marriage practices, choices for charitable and philanthropic activities, socialization practices, memory—what we can summarize as "the Armenian tradition," had to spring from the homespace whose heart was a mother.

Since the late nineteenth century Armenian feminists, who had been equally invested in the Armenian national project (of improving Armenians, of preserving Armenians, of liberating Armenians), objected to the limiting ways women could be subjects of/for the nation. They demanded that women *as Armenians* trespass the line dividing the homespace and public space and act in the realm of politics, decision making, and future-planning. Before turning to the parameters of the challenge that feminists faced, it is necessary to see how and why a gendered division of national/communal labor came into existence in the first place. We can then see how gender, the social organization of relations between the sexes and the social regulation of sexual relations, has been key to the survival of Armenianness after major catastrophes.

Gendered Endurance and the Endurance of Gender

While the gendered roots of Armenian self-understanding and organization must be connected to Christianity and religious tradition (and perhaps even to pre-Christianity), for our purposes in this book four specific processes of Ottoman domination need to be highlighted in trying to understand how gender became a survival kit for Armenians.

The Ottoman Muslim state under which Armenians had lived since the fifteenth century had always found sexual difference meaningful in its management of religious diversity. Similar to how the rights and duties of the *dhimma* (plural of *dhimmi*) differed from Ottoman Muslims, dhimmi women had a different legal standing than dhimmi men. The most important rule pertained to interfaith marriageability. Muslim men were allowed to marry dhimmi women but dhimmi men were forbidden to marry or fornicate with Muslim women.[23] In this patrilineal society, rules governing reproduction were meant to ensure the demographic advantage of Muslims over non-Muslims and sustain the symbolic superiority of Islam over other religions, rules that emerged in the earliest centuries of Islam's expansion in Arabia. From the perspective of dhimmis—who had to submit to the Muslim state's laws at all times—this sex-specific law, as one would expect, put additional burdens on women, increasing their importance for the maintenance of grouphood. Because Muslim males were legally allowed to pick dhimmi women as wives, women's appearance, interactions, and mobility came under constant surveillance by the religious and lay leaders of non-Muslim communities who would not want to lose their women, their childbearing potential, and their symbolic value to the dominant Muslim group. In short, the gendered ways the Ottoman legal universe orchestrated a hierarchy between Muslims (high) and non-Muslims (low) reinforced a gender-aware mentality among its subjects. This awareness remained relatively intact even after the Turkish Republic outlawed Islamic law. The new Civil Code introduced in 1926 made interfaith marriage for the first time legal for all Turkish citizens irrespective of sex. But because patrilineal descent rules remained largely the same for the state and for the Armenian Church, and given the legacy of long centuries of state meddling in who could marry out and who could not, endogamy has remained the norm among Armenians in Turkey to this day.

Second, nineteenth-century discourses and practices associated with nationalism and modernity played an important role in the prominence of gender in Armenians' postwar communal self-understanding. In the late nineteenth century the Armenian "awakening" to a national consciousness implicated women in the project of nation formation in certain ways. Thanks to the compelling body of literature on gender and nationalism that has developed in the last twenty-five years covering a wide-ranging geography, we now know that all modern nationalisms employ familial tropes (fatherland, mother tongue, brotherhood of revolutionaries) and imagine the members of the nation as sexed bodies (the mother/father of the nation). While they assign atavistic continuity to women as preservers of timeless "tradition," they allow, and even require, men to change in the name of "progress," "modernity," and/or accommodation to a perceived external threat.[24] Moreover, the dichotomous formula for Armenian survival along the "world" vs. "home" axis resembles how, from Bengal to Cairo, anticolonial nationalists located the nation's "inner core"—that which has to remain the same in the face of humiliating outside intrusion—in the realms of spirituality and "tradition."[25] The nationalists perceived women as the storage vessel for this "inner core," which made mothers constitutive elements and transmitters of the nation's critical difference, a common good otherwise known as "culture," constructed as a fortress against penetration from the "world."

Like their anticolonialist peers elsewhere in the world, the educated Armenian elite early on recognized the maternal role of women as an indispensable tool for the patriotic socialization of the new generation and for the enlightenment and the modernization of the Armenian masses. Mothers, both in urban centers and remote rural corners, had to be educated so that they could raise the new generation with a new national consciousness. Paradoxically, women had to be educated but not transformed too fundamentally because they, in their songs, lullabies, food, garb, and crafts, stood as the nation's uncontaminated, unique core, that which differentiated Armenians from other nations.[26]

This defining feature of nationalisms' gendered character and its attending paradoxes served feminism well. The roots of feminism go back to revolutionary France when women, *as citizens*, demanded to be included in the body of the nation as participating members, full political subjects eligible for a voice and a vote. Nationalism is the horizontal, nonhierarchical, and secular conception of national membership in which every member should be the same before the nation and before the law. This new way of thinking about Armenianness (now not just a religious community but a national one) led Armenian women of urban, elite backgrounds to claim new rights that did not confine them to home and motherhood. From the 1860s on a new Armenian female intelligentsia, many educated in new, modern girls' schools, appropriated nationalism's inherently gendered and paradoxical logic. Like other nationalists, Armenian feminists started a press, opened up schools, and built associations in order to remake women into scientific homemakers, patriotic mothers, and educated wives.[27] As they reproduced this gendered imagination, however, feminists asked for reciprocity in return for their involvement in the national project.[28] Their demands for representational rights, which they labeled "women's emancipation," left a feminist legacy for postwar Armenians and gave women's activists a language in which to relate to larger Armenian agendas and work to change their parameters and goals.

Third, the Medz Yeghern was a gendered and age-conscious event; therefore it left a gendered and age-conscious legacy. An integral though nonlethal aspect of the Young Turk final solution to the Armenian problem involved the transfer of women and young children from their natal families to Muslim households and orphanages for eventual Islamization and incorporation into the Muslim community. The implementation of this policy relied on a number of preconditions. First of all, the difference between the perpetrators and target group was not conceived on the basis of fixed, blood relations but instead relied on religious difference, which was open to metamorphosis. But that metamorphosis was not permissible for adult males, who could, given the patrilineal descent rules and the sharia rulings mentioned above, transmit religious identity to their offspring. Since the grand Young Turk goal did not involve eradication of every single Armenian but the removal of the Armenian demographic threat, it was not necessary to kill all Armenians; those deemed reprogrammable could be neutralized by making Muslim Turks, Kurds, Arabs, etc., out of them. This is not to say that women and children were not killed during the Armenian genocide. Generally, massacres were more systematic and gender blind in the east, where Armenians were concentrated. In many other parts, however, while adult males were killed, women and children were ordered into deportation marches during which they were made available for rape and abduction. Because women were conceived as being devoid of the agency to organize political resistance, and because they could not reproduce Armenian children without their men (who were separated from them and killed), they were better recycled than discarded.

In the immediate aftermath of the Ottoman defeat, and under the Allies' protection, surviving Armenians organized rescue operations to bring kidnapped women and children back into the Armenian community. These operations had expectedly assumed a masculinist language of protection, honor, and vengeance. Therefore they amplified Armenians' gendered sensibilities. The gendered orchestration of the genocide meant that the majority of the survivors would be women and children. Some of them remained in Muslim households and died as Turks, Kurds, and Arabs. Others were liberated into their natal communities. That *Turke* ("The Turk" in Armenian, a common way of referring to Ottoman Muslims) "stole" them during the genocide reinforced women's and children's already important role in the eyes of surviving Armenians.

A fourth factor relates to the particular processes that attended the transition from the empire to the republic and the ways the Turkish state engineered its new society. In 1923 the Ankara-centered Kemalists signed a peace treaty with the Allies. The Treaty of Lausanne recognized Turkey's sovereignty in Anatolia, including eastern Anatolia, which Armenians had claimed as their own homeland. At the insistence of the Great Powers, Turkey gave official minority status to non-Muslims who remained inside the new country's borders. The treaty stipulated that minorities would have freedom to conduct their religious affairs, use their mother tongues freely, continue their press, conduct the affairs of their educational and charitable institutions, and continue following their customs in personal status law. Even though Turkey breached many articles of the treaty, minorities have until this day retained some room for self-governance.

Many of these new minority rights eerily resembled the entitlements *dhimma* enjoyed under the Ottoman Empire, rights they received in exchange for their agreement to defer to Muslims at all times and not aid the enemies of the state. Such similarities allowed for continuities in how Armenians conducted their everyday lives and how they positioned their community vis-à-vis the state and the dominant group. This was a spherical imagination in which the borders of concentric circles were formed according to the existence and intensity of the state's interference. The *in*-side of the community was composed of Armenian families, homes, and kinship networks. The *mid*-side of the community was made up of churches, schools, charitable organizations, and cemeteries in which Armenians related to other Armenians but by law and regulations, these spaces were under state surveillance. The *out*-side of the community was the realm of non-Armenians, the Turkish public sphere, and the state. This enclave-like existence did not negate or exclude intercommunal interaction between Armenians and other ethnic and religious groups in Turkey. The foundation for this type of communal life had been laid during Ottoman times and was reinforced by the minority protection clauses that the Allies forced on Turkey and other postwar countries such as Hungary, Romania, and Czechoslovakia, among others.

Homespace included kinship and friendship networks of one's "private life." This site thus became the only space where Armenians connected with other Armenians free of the state's scrutiny.[29] Homespace was made possible by women and activities traditionally associated with them as mothers, homemakers, and transmitters of traditional ways of being. This tendency was buttressed with yet another context, which was the new Turkish state's modernization project. Like many other newly formed postwar states, Turkey aimed to standardize its population through nationalizing, secularizing, and Westernizing reforms. In 1927 Prime Minister İsmet İnönü summarized this goal by declaring that the state rejected a nation made up of "confederated civilizations" and instead was committed to creating a monolithic mass (*yekpâre kütle*).[30] The universalism of the republic's public had to exclude many particularisms, including that of the Armenians. Much like Jews in nineteenth-century liberal-secular regimes of Europe who advocated being "a man in the street and a Jew at home,"[31] Armenians increasingly "privatized" their difference—and they knew how to do it.

Under such conditions in which Armenianness relied on protectionist traditionalism and where "tradition" centered on norms and ideas associated with "women," how could feminists reconcile their demand for gender equality with their wish to perpetuate Armenianness? How could one be an Armenian *and* a feminist after genocide and minoritization in Turkey? This is the question that drives this book.

Sources of Knowledge

In September 1922 when the news of the Kemalists' victory in western Asia Minor and the ensuing burning of Smyrna/Izmir reached Constantinople, the Armenian patriarch, Archbishop Zaven Der Yeghiayan, the head of the Ottoman Armenians, felt a keen sense of alarm. Kemalists could enter Bolis anytime and repeat the carnage wreaked in Zmiurnia (Smyrna). As he began packing, the first thing he thought of taking out of the city was the archive. He squeezed the patriarchate's correspondence of the last four years inside twenty-four boxes and shipped them to Bishop Grigoris Balakian, pastor of Armenians in Manchester, England.[32] In a few weeks, the patriarch packed his own belongings as well and left the city, never to return.

The archives Patriarch Zaven wanted to protect contained various important documents, such as the minutes of the Armenians' National Assembly meetings and the patriarch's exchanges with the Armenian National Delegation at the Paris Peace Conference. The patriarch knew that that past would not sit well with what was to become of Armenians after the Kemalist takeover of Bolis. The future, the patriarch must have thought, could only be saved if some of its parts remained in the dark.

The archives of the Armenian patriarchate, the semi-formal center of the Armenian community in Turkey, remain closed to this day. There are many unknowns surrounding why, on whose orders, and how exactly the archive was closed and when and if it will ever be opened. This is a way, I think, that the Armenian community, an ever-precarious entity in Turkey, exercises control over its history and therefore its present. In a Turkey in which referring to the "events" of 1915 as "genocide" is still considered "insulting Turkishness" and is technically punishable by law, this attitude on the part of the Turkish Armenian community is understandable. For the researcher, however, the absence of this archive is restraining. Without this archive, which could have helped historians detect how the relations between the Turkish state and the patriarchate evolved in the formative years of the republic and how Armenian representatives internally discussed questions pertaining to their community, it is difficult to fully reconstruct Turkish Armenian history after World War I.

On the other hand, the absence of a traditional, formal archive and a near complete absence of secondary sources intensify the importance of the primary sources that are available. The availability of certain kinds of sources, in turn, frames the research questions that can be asked. In writing this book I have consulted Armenian memoirs, institutional reports, published and unpublished correspondence among intellectuals, Turkish state archives, and Turkish newspapers. My main source, however, has been the Armenian press, a hugely important archive for the history of Turkish Armenians.

The Armenian press, whose history goes back to 1794 in Madras, India, sat at the center of Armenian public life in various parts of the Ottoman Empire since the 1830s. Newspaper publishing, however, like almost all other political, social, cultural, and intellectual activities among Armenians, largely stopped during the war. In many places it never resumed. In Constantinople, only four newspapers continued to be published—subject to close government surveillance—during the war years. After the war and with the entry of occupation forces, Bolsahays rushed to revitalize almost all aspects of their lives, including their newspapers. In Bolis alone, sixty-five Armenian periodicals began publication between 1918 and 1922.[33] Some were brand-new periodicals, others, a continuation of prewar publications. Together they served the needs of the roughly 150,000 Armenians of the Ottoman capital.

At this time Armenian numbers increased because in the aftermath of the Armistice about 35,000 survivors from Mesopotamia and the Levant sought refuge in the city.

Post-genocide Armenians read newspapers not just to get informed about their community and the world. Newspapers have been part and parcel of reclaiming normalcy. Some newspapers, the ones that were the publications of political parties (and four reopened in the city after the war), offered a place where people could meet, reconnect, and discuss current events. Moreover, periodicals were the primary medium that connected the dispersed Armenian communities with each other. Almost all newspapers featured long "missing" columns where people searched for their family, relatives, and friends lost during the war. These columns became a staple of Armenian newspapers worldwide and helped many survivors reconnect.[34] Weeklies, monthlies, illustrated magazines, satirical journals, and almanacs targeted a variety of audiences such as youth, children, leftists, republicans, the religiously conservative, medical doctors, lawyers, scouts, athletes, cinema lovers, and, feminists.

Hay Gin (Armenian Woman), the fortnightly that Hayganush Mark edited as the organ of the Armenian Women's Association, began publication in 1919 in this hopeful, lively Armenian atmosphere. Even though the timing of its commencement was not particularly special, *Hay Gin* would prove to be extraordinary in terms of its duration and its termination. After the Allied evacuation and Turkish takeover of Istanbul, when a significant number of Armenians left the city, many periodicals were automatically closed. Some of them reopened in places where their editors moved, such as Cairo, Corfu, and Paris. *Hay Gin* became the only Turkish Armenian periodical that continued publication almost without interruption, without changing its name, and with the same editor from the occupation years through the first decade of the Turkish Republic. It thus makes for a perfect archive to trace changing Armenian discourses in these eventful transition years. If this is one reason why the whole run of *Hay Gin* is an indispensable source for this study, the second is related to the fact that it is the place to find feminists who offered an alternative to the mainstream discourses of how to be an Armenian in Turkey.

Initially *Hay Gin* was the organ of the newly formed Armenian Women's Association. Even though the association closed its doors and most of its members fled the country during the exodus of fall 1922, Mark continued the journal, probably thinking that since hers was *merely* a women's journal she could evade the radar of the incoming Kemalist leadership. And she did. It wasn't until January 1933 that the state ordered *Hay Gin* closed. The new press law had declared that people who had served the "enemies of the Turks" during the occupation years would not be allowed to publish periodicals. *Hay Gin*'s support of the Allies in the 1918–1922 period thus caught up with Mark in 1933. The folding of *Hay Gin* is emblematic of how history became destiny for Armenians in the new Turkey and it is the reason why I end the book in 1933.

Because this study focuses on public figures and the public discussion about Armenianness, it does not directly engage with what individual Armenians thought, felt, remembered, forgot, and discussed inside their households, with their friends, and among their kin.[35] This is not only a question of personal choice and availability of sources, but also is one dictated by my disciplinary background in sociology and history. Yet, given the nonexistence of a scholarly field, I felt the urge to hear from people who lived at least some parts of my book's focus. I conducted oral history interviews in the United States with several Armenians born in late 1910s and 1920s Istanbul. Given my focus on published materials and public discourse, I did not include these interviews in the body of the book but instead have highlighted these people's voices either in the notes, and very occasionally, in the text. This does not mean that my interviewees did not affect my thinking about this era. On the contrary, their words, gestures, Armenian accents, accents in Turkish, the smells of their houses, and even their clothing influenced the way I read my "real" primary sources, the text. For instance, I was initially alerted to the perceived positive aspects of Kemalism by hearing how more than one senior Armenian told me how much they wept out of sorrow on the day Atatürk died. Similarly I was startled to hear the late Madame Knar, then a 92-year-old resident of Cliffside Park, New Jersey, tell me that she had not felt discriminated against in the Bolis of her childhood and youth. When I asked, in Armenian, what language she spoke with her mother in the streets, she noted, without hearing any contradiction in her narrative, that "of course we could speak *only* Turkish."[36] Their life narratives, as well as the stories of my grandparents and parents, and my intuitions as a sometime member of this community, helped me find my way and understand the multiple possibilities of belonging to a place that is home, but not quite.

∾

The book progresses chronologically. The first two chapters discuss the years from late 1918 to late 1922. Chapter 1 analyzes the gendered ways and familial vocabulary in which Armenians imagined how they were going to survive the recent catastrophe, and Chapter 2 focuses on Armenian feminism of the time and feminists' struggles to partake in the decision-making bodies of their community. Chapter 3 is about one single year, late 1922 to late 1923, during which the Kemalist movement finalized its military and diplomatic victories. As thousands of Armenians left Istanbul for foreign lands, those who remained came to be legally defined as "minorities." Chapters 4 and 5 cover the years from 1923 to 1933. Chapter 4 includes two layers of analysis. On the one hand, it discusses the state's approach to the remaining Armenians, which was somewhat paradoxical. On the other hand, the chapter discusses Armenian responses to simultaneous exclusion from a Turkhood in which they were sometimes included. I call this kind of state-minority relationship "secular dhimmitude." The fifth and last chapter returns to feminism to examine the particular blows that gender equality had to endure if Armenianness was going to survive the new Turkey.

Figure 3. Cover page of the almanac *Sargavakin Daretsuytse* showing Armenian children defending their newly acquired fatherland, an Armenia they hoped to expand. *Sargavakin Daretsuytse* (n.p., 1921).

(CHAPTER 1)

THE REBIRTH OF A NATION

In 1921, an untitled and unsigned picture appeared on the cover page of the *Deacon's Almanac* (*Sargavakin Daretsuytse*) (Figure 3).[1] The image features a young boy and a girl standing next to each other, ready to defend themselves and their nation. The rock in the image, which represents Mother Armenia (*Mayr Hayasdan*), is protected by the boy's masculine power, his rifle, and his readiness to die for his homeland and his people. The girl, possibly his sister, embodies "the nation," not only because of her location—on the land—but also because she holds the tricolor flag (red, blue, and orange) that the newly founded Republic of Armenia adopted in 1918. The flag signals the identity of the nation in its distinctiveness and history, depicted here as larger than the girl and the boy, and capable of engulfing them both. These two figures complement each other by dividing the national labor along traditional gendered and familial lines. He is in a soldier's uniform; she wears its counterpart, a Red Cross uniform, attesting to her readiness to come to his aid if he falls wounded. She is the caregiver: a future mother, an apprentice in the service of the nation. The color of their outfits, and the girl's headgear, might even allow this picture to be read—however faintly—as reminiscent of a wedding photo. She is dressed in white and veiled, he is in formal black; she touches him, he holds a firearm at the ready; they are capable of reproducing the nation. Alternatively, the girl, who stands above the boy, can be viewed as a miniaturized mother. The determined mother touches a son to pass on to him courage, knowledge, and memory. Even without going into its subconscious layers, however, we can safely assume that in the year 1921 this illustration was accessible to the Armenian public in a certain way: a nation that had just survived a major attack against its very existence belies defeat by relying on its children, who are ever ready to face the future whatever it might bring.

Like their non-Armenian counterparts, Armenian spokespeople had long understood their nation as one big family and told its story through gendered children's bodies. However, at this immediate post-catastrophe moment marked by high hopes for Armenia's territorial expansion, children and their mothers gained even more important roles, literally and metaphorically. The figure of the child instilled an exceptional sense of temporality. He or she symbolized the past (suffering), the present (unity and self-help), and the future (Greater Armenia), all at the same time.[2] Public figures of all standings made strong, persistent claims that the desired sort of bridging from the past to the future could happen only through surviving children's bodies, memories, emotions, and actions; and that women, as carriers of babies and caregivers of children, family, and thus the nation, had the primary role in bringing about that future.

This emphasis on children was part and parcel of a larger political, social, cultural, and affective repertoire in which the Bolsahay elite processed the damage the Great War did to their group and imagined its recovery. They referred to the era in which they lived with a number of terms that expressed recovery. Usually capitalized, these terms were National Rebirth/Restoration/Revival (*Azkayin Veradznunt*) and National Reconstitution (*Azkayin Verashinum* and *Azkayin Veraganknum*). The ultimate goal of recovery was to bring the Armenian people and resources to their prewar levels and to reclaim the western parts of the Armenian historical homeland. These two legs of the recovery project were seen as the ultimate revenge that the Armenians would exact on "the Turk." Despite multiple internal disagreements on the specifics of how to bring about that recovery and what Greater Armenia should look like, Armenian spokespeople were in basic agreement that the institution of the family was to play a fundamental role in national restoration. *Turke* had attacked the Armenian family, violated mothers, sisters, and wives, kidnapped daughters and sons, and killed husbands, fathers, and brothers. Therefore, National Rebirth had to start by reconnecting the broken pieces of the nation. Remnants had to find each other and form new families. The new families would reproduce new Armenians, who would then inhabit the soon-to-be-established Mother Armenia. This familial vocabulary and imagery—always necessarily gendered—enabled Armenian leaders to make sense of the recent catastrophe, organize for the care of the survivors, and mobilize hope that Armenians as a nation would survive, even thrive, despite recent attempts to destroy it.

While the body of a minor child symbolized the hope for repair, remembrance, and revenge to the Bolsahay elite, the same bodies had different meanings for a subsection of survivors who had been kidnapped into Muslim households during the war. Some of these women did not want to give birth or mother babies conceived during captivity and as a result of rape by the enemy. Given their disempowered state, however, they frequently had to yield to the demands of the Armenian authorities and relief institutions, which typically approached *all* children, regardless of their (Muslim) fathers, as the future of the Armenian nation. These reluctant mothers were among the survivors who found their way to the capital in the aftermath of the war and depended on Bolsahay relief societies for their everyday sustenance. They did not write their stories and the mainstream press did not report on them. Their perspectives would have remained completely submerged within the hegemonic narratives had the Bolsahay feminist press not highlighted their existence and had individual feminists not included their *darapakhd kuyrer* (unfortunate sisters) in their memoirs written years later.

The National Government of Armenians in Constantinople

Soon after the Ottomans' acceptance of defeat with the signing of the Armistice of Mudros on October 30, 1918, Armenian survivors who had been dispersed to Mesopotamia and the Levant began to return.[3] However, given that the Allies did not occupy all Ottoman territories, and because the situation was uncertain and potentially still dangerous for Armenians in unoccupied places, most of the survivors went to French-occupied Cilicia (contemporary southern Turkey) and to Constantinople, which the Allies jointly occupied beginning in November 1918.[4] The Armenian leadership and the press referred to the incoming survivors as *darakir* or *darakryal*, meaning exiled or expatriated people, usually translated to English as "deportee."[5] Because the genocidal policy primarily (though by no means exclusively) targeted adult males for killing, women and children composed the majority of the survivors.

From 1919 until 1922, approximately 35,000 deportees entered Constantinople and joined the 120,000 Armenian residents of the city.[6] Bolsahays immediately rushed to help these mostly sick, emaciated, and traumatized people. Because the Ottoman capital had not experienced the war years in the same way as the rest of the empire, its Armenian infrastructure—people, churches, schools, orphanages, charitable institutions, hospitals—had remained more or less intact and ready to be put in the service of the needy. In 1912–1913, the city was home to 42 Armenian parishes, 42 neighborhood elementary schools, 10 secondary schools, and a dozen Catholic and Protestant middle and high schools, with a total enrollment of about 25,000.[7] Bolsahays opened thirteen refugee stations (*gayan*) to shelter and feed the refugees (Figure 4).[8]

Given their experiences as a semi-autonomously governed *millet* under the Ottomans, Bolsahays knew how to organize for communal self-help and because of the previous massacres in the provinces (i.e., the 1894–1896 Hamidian massacres and the 1909 Adana pogrom) they knew how to organize for self-help even during such emergencies. Although the Great War had wrought damage on an unprecedented scale, they tried and largely managed to provider deportees with shelter, food, clothing, medical treatment, and when possible reconnected them with surviving family members and/or facilitated their emigration abroad. Some of the deportees left almost immediately for other countries, some became self-sufficient after a short time, some stayed with their relatives in Bolis, and many remained housed in orphanages, hospitals, former barracks, schools, shelter homes, and refugee camps. Western aid organizations such as the British Lord Mayor's Fund, the Swiss-Armenian Society, and most important, the American Committee for Relief in the Near East, commonly known as Near East Relief (NER), also provided relief.[9] Among Armenians, while the initial aid efforts were organized at the neighborhood level, the Armenian patriarchate soon managed to centralize the care that the Bolsahays offered to their less fortunate *azkayin*s, nationals or members of the same nation.

Established in 1461 at the request of the Ottoman Sultan Mehmed II after his conquest of the city, the Armenian patriarchate of Constantinople had functioned as the administrative and spiritual center of Ottoman Armenians.

The patriarch acted as the liaison between the state and his Armenian congregation, almost all of whom were Apostolic Christians until the eighteenth century.[10] In the early nineteenth century and in response to conversions and the interference of France and Britain, two separate Armenian *millet*s came into being. While the Ottoman government approved an Armenian Catholic *millet* in 1830 and one of Armenian Protestants in 1857, the overwhelming majority of Armenians continued to practice Apostolicism. Given this history

Figure 4. The Haydar Pasha Refugee Station, the biggest of the thirteen refugee stations operated by the Constantinopolitan Armenian community for survivors who arrived in the Ottoman capital from all over the empire. Women, children, and elderly made up the majority of survivors. In October 1919, about 1,200 people lived in this refugee station. *Azkayin Khnamadarutiun: Enthanur Deghegakir Arachin Vetsamsya, 1 Mayis 1919–31 Hogdemper 1919* (Constantinople: M. Hovagimian, 1920), 101.

and the demographic differences, when one talked about "the Armenians" in the Ottoman Empire one meant Apostolic Armenians; qualifiers such as "Armenian Catholics" and "Protestant Armenians" were necessary when one referred to these non-normative populations.

During the mid-nineteenth century, as part of the Ottoman state's Tanzimat (Reorganization) modernization program, each non-Muslim community reformed its internal organization by making it more participatory and democratic. In the process, each *millet* came up with new rules and regulations pertaining to self-administration and legalized these procedures in a written document that had to be ratified by the Ottoman center. The state approved Armenians' *Azkayin Sahmanatrutiun Hayots* (National Constitution of Armenians) in 1863.[11] The Armenian constitution instituted a National Assembly (*Azkayin Zhoghov*) of 140 members made up of elected clerical and laymen. In the coming decades, this National Assembly effectively served as a parliament and was understood by the population as such. In the period under study, the Armenian press called the members of the National Assembly *yerespokhan*, meaning, parliamentarians or deputies. While the clerical members (20 people) were elected by other Armenian Apostolic clergy in Constantinople, the lay members (120 people) were elected by popular (male) vote.[12] The assembly's various duties included the election of the patriarch, who served as the head of the assembly. The assembly also appointed the members of the commissions that dealt with specific issues related to the everyday lives of Ottoman Armenians both as individuals and as a community. These commissions were responsible for finances, education, personal status law, endowments, hospitals, and church buildings, and so on. Ottoman Armenians referred to this whole system as their National Government (*Azkayin Ishkhanutiun*) or National Administration (*Azkayin Varchutiun*).

During World War I the Ottoman government exiled the Armenian patriarch, Zaven Der Yeghiayan, to Mosul and ordered the patriarchate closed.[13] The National Assembly, which traditionally convened in the patriarchate building, ceased functioning. The patriarchate reopened only after the war. In February 1919 the patriarch returned to office and the National Assembly resumed its work but with a reduced number. Many of its former members, especially representatives from the provinces (*kavar*), had fallen victim to the genocide. For the first time in its history, the Armenian patriarchate and the National Assembly unilaterally cut their ties with the Ottoman government.[14] Relying on the Allies' support, the patriarchate openly condemned the government for the massacres during the war. In Allied-occupied Constantinople, Zaven Der Yeghiayan, the ultimate head of the Ottoman Armenian community, cooperated with occupying forces and worked for the partitioning of the Ottoman territories out of which he hoped a new and free Armenia would be born. This post-genocide moment of crisis and the necessity to present a united front in the struggle for the establishment of Greater Armenia led to another unprecedented development. The patriarchate of the Apostolic Armenians together with the All-Armenian Catholic patriarch and the leader of the Armenian Protestant community formed an All-Armenian Assembly (*Hamazkayin* or *Hamahaygagan Zhoghov*) and cooperated in finding solutions to the problems that beset all Armenians regardless of their religious affiliation.

One of the first steps taken by the reestablished National Assembly was to command the establishment of an umbrella organization to respond to the refugee crisis. The ensuing Armenian National Relief Organization (*Hay Azkayin Khnamadarutiun*) was run by twelve members, four from each Armenian *millet*.[15] Like almost all other Armenian initiatives at this time, the Relief Organization remained an all-inclusive endeavor extending its help to Apostolic, Protestant, and Catholic Armenians alike. In his memoirs, the chairman of the society explained this unity simply by saying that "since the Turk massacred all Armenians without distinction," acting together was essential.[16]

Initially the budget for the Relief Organization was drawn from wealthy donors, but in September 1919 the National Assembly's Civil Council (*Kaghakagan Zhoghov*) decided to standardize fundraising and share the burden of the relief work with the whole community. Every Armenian, male or female, with a source of income was to pay a new monthly tax.[17] The revenue from the new tax would be used for two purposes: to care for orphans and deportees, and to fund the patriarchate's political and diplomatic efforts among the Allied powers in Constantinople and in Europe. That the new tax was called a Fatherland Tax (*Hayreniki Durke*) was indicative of how the postwar Armenian leadership understood the terms of their nation's recovery. Rehabilitation of the survivors and the reclamation of territory constituted the two halves of the same project of National Rebirth.

Survival of the Weakest

While the Fatherland Tax created a fund for the care of the deportees, resources never sufficed to meet the demand. Although deportees as a general category received attention, the Bolsahay organizations, press, and the leadership paid the most attention to the care of the orphans. It is not clear what the age limit was for being categorized as an "orphan" (*vorp*). My reading of the institutional reports, periodicals, and memoirs suggests that unmarried girls and boys, regardless of their age, were considered orphans if they had lost one parent, usually the father, and if they had no male relative on whom to depend. Often women without a male relative were also considered orphans. Armenians have a term for such women: *vorpevayri*, meaning "orphan and widow." Orphanhood and the disintegration of the known family structure were closely related. To a certain extent, orphanhood meant an absence of the support of a family on whom one depended for everything before the catastrophe.

Armenian orphanages in Constantinople in the immediate aftermath of the war housed about 4,000 orphans.[18] To encourage people to donate money to orphan care and volunteer their labor and time, periodicals frequently reprinted before-and-after photos of orphans. A typical example appeared in the 1922 issue of the famed intellectual Teotig's *Amenun Daretsuytse* (Everyone's Almanac). Two photos show the same group of orphans at different times.[19] In the first photo, the children look miserable, angry, and sad. Lacking shoes, wearing rags and unattractive outfits, they shiver in the cold. In the second photo, captioned "The same orphans after they have been saved by our efforts," the children have hats and decent, clean clothing, and they look confident.

The transformation of orphans instilled hope in the Bolsahay elite that the Armenian nation too would soon rehabilitate itself. The anthem of one of the orphanages in the city assured the adults that:

> Having been freed from the painful black days of the past,
> We are in our home now.
>
> . . .
>
> We are the sparks of the Howard Karageuzian Home Orphanage;
> We are the hope of the Armenian world.[20]

Orphans represented the hopes of the Armenian world also because they personified a certain kind of revenge (*vrezh*). In this period, Armenians associated "living" with vengeance. Existence—as an individual, as a community, as a nation, and as a state—had become more than a state of being; it had turned into a political act.[21] *Abril* (living) as a trope permeated both the survivor narratives and the postwar articulations of the present and the future. One deportee in Constantinople, Madame Hisarlian, narrated to Zaruhi Bahri (a feminist social worker who later included the episode in her personal memoir) the story of how she managed to escape from the interior provinces to Bolis during the war. Madame Hisarlian's husband, a prominent doctor in Tokat, had been murdered in 1915. On the death march, along with a group of women, she had been gang raped but not kidnapped. After the incident, she recognized that a nearby river was running red because of the blood of the Armenians who had been killed and thrown into it. Resisting her thirst for a long while, she finally gave in and drank from the red river. When she told her story to Bahri in postwar Constantinople, where she arrived after episodes of being sold as a slave and enduring typhus, she looked remarkably put-together, with her nails and lips in shining red. Seeing Zaruhi's bewilderment, she explained:

> Madam, I know that you are surprised to see me in such good shape. But, if you knew what I (with bleeding wounds) had felt when I put my lips in the river which ran red with Armenian blood, you would understand that at that moment my inner world was dominated by one strong feeling: Do they want to kill us all? If so, then, we have to live. The more we live, the more we survive, the more we will be able to secure our revenge and victory. And I did. . . . I lived.[22]

One of the first published eyewitness accounts of the Armenian genocide was written by a teacher in Samsun who, before embarking on the deportation marches, entrusted her two children to a Greek family because she did not think she would survive. Similarly, her sister distributed her four children to Greek neighbors to keep them while she was away. After detailing the unbearable pain of separating from her children, Payladzu Captanian wrote,

> We were driven by immeasurable motherly love and the cause of *national existence* [*azkayin koyutiun*]. We were sure that even if we managed to keep three children alive, we would have already taken our revenge on the enemy. There

would be established three families on the ruins of one ruined family, and that's how the Armenian Nation would come back to life and reconstitute itself [*gentananar yev veragankner*]. Then, it was not important that we would die. They had to live. We would survive in them.[23]

It is impossible to retrace what Madame Hisarlian's *real* motivation was in drinking the water of the red river, or if Payladzu Captanian really thought in those terms when she handed her children to Greeks. The former might simply have given in to thirst (a less heroic explanation certainly), and the latter's sole motivation could have been the physical well-being of her children, were they to become Greek, Armenian, or even Turkish. Given the mediated and after-the-fact nature of these and many other such accounts, we cannot assume authenticity. But for our purposes, the original intentions do not matter. What matters is how those acts were talked about and given meaning in the immediate postwar years, and it is certain that a vocabulary of "surviving in children" as a way of taking revenge and restoring the nation was commonly employed. Indeed, the oneness of the dead and the surviving, especially children, in connection with a desired revenge is a common post-genocidal reaction. In her study of Jewish displaced persons (DPs) in the Allied-occupied zones in post-Holocaust Berlin, Atina Grossmann argued that the visible and well-documented baby boom was, "beyond a 'manic defense' against catastrophic experience and overwhelming loss," a means to consciously assert Jewish life and presence, especially in Germany. The presence of pregnant women, babies (in their names and bodies), and baby carriages that filled the dusty streets of Jewish refugee camps in Germany was imbued with deep emotions related to mourning and revenge.[24]

Even though we lack the necessary statistics to judge if there was a similar "baby boom" among post-genocide Armenians, natalist calls were common, and they predictably placed women at the heart of the discourse; this was true for both mainstream publications and the feminist biweekly *Hay Gin*.[25] The journal wholeheartedly embraced the maternalist discourse in the formulations of how Armenianness could survive and revive after the catastrophe. Resumption of family meant the resumption of the figure of the traditional mother, the mother who gave birth to many children and devoted herself fully to raising them into happy, healthy, and patriotic adults.

Hay Gin organized pretty baby contests that featured robust Armenian children as future Armenians and the future of Armenianness (Figure 5). These contests also encouraged motherhood and mothering. Pretty baby contests were a novelty in Constantinople of the time and in her autobiography Hayganush Mark took pride in the fact that *Hay Gin* was the first to feature such events.[26] In the early 1930s, Turkish periodicals would start similar contests. Even though Turkish and Armenian baby contests shared a

Figure 5. Hay Gin's "pretty baby contest." The journal organized these baby contests to instill in the survivor-nation the conviction that Armenians had a bright future. People from Cairo, Fresno, Paris, Brussels, Ethiopia, New York, Beirut, Tbilisi, and Yugoslavia, and elsewhere, sent pictures to the journal. *Hay Gin* 1, no. 7 (February 1, 1920).

similar logic of showcasing robust children to instill hope in a postwar population with a large number of orphaned and destitute children, the Armenian case featured a difference.[27] During the period that *Hay Gin* continued the contest (1919–1928) people sent photos of their children to the journal from all over the world, from Cairo, Fresno, Paris, Brussels, Ethiopia, New York, Beirut, Tbilisi, and Yugoslavia, among others. The postwar Armenian reading public was very much aware of this dispersal that was largely an effect of the genocide. Survivors all over the world cultivated various mechanisms to fight against the disintegration of the Armenian nation and the Armenian family. *Hay Gin*'s pretty baby contest was one such medium by which Armenians endeavored to defy dispersion and revive their nation regardless of where its members might be anchored territorially. As long as Armenian families reproduced themselves (and the pretty babies were proof that they did) the nation would survive.

That the biological and social reproduction of the family (thus Armenians) received such central attention put additional and national burdens on the female body. The way the journal *Hay Puzhag* (Armenian Healer) discussed the issue of abortion was typical of the general mood. This medical journal, which found it necessary to publish regular reports on how many marriage certificates the patriarchate had issued each month, characterized abortion-seeking women as "egoistic and undutiful." Equating abortion with infanticide, it addressed the Armenian woman: "Keep away from all thoughts and principles of degeneration. Devote yourself to procreation, which is your *sole duty*. It is the complete fulfillment of this duty that will realize our ideal."[28]

The word "ideal" in the unsigned *Hay Puzhag* column referred not only to an abstract idea of survival and multiplication, but also to the concrete goal of securing an Armenia free from the Ottoman yoke. Given the international political context of the time, *Hay Puzhag* was correct in linking fetuses to territory. The Paris peace settlement negotiations, with their emphasis on Wilsonian "self-determination," came to an agreement that the nationality of a region was to devolve to the group that made up the majority of the population.[29] Even though demographics had been in the forefront of competition for land and sovereignty since at least the early nineteenth century, the primacy of the principle of self-determination in the aftermath of the Great War escalated the importance of numbers and statistics. The Allies made sure that the Armenians understood the intricacies of international diplomacy. For instance, in London, during Patriarch Zaven Der Yeghiayan's European tour, which he undertook in support of the Armenian National Delegation at the postwar peace conferences, the commission charged with Armenia's future borders told the patriarch, "The more people you have the more land you will get."[30] British Foreign Secretary Lord Curzon's assistant also advised the patriarch to "hearten the dispersed Armenians to immediately return and populate Armenia." The patriarch assured him that the survivors living in foreign lands intended to return to the fatherland at the first opportunity, and were not even trying to improve the condition of their (temporary) homes.[31]

By mid-1919 a resistance movement emerged in non-occupied Ottoman territories. Mustafa Kemal led this movement of Ottoman Muslims that opposed the partitioning of Anatolia into Greek, Armenian, Turkish, and Kurdish states and into spheres where the British, French, and the Italians would exercise "influence." These were the terms the Ottoman sultan accepted by signing the Peace Treaty of Sèvres with the Allies in August 1920. The Kemalists rejected this treaty and thus the representatives of the Ottoman sultanate and government that signed it. They had already chosen Ankara as their base and instituted a Grand National Assembly (which would later become the Turkish parliament) that used Wilsonian language to claim that they represented the popular sovereignty of the people (i.e., Ottoman Muslims).

However, given the emphasis Wilsonianism put on demographics, one of the most important tasks of the emerging Turkish nationalist defense committees was to prove, by "scientific means," that Muslims had always constituted the majority in the regions that Armenians claimed as their historical homelands—places that the Armenian delegation in Paris attempted to prove, also statistically, belonged to Armenians.[32] In such a climate in which population numbers were expected to translate into territory, Armenians, who had just come out of an assault against their very numbers, were at a disadvantage. The Armenian leadership in various parts of the world knew that they had to come up with numbers, and quickly. If one way of doing this was to reproduce new Armenians and take good care of the existing ones, another and much quicker way was to locate and retrieve young children and women kidnapped into Muslim houses and institutions during the war. Their retrieval was also imbued with deep meanings of revival, restoration, and revenge.

Reconstituting the Stuff of the Nation

During World War I, the ruling Ottoman party created the conditions for, allowed, and openly encouraged Ottoman Muslim households (Turks, Kurds, Arabs, Circassians, Chechens, and émigrés from the Balkans) to incorporate Armenian women and children, and to a lesser extent, women and children of other Christian groups such as Greeks and Assyrians, into their households. Armenian orphans were also housed in Turkish Muslim orphanages and many were forcibly Islamicized.[33] Following a conversion complete in name, religion, and language all these women and children would be remade into proper Ottoman Muslims and cease to threaten the Young Turks' ultimate goal: population homogeneity based on religion.[34]

The signing of the Armistice of Mudros initiated a new political climate in which Armenians could rescue kidnapped Armenians or rescue themselves. The armistice stipulated the release of Ottoman prisoners of war, a clause that Armenians and the Allies interpreted to include Islamicized women and children. When Patriarch Zaven returned to his seat, one of his first jobs was to begin the liberation (*azadakrum*) of Islamicized people of Armenian origin in the Ottoman capital and its environs. The patriarchate initiated an effort called *vorpahavak* (literally, the gathering of orphans), a campaign to retrieve and reintegrate children and women sequestered in Muslim households and orphanages.[35] While the *vorpahavak* in Constantinople began after the Mudros Armistice, Armenians had initiated similar efforts in Sinai, Palestine, Syria, and Iraq in late 1917, after the British arrived.[36]

In Constantinople, the *vorpahavak* caused many conflicts between Armenians and the Ottoman government because Armenians frequently "rescued" children and women who claimed, or whose parents or husbands claimed, they were true Muslims. Both sides accused the other of kidnapping and forcible conversion. Disputes reached such levels that at the initiative of the British, "neutral houses" (shelters of some sort) were established to determine the true origins of orphans with unclear identities.[37] According to the memoirs of the patriarch, until the end of 1922 Armenians managed to reclaim three thousand of the five thousand kidnapped women and children.[38]

Demographic and territorial concerns, feelings of revenge, and the need to recapture the virility of the nation influenced the Armenian rescue effort, which was seen as an indispensable component of the overall goal of National

Revival. Although it is hard to say that Armenians purposefully Armenianized Muslim children, it is evident that the *vorpahavak* agents usually erred on the side of the potential Armenianness of anyone. Indeed, authorities at times forced confessions (true or possibly false) and occasionally looked the other way when Muslim children were Armenianized. In his memoir, Aram Haygaz, a teenager at the Esayan Orphanage at the time, told of a ten-year-old boy who, unlike many others, would not admit his Armenianness. Even after some time at the orphanage, and after suffering threats and pressure, the boy continued to insist that he was a Turk. Ultimately, Haygaz and his friends believed the boy, but they decided that "even if he was a pure-bred Turk, we would keep and Armenianize him gradually." One of the orphans who worked on this "case" with Haygaz maintained, "They Turkified thousands from among us. Now it is our turn to at least Armenianize one among them." Haygaz—the sole survivor in his family—who had spent the war years in Ottoman Kurdistan, where he was converted to Islam and adopted by Muslim families, noted that the issue here was one of "reprisal" (*pokhvrezh*).[39]

Demographic and other sorts of anxieties reached such levels that the Bolsahay elite found it justifiable to ignore paternity in determining a baby's ethnic and religious origins. Despite the established patrilineal logic of both Armenian canonical law and sharia, the patriarchate and its *vorpahavak* agents decided that anyone with an Armenian mother, regardless if the father was a Muslim, would be officially considered a full-fledged Armenian. As such they would be eligible for a place in the orphanages and shelter homes run by Armenians and for Armenians (Figure 6). The Armenian Church baptized babies (of Muslim fathers) who would have been considered full Muslims in the pre-genocide era.[40]

The ultimate *vorpahavak* agenda for babies and children was to place them with Armenian families as foster children and adoptees. For women and girls, the *vorpahavak* goal was to marry them to Armenian men. This represented an ideal solution: Armenians retrieved what the Turks had stolen from them and employed the women and girls to reproduce Armenianness. Given the pre-genocide ideas about purity and propriety, however, Armenian leaders had their work cut out for them in packaging rescued women, most of them rape victims, as proper marriage candidates and future mothers. As early as 1916, *Hairenik* (Fatherland), a daily Armenian American newspaper

Figure 6. "Our Orphans at the Armenian Red Cross Dispensary in Pera." Armenian relief organizations accepted babies of Muslim fathers as full-fledged Armenians. The mothers were newly rescued Armenian women who gave birth to babies conceived in captivity. *Azkayin Khnamadarutiun: Enthanur Deghegakir Arachin Vetsamsya, 1 Mayis 1919–31* Hogdemper 1919 (Constantinople: M. Hovagimian, 1920), 154.

published in Boston, announced: "An Armenian man should not reject a woman who has been abducted since she is an innocent victim who cannot be held morally responsible for her condition."[41]

Patriarch Zaven himself, suiting his function as *parens patriae*, took the guardianship of his unprotected flock seriously.[42] He considered all the rescued women, even the prostitutes he had saved in Mosul during the last months of the war, as the nation's "unfortunate sisters." For the patriarch, these women still represented the honor of the nation, the precious Armenian national honor that men had to protect by marrying them.[43] Marry they did, but not all of them. The available evidence, including oral history interviews, suggests that these "orphaned women" did not constitute appropriate marriage candidates for elite Bolsahay families who preferred to marry among themselves.[44] Men from abroad, however, seemed to be willing to take orphaned girls or rescued women as wives. In 1919, out of the seventy women sheltered in the Scutari Women's

Shelter for the Rescued, twenty-one married within their first year of entering the institution (Figure 7).[45] Most went to America, many as picture brides. Everyone hoped that once Greater Armenia was established they would return and settle down in the fatherland. Many of the grooms had settled in North America before the war, and had lost their families in the Ottoman lands during the war. A survivor observed that men "returned from America for the sole purpose of marrying orphans and widows to help heal and make them forget

Figure 7. Armenian Red Cross Scutari (Üsküdar) branch shelter, which served as a temporary home to women and girls rescued from Muslim households. In 1919, twenty-one of the seventy women it sheltered married within their first year of entering the shelter. Many went to America, mostly as picture brides. *Yergamia Deghegakir H. G. Khachi Getr. Varchutyan, 1918 Noy. 18–1920 Teg. 31* (Constantinople: M. Hovagimian, 1921), 24.

their tragic past, to give them a new home, and to create new hope—this was the least they thought they could do for those who had survived."[46]

For men who rescued women and married them, these acts were patriotic. But they also helped them, and in the process, the Armenian nation, rescue its power, honor, and masculinity.[47] Armenian men who were made to witness violations of their families, or were away when the violations occurred, now had a chance to do what they felt they should have been doing before: protecting their women and children. While saving the women, either literally or by marrying them despite their so-called defiled state, these men probably tried to save themselves from feelings of guilt and emasculation. In addition to the chance to regain people and land, then, *vorpahavak* offered an opportunity to reclaim manhood, and this was an important dimension of the overall goal of National Revival.

Feminists' Object of Relief

For a project that had such masculinist undertones, feminists' wholehearted involvement in the *vorpahavak* might at first appear perplexing. The rescue squads that searched Muslim households in order to find Armenians included women members.[48] Armenian men's entry to harems (women's quarters in Muslim households) was not seen as appropriate even for *vorpahavak* agents who otherwise did not shy away from using force, frequently under the protection of British or French soldiers. Bolsahay women ran the shelters that housed the formerly kidnapped women and children. These elite women were frequently involved in the feminist movement and wrote for *Hay Gin*. A group of them helped found the Armenian Red Cross of Constantinople, which was run mostly by women; the Red Cross was one of the main organizations that took care of pregnant refugees and the sick.[49] The Armenian Women's Association (AWA), which was founded in 1919 with the larger goal of working for women's equality, operated its own shelter for rescued women and was responsible for the management of the orphanage inside the Armenian National Hospital in Yedikule.[50] In addition, Patriarch Zaven himself explicitly called on Armenian feminists to "save their sex's honor." In his talk at the Armenian Women's Association, the patriarch asked Bolsahay women to rehabilitate refugees who had to turn to prostitution, and sponsor workshops so that these "fallen women" received training in various crafts, such as needlework, to be able to earn an honorable income.[51] It was Patriarch Zaven himself who asked Zaruhi Bahri, a feminist, a founding member of the Armenian Red Cross, and regular *Hay Gin* contributor, to manage the neutral house in Şişli, where women and children of ambiguous ethnicity were brought in order to determine whether they were Turkish or Armenian. Zaruhi Kalemkearian, another *Hay Gin* writer and an active member of the Armenian relief machinery, was involved in the day-to-day management of the Armenian Red Cross branch hospital in Şişli. This hospital included a special maternity ward for refugees expecting babies fathered by Muslims (Figure 8).

Figure 8. The Armenian Red Cross Şişli Branch Hospital, which included a special maternity ward for newly rescued women. *Yergamia Deghegakir H. G. Khachi Getr. Varchutyan, 1918 Noy. 18–1920 Teg. 31* (Constantinople: M. Hovagimian, 1921), 6.

Vorpahavak appealed to these feminists for various reasons. First of all, it offered them a chance to partake in the national project as active, public agents and not just home-bound mothers. Moreover, practices associated with the reclamation of the kidnapped only rarely used an explicit language of masculinity. Instead, the discourse employed a vocabulary of protection (*der ganknil*), benevolence, national honor, and revenge. These were goals Armenian feminists could easily relate to. In any case, at this post-genocide moment, when feminists' commitment to the revival of their nation conflicted with their dedication to their sex (as equals of men), they chose Armenianness over womanhood. At the time, they did not verbalize such a conflict but in their memoirs written years after, they signaled resentment, sometimes even regret. The main source of conflict pertained to the issue of abortion and kidnapped women who did not want to be "saved" from Muslim households.

That the Armenian administrative apparatus rendered paternity irrelevant in determining group belonging at first looks like an inclusive, even progressive approach. It certainly worked to the benefit of many raped women who embraced their children regardless of their biological father's background and offenses. However, many women who were pregnant at the time of their rescue did not want to give birth to what they considered to be children of the enemy. Yet, the Armenian authorities, including feminists who were involved in the management of shelter homes and hospitals, denied these women's requests for an abortion. In one case Zaruhi Kalemkearian admitted that they imprisoned a pregnant survivor in the Armenian Red Cross special maternity ward in Şişli because they were afraid that the mother, who had been asking for an abortion for months, would purposefully harm the fetus. Even though this woman gave birth to a healthy boy, she took her own life hours after childbirth.[52] In another case, Kohar Mazlemian related to *Hay Gin* readers the story of a recently liberated woman named Nazeni whom she met at a refugee camp. Nazeni gave birth to a healthy baby but soon, for unknown reasons, the baby died. Mazlemian alarmed readers by mentioning that instead of feeling grief, Nazeni felt relief after the death of her baby, whom she had called a "fetus of suffering."[53] It does not look like Nazeni's feelings were isolated. Dr. Yaghubian, a prominent physician in charge of the Armenian Red Cross Şişli hospital, brought up a similar issue during his talk at the Armenian Women's Association. Yaghubian warned about pregnant survivors who were trying dangerous self-abortive techniques. He encouraged the members of the Armenian Women's Association to train nurses and midwives so that they could prevent abortion and infanticide among survivors who had fallen victim to the "savage race's lust."[54]

Clearly, then, some rescued women's understanding of survival disrupted what the elite and intellectual Bolsahay leadership understood as national revival and reconstitution. The latter's natalist emphasis located resistance and vengeance in life, living, and multiplying. Some of the survivors refused to bear the brunt of this project that asked so much from their already worn-out bodies.[55] Instead, many mothers on whom motherhood was forced (during the war by Turks and after the war by Armenians who claimed to have saved them) must have found "rescue" and perhaps even revenge in refusing to give birth or mother "wrong" children.[56] Such a dissonance created tension not just between the leadership of relief work and the people who were at the receiving end but also between elite feminists who had *not* been deported, orphaned, and kidnapped and refugee women who had experienced misery in all of its forms. V*orpahavak* practices were frequently illiberal in the sense that they prioritized group maintenance over individual freedom and choice.[57] Therefore they were at odds with feminism, which is by definition a liberal ideology that demands equality on the basis of women's humanness, thus their right to decide on their bodies, representation, and governance. Therefore, this conflict is telling in terms of feminism's limits for a postgenocide nation trying to come up with numbers so that it can reclaim normalcy as well as security in the form of a nation-state.

It would be wrong, however, to characterize the relationship between Bolsahay feminists and refugee women as one of pure conflict. At the most basic level, we learn about these women from the feminist press and feminists' memoirs.[58] Refugee women either did not write their memoirs or when they did, they did not tackle the issue of unwanted motherhood and babies.[59] Remarkably, the many men at the highest ranks of the Bolsahay refugee aid mechanism who wrote their memoirs did not mention the existence of reluctant mothers. The mainstream press of the time, which was in general so attuned to the suffering of orphans and rescued women, did not mention survivors who were disenchanted by the promises of the National Revival.

It is only in the pages of *Hay Gin* that one learns about Nazeni, the young woman relieved by the death of her newborn. Moreover, that Kohar Mazlemian did not finish Nazeni's story at that moment alludes to feminism's potential even in fraught national contexts. During the Medz Yeghern, as Mazlemian narrates, Nazeni was thirteen. Kurdish men kidnapped her and soon she was incorporated into the household of Kör (blind) Hüseyin, an infamous perpetrator. Nazeni was raped, abused, and enslaved for years until, after the war, a young Armenian man helped her escape and took her as his wife. They found their way to Bolis where they began living in the Haydar Pasha Refugee Station. Even though Mazlemian clearly grieved over the loss of Nazeni's newborn baby (it is not clear if the father was the Kurdish rapist or the Armenian husband), she also sympathized with the mother. This was because Nazeni's husband beat her every day. Mazlemian warned that even though she had long endured this abuse, considering it as her destiny, if one day Nazeni decided to leave the husband, the camp, and her Armenian honor, and turn to prostitution, no one could blame her. The article ended:

> With pen in my hand, I pause for a moment. At this time, in every developed country feminists are struggling to better women's conditions. The Armenian woman too wants the same thing but she has to submit to sheer force [...]. We are so far away from feminism; we need to wage a long fight if nothing else in order to prevent women being beaten.[60]

It should be noted, however, that even among feminists Mazlemian's was a rare voice of self-criticism. Even though since the 1860s Armenian feminists criticized marriage practices that were unfair to women, in the aftermath of the genocide they saw marriage as a goal in and of itself and did not concern themselves much with what happened after the materialization of the union. Here, too, a class issue came to the fore. Hayganush Mark and other *Hay Gin* writers did continue their criticisms of unequal, traditional marriage, for instance by referring to husbands as masters and wives as slaves. But when the bride was a refugee, orphan, or a formerly kidnapped woman, the aftermath of the wedding union did not matter; these women were saved and with them, the Armenian nation.

The majority of feminists aligned themselves with the general *vorpahavak* ideology that saw the reunification of Armenians as the bulwark of National

Revival. The Armenian Women's Association proudly reported the number of orphans and the previously kidnapped women that they married off to proper Armenian men. *Hay Gin* considered these bridegrooms' acts as benevolent and encouraged other men to do the same. In January 1920, there were 87 women and girls, mostly recently reclaimed from Muslim households, who were being housed in the AWA's building in Pangaltı. They were attending a workshop in Pera every day to learn needlework so that they could earn a living for themselves and attain independence. When, in April 1920, one of these girls was married off to an Armenian man—the second such match—*Hay Gin* proudly announced the news and called on Armenian youth to emulate them: "You, Armenian young men! You, too, should follow these examples and marry these unfortunate girls."[61] In another instance, a carpet dealer from Iran attracted *Hay Gin*'s appreciation for having married a girl from an orphanage in Bolis (see Figure 9).[62] Typically, the association's members prepared the dowry of such brides. During the church ceremony, just so that the bride did not feel desolate on such a beautiful day, the association's members sat on the benches that are traditionally reserved for the bride's relatives. This was indeed an important symbolic gesture: for their "unfortunate sisters," feminists were willing to take up the role of the natal family, the ultimate source of support for a newlywed woman that these brides lost to the Medz Yeghern.

In one of the rare studies on these refugee women, Isabel Kaprielian-Churchill conducted interviews with mail-order brides who were married off to prewar male settlers in North America. She maintains that marriage was the immediate goal of refugee girls and women for reasons ranging from the hope of bringing their surviving family members to the New World "to save them," to a desire to end a life "in transit."[63] In her memoirs, Anayis (Yevpime Avedisian), a member of the Armenian Women's Association, contributor to *Hay Gin*, and volunteer in relief organizations, recounted the first wedding between a rescued young woman and a Bolsahay man. The wedding celebration took place nowhere other than in a neutral house, and it was Patriarch Zaven who presided over the ceremony:

> Only rarely has a wedding been this serious and impressive. When the priest, amidst the fragrance of incense, was blessing the young groom and the bride

in white, we felt as if we recognized the smells of martyrs' souls, who (forgetting their tortures, the suffering of exile, the blood-filled lakes that they had seen, and the whip of the merciless Turkish sergeant) came, in the company of little angels, to witness the wedding of a sweet budding flower who was going to sprout on top of embellished mountains and give beautiful flowers so that the nation/race [*tsegh*] will invincibly continue.[64]

Figure 9. "A Dignified Marriage from the Kalfayan Orphanage." Weddings of orphaned or rescued girls were a source of happiness for the Constantinopolitan Armenian community. Here an Iranian Armenian carpet dealer marries an orphaned girl. *Hay Gin* congratulated the groom for choosing his spouse from an orphanage, an act "that proved to everyone how benevolent he was." *Hay Gin* 4, no. 20 (October 1, 1923).

Remarkably, the bride wore the color of purity despite having been rescued from a Muslim household where she probably served as a wife or concubine. Her dressing in white negated her previous experiences, thus denying, both literally and figuratively, her kidnapper the right to violate an Armenian girl's virginity, and by extension, the capacity to dishonor what she represented: the honor of her nation. This was also a retaliation ceremony that the martyred dead would have watched with satisfaction: the wedding of two Armenians, including one who could have been lost to the Turks forever, meant that Armenianness would continue despite the enemy. That this sweet budding flower was going to sprout atop "embellished mountains" takes us directly to the issue of land. Given that the ultimate territorial symbol of the Armenian historical homeland had long been Mount Ararat, the reference to mountains connected the reclamation of land to the reclamation of people, the two sides of the overall Armenian cause.

Mother Armenia Avenges Her Enemies

In order to further grasp the connections between the goal of establishing a Greater Armenia, orphans, marriage, and vengeance it is important to remember that the Ottoman state had justified the official authorization of the mass deportation of Ottoman Armenians as a temporary wartime measure to prevent Ottoman Armenians' alliance with Russians, and to thwart the danger of an Armenian state being carved out of Ottoman territory, much as the Christian states in the Balkans had been created in the preceding decades. In the aftermath of the war, for Armenian spokespeople a state of their own meant Turkish failure and Armenian victory. In other words, Greater Armenia was the embodiment of revenge.

In May 1918 when Bolsahays heard about the establishment of the Republic of Armenia in Transcaucasia they did not have the chance to collectively and openly celebrate. But in 1919, the Allied occupation made them feel secure enough to pour out into the streets to celebrate the first anniversary of the republic. It is telling that a Protestant clergyman employed the language of revenge to describe the day. Reverend Khachadurian, in his piece called "The Revenge of the Armenian," wrote,

> How big a revenge it is for Armenians to celebrate the anniversary of the Republic of Armenia's independence in Bolis, a city where the plans of annihi-

lating Armenians were hatched and a city that became the center of the realization of that annihilation. For the intolerant enemy, it must be such an intolerable pain to see the Armenian tricolor cover up Armenian buildings and fly in the hands of Armenian children. The joyfulness of Armenians should be an unimaginable grief for all the neighbors [Turks]. If they had lost all Turkey to Europeans, they would not be in as much pain as when they are witnessing the anniversary of the independence of that nation which only yesterday was their slave, something they had decided to annihilate at any cost.[65]

The reference to Armenian children holding the Armenian tricolor takes us back to the opening illustration of this chapter (Figure 3). Most Armenians who penned articles in the press were confident that children celebrating the anniversary out in the streets would soon rejoice at the news of the establishment of an even bigger Armenia. Reverend Khachadurian acknowledged that there were many who aspired to take truly violent revenge, and "to do the exact same thing that the Turk did [to them]," but he assured them that they were mistaken. "The role of the Armenian nation is neither massacring, nor plundering," he noted; and he urged everyone to instead turn their eyes toward an independent Armenia, "a centuries-old dream," so that "it is classified among the civilized nations."[66]

Calls for revanchist reprisal were rare in the press, and although this might be partially explained by censorship, another reason was how Armenian intellectuals imagined their nation and wanted to represent it to the Western world, to those who were going to decide their fate. Even though survivors' diaries (at the time unpublished) mention the need to take aggressive revenge and formulate this as a response to the Turks' violation of the sanctity of their families,[67] and notwithstanding the occasional entries in the press, for example, when men were encouraged to shine their "Armenian swords" to make the "enemy shake in fear,"[68] tropes such as Armenia-as-revenge, reproduction-as-revenge, or rescue-as-revenge were far more common than violent reprisal.[69]

The Armenian delegation to the Paris Peace Conference employed a discourse of dichotomy. Armenians belonged to the peaceful, productive, enlightened, tolerant, and superior Western civilization, while Turks were of dark Asia: ignorant, parasitic, violent, and barbaric. Therefore, Armenians were *like* the West and *unlike* the Turks—yet another reason that Armenians deserved that land, a piece of territory on which they would rule and keep the peace of the Orient.[70] In February 1919, an editorial in the *Arakadz* weekly described the Ottoman (*Trkagan*) government as "a shame for civilization and a curse to humanity."[71] Once Armenians gained their Greater Armenia, they would become "their [the Turks'] teachers and leaders [...] by disseminating the ideas of Western civilization in the depths of Asia." Armenians were capable of doing this, the editorial explained, because they had recently proved how strong they were by surviving the campaigns "to irreversibly annihilate [their nation]." It was clear that Armenia was a nation "bound to live," and everyone wanted to live in this Greater Armenia, whose establishment and repopulation by orphans would constitute revenge.

The press frequently referred to the Republic of Armenia as an infant or newborn. "Infant Armenia" (*manug Hayasdan*) was a precious little thing that was conceived after centuries of Ottoman and Russian rule. As in the orphan rehabilitation efforts, all Armenian energy had to be directed to collectively transforming this infant into the mother—and motherland—for all Armenians, that is, their *Mayr Hayrenik*, literally, "mother fatherland" but also "the main homeland."[72]

In raising this "Infant Armenia," women had special duties that went beyond making babies to populate the land. One such duty was to become a nurse. Girls were encouraged to be trained in nursing so that they could educate refugee women in modern, scientific methods of child care and offer lessons in hygiene, and would be ready to serve as medical personnel in the soon-to-be-established Greater Armenia. Through these efforts, infant, juvenile, and maternal mortality rates would decrease, and birth rates would increase. Both the Armenian Doctors Association and the Armenian Red Cross offered girls courses in nursing.[73] Similarly, the Near East Relief Child Welfare Clinics in Constantinople trained young Armenian women to assist doctors in child welfare clinics.[74] Both *Hay Gin* and *Near East* (NER's journal) proudly reprinted the photo of these newly trained nurses under the caption "The Little Army against Disease" (Figure 10).[75]

These examples demonstrate that it was no coincidence that the girl in the illustration at the opening of this chapter was depicted as a nurse in a Red Cross uniform. She embodied the medically informed future Armenian

Figure 10. "The Little Army Against Disease." Both Armenian medical organizations and Near East Relief trained Armenian girls in nursing in order to meet the ever-increasing need among orphans and refugees. *The New Near East*, September 1922, 12.

woman, who superbly nurtured her own family while caring for all the nation's children as well as the soldiers fighting to provide a secure homeland for Armenians. She was the she-soldier, a member of the "army against disease."

For the Bolsahay elite, children were important also because their bodies and minds would store collective memory. Intellectuals considered remembering to be crucial for the restoration of national unity. The desired future depended on a present consciousness about the recent past. As the main caregivers of future generations, mothers were expected to ensure the transmission of memory, through published volumes and also through their bedtime stories, lullabies, and various other parenting practices. The interaction between the mother and the child was perceived to be a particularly important relationship through which the child would be imbued with national aspirations. In March 1920 Nargiz Kipritjian wrote in *Hay Gin* that "by their sweet voice," mothers were "not going to sing lullabies to their children anymore," but would "put them to sleep with military songs." She went on to advise mothers accordingly:

> At an early age cultivate patriotism deeply in their young hearts, tell them the glorious history of Armenians, explain to them the limitless suffering that Armenians endured, tell them the life of our miraculous and unparalleled heroes such as Antranig, Serop, Murad, and teach them to be brave,

valiant, and ready for self-sacrifice. Mothers! Your children should not go to light candles for the saints. Instead, take them on a pilgrimage to that big temple, that huge cemetery where the relics of our hundreds of thousands of martyrs are dispersed. [...] Our whole hope is in them. They are the ones to reconstruct tomorrow's glorious Armenia on the soil on which our martyrs' bodies molder, on the heap of unburied corpses.[76]

Mothers were also expected to read "educational texts" to their children that included eyewitness testimonies of the genocide. Even during the war, as soon as they understood the systematic nature of deportations and liquidation, Armenians began recording their experiences and collecting personal histories. They consciously collected evidence to bear witness for the future. Though eyewitness testimonies by Armenians and Western observers were first published abroad, immediately after the armistice the Ottoman lands too saw a surge in personal narratives of the war years, along with graphic photographs of the starving and tormented victims and presumably original documentation proving the Ottoman intent to exterminate Armenians.[77] In April 1919, the first ceremony of commemoration was organized in the Ottoman capital. To mark the anniversary of the initial deportation of Armenian leaders from Istanbul on April 24, 1915, Bolsahay intellectuals convened several ceremonies and published a book that included the names and biographies of all the intellectuals, public leaders, and professionals who had been deported that day.[78]

Beyond fulfilling a human need to cope with a recent trauma, these publications and ceremonies served at least two other purposes. First, they were used as propaganda tools to influence Western public opinion by demonstrating the extent to which Armenian survivors were in need of humanitarian aid; to prove that after their limitless suffering, Armenians now deserved a homeland of their own, and that the perpetrators of such monumental war crimes had to be punished immediately.[79] Second, these publications served as pedagogical texts for new generations of Armenians about the national anguish so that they would never put revenge out of their minds. Henry Morgenthau, the US ambassador to the Ottoman Empire from 1913 to 1916, published a memoir of his years in the empire, including his eyewitness account of Armenian massacres and deportations.[80] In 1919, two Armenian translations of the book were already in the bookshops and newsstands of Constantinople.[81] The memoir was commercially advertised in *Hay Gin* as a book that "every [Armenian woman] has to read herself and to her children."[82] Another book, titled *The Whole History of the Massacre of One Million Armenians*, which included official documents and eyewitness testimonies, was advertised in the journal with the following words: "Armenian Women! In order for the fire of national revenge to be forever alive in your and your children's hearts, read this book and recommend it to your aquaintances."[83]

༶

Historical developments unfolded such that Armenians failed to achieve their postwar political goals. A Greater Armenia was never established and the Republic of Armenia became part of the Soviet Union in December 1920. The western part of the historical homeland remained inside Turkey, which the international community recognized with the signing of the Treaty of Lausanne in the summer of 1923. The same treaty declared amnesty for war crimes committed from 1914 to 1923, thus extending immunity to the perpetrators of the Medz Yeghern. The military tribunals that the Ottoman government established right after the war to punish the perpetrators ended up being largely ineffective, not even punishing a fraction of the perpetrator population.[84]

In September 1922, when the Kemalists won their ultimate victory in western Anatolia, Armenians in Constantinople understood the game was over; thousands fled the city in anticipation of retaliatory massacres. Before turning to this wave of exodus, in the next chapter we look at the Bolsahay feminist movement, which reached its heyday, paradoxically, in post-genocide Istanbul.

Figure 11. Hayganush Mark, the leader of Armenian feminism in post-genocide Turkey, depicted as a suffragette holding the banner of the Armenian Women's Association in her right hand and the banner of *Hay Gin* in her left. Dzablvar Darekirk (Istanbul: n.p., 1921), 39.

(CHAPTER 2)

CAN FEMINISTS REVIVE A NATION?

"From the perspective of our National Reconstitution which woman is preferable, the old woman or the new woman?" asked a 1921 issue of *Hay Gin*.[1] The answers published in ten consecutive issues varied, but they agreed on the characteristics of the "old woman": multiple children, domesticity, hard work, and conservative traditionalism. If, Mr. Mikaelian of Izmir argued, "National Revival means physical existence," then Armenians undoubtedly needed the old woman.[2] Mrs. Hripsime Hashashian agreed that for the "numerical superiority of the race" and for the "healthy organization of the family," the old woman was an asset.[3] Even though these ideas might have represented the mainstream approach among the Bolsahay elite, the majority of answers came from people who argued that the new woman was more desirable for the national cause because she was not only a better (meaning, educated) mother but also an active member of the broader public. Zaruhi Bahri noted that the new woman demanded equality and that's why men felt threatened by her. She assured readers that the new woman did not want her rights in order to compete with the man but to complement him. The new woman, Bahri argued, was a feminist not because she aspired to be the superior of men or withdraw from domestic life, but because her equality would make humanity better in all possible ways. All that the new woman wanted was to do what she was capable of doing, both in private and in public.[4] Vartuhi Kalantar, a young *Hay Gin* writer, agreed with Bahri but emphasized that the National Revival included the project of creating "tomorrow's woman," who would in herself synthesize the old and the new. She cautioned that "even the old woman did not only busy herself with her household and dolmas, but she also shared her husband's and father's responsibilities in the field or in the forest." Kalantar concluded: "Revolutions cut out only the deadwood. Those who are good or necessary remain intact."[5]

Perhaps uniquely in its history, feminism among Armenians reached its zenith in the immediate aftermath of the genocide and in the capital of the perpetrator state. A combination of factors engendered this dynamic movement, which was acknowledged even by one of the most antifeminist men of the time as "an undeniable chapter of the revolution that characterized the post-Armistice years."[6] Most significant, the goals related to the National Revival put extraordinary emphasis on women's duties to the nation, not only as reproducers and nurturers, but also as relief workers, financial contributors, and lobbyists. In addition, the Republic of Armenia gave suffrage to women, which in turn emboldened Armenian women in different parts of the world, including those in Allied-occupied Constantinople, to demand representation in the governing bodies of their communities. Last but not least, the existence of one energetic and experienced leader made a difference. Hayganush Mark remained at the forefront of the battle against "women's enslavement" and took it upon herself, along with her comrades in her journal *Hay Gin*, to convince "the nation" that women's emancipation would not detract from but complement its revival.

Working for the National Cause

Since the mid-nineteenth century, elite women of Constantinople had established self-help organizations, such as charitable associations to aid the poor and educational organizations that founded girls' schools and teacher training colleges for women.[7] It was only in the postwar era, however, that women formed an association that did not have a specific goal attached to its name. The Armenian Women's Association (alternatively Armenian Women's League, *Hay Ganants Engeragtsutiun/Liga*, hereafter AWA) was established on June 25, 1919, and continued its work for three or four years. It is not certain when the activities of AWA ended, for its archives did not survive the Kemalists' entry to Istanbul in the autumn of 1922. Our knowledge about the AWA derives from the press and members' memoirs.

Together with Garabed Nurian, a member of the National Assembly, Patriarch Zaven initiated the formation of an Armenian women's organization to "make [Armenian] women's voices heard in the diplomatic world and in the League of Nations."[8] Nurian was one of the three members of the patriarchate's Information Bureau, whose goals included doing propaganda work among the Great Powers in Paris and their representatives in Istanbul. Moreover, Nurian was one of the two directors of the French language daily *The Renaissance*, an organ of the patriarchate that targeted the Allied occupation forces and their families in Istanbul with the goal of cultivating in them a pro-Armenian public opinion.[9] Both the patriarch and Nurian must have thought of putting the energies of well-educated, multilingual, and presentable Armenian women of Bolis to good use. They were certainly aware of the competition for the Allies' attention.

In the Armenian press of the time and in many of the memoirs about the era, Turkish women are blamed for "deceiving" the Allied forces with their so-called Oriental, female allure. While Kohar Mazlemian likened charming Turkish women's deception of naïve Allied officers' to the centuries-long Turkish diplomatic trickery of Western powers,[10] Grigoris Balakian, an influential member of the clergy, argued that when "the Turks" saw that they lacked any other means to recover after their severe losses,

> these fanatical apostles of *jihad* opened the well-fastened gated windows and doors of the harems. To the foreign officers they offered Turkish girls made up with rouge and redolent of perfume, thus winning an easy victory. Turk-haters became Turk-lovers, while judges became advocates. Encouraged by how they were received, the Turkish women perfected their tactics with foreign officers, and the Turks presented their heroines to the latter as the houris of pashas, beys, or noble Turkish families. And so the victors entering the Turkish capital city soon forgot whether they had come to punish or reward.[11]

Even though these orientalist depictions mistake the reasons for the Turkish victory over the Allied forces, they nonetheless conceive of women as actors capable of influencing political outcomes. Indeed, Turkish politicians seem to have really relied on the help of women. For instance, Princess Mevhibe

Celalettin, a niece of Sultan Abdülhamid II, recounted that in the immediate aftermath of the war, when Mustafa Kemal was in the capital and planning his departure to Anatolia, he asked Mevhibe, an attractive, capable woman who knew multiple Western languages, to find a way to get invited to the upcoming charity ball that was certainly going to be attended by many Allied diplomats and their liaisons in the city. Mevhibe Celalettin accomplished the mission successfully, attending the ball and informing Kemal of who attended and what was discussed.[12]

For Armenians, it was surprising to see the superb dancing styles and overall "coquetterie" of Mevhibe and women like her, whom they had previously considered "harem-confined creatures who run away from men."[13] If even Turkish women could be used as political liaisons, the patriarch and Nurian must have thought, Armenian women would certainly make great liaisons and this was exactly the point of the AWA. Its list of goals concluded with the following:

> Taking into consideration the imperative demands of the present day, the *immediate* aim of our association is to defend the Armenian Cause by the voice of the Armenian woman and together with the National Assembly, to assist in the reconstruction of the Mother Fatherland [*Mayr Hayrenik*].[14]

The AWA remained in dialogue with the local YWCA chapter in Constantinople, Near East Relief personnel, and the British, French, and American consulates and high commissions. AWA members managed to frequent diplomatic gatherings, including Fourth of July celebrations, and threw tea parties in honor of influential diplomats such as Admiral Mark Bristol, the United States high commissioner in Turkey.[15] In early 1920, the AWA sent telegrams to the wives of European leaders protesting the Kemalists' massacre of Armenians in Cilicia in February.[16] The organization also sent telegrams to various European prime ministers asking for a solution to Armenia's problems.[17] Other women's organizations in the pre-genocide era involved in philanthropic causes joined the AWA in its propaganda effort. For instance, in 1920, the Armenian Women's Patriotic Association (*Azkanver Hayuhyats Engerutiun*) published a French volume titled *Unpublished Testimonies about the Atrocities Committed by Turks in Armenia, and a Narration of the Epic of Shabin-Karahisar*.[18] Published in Paris, the book was dedicated to the Allied powers so that they would intervene in the fate of the Armenians. A year earlier, Armenian female students of the American College for Girls in Constantinople had organized a special celebration in the school to raise awareness about the situation of Armenians worldwide.[19]

In 1920, the former prime minister of the Armenian Republic visited Constantinople for five days on his tour of diaspora communities to collect financial aid for the Republic of Armenia, whose economy was in dire straits. Armenia needed to borrow money from the diaspora to strengthen its military. The young republic was going through a particularly hard time as half the population, approximately 300,000 refugees from the Ottoman Empire, were starving. Moreover, the harsh winter of 1920 together with a typhus epidemic killed about 20 percent of the population.

Bolsahays received Alexander Khadisian, the former prime minister of the Republic of Armenia, and his campaign for an "independence loan" (*Angakhutyan Pokharutiun*) with warmth and enthusiasm.[20] A newspaper editor began an interview with Khadisian by emphasizing that even uttering the words "[the former] Prime Minister of the Armenian Republic" was the realization of a dream.[21] Zaruhi Bahri wrote in the *Jagadamard* (Battle) daily a piece entitled "The Fatherland Is in Danger," arguing that since Armenian sons outside of Armenia were not conscripted into the Armenian military, they should financially compensate the state. To set an example, she sent 100 golden liras to Armenia on behalf for her two sons, Krikor and Zhirayr.[22]

As the leaders of the women's national movement, the AWA and *Hay Gin* representatives were invited to meet with Khadisian during his 1920 visit. Besides meeting with businessmen, religious leaders, and lawyers, Khadisian devoted some of his limited time to visiting with a group of Armenian women because he announced his belief that women should have a bigger share in his campaign. In his above-mentioned interview with the *Zhoghovurti Tsayne* (Voice of the People) Armenian daily, Khadisian mentioned that women of the Armenian communities in Batum and Tbilisi initiated a "Gold Fund" to which they had contributed their gold coins, rings, watches, necklaces, earrings, bracelets, and other jewelry. Similarly, in a visit to the Armenian National Hospital during which he had a chance to converse with Hayganush Mark, Khadisian encouraged a similar initiative by Bolsahay women.[23] *Hay Gin* led the way by organizing a "Gold Fund" day.[24]

Additionally, an Armenian housemaid, Dikranuhi Der Minassian, met with Khadisian in the Armenian patriarchate to offer her life savings, totaling 50,000 francs, to the campaign. Her donation was earmarked for the construction of a school in Armenia. *Hay Gin* was thrilled with her example. The journal not only published a news piece, entitled "The True Armenian Woman,"[25] in which Mark suggested that Armenia should save a place for this selfless woman so that in her old age she would be taken care of, but it also featured Der Minassian's photo on the cover page with the caption: "She is a woman who is originally from a modest strata but in fact, with her heart, she belongs in the highest. Her example is very inspiring."[26]

Women were encouraged to participate in Khadisian's campaign to "prove that they are competent patriots and that they can make great sacrifices" since "in a faraway land, [their] brothers are fighting to guarantee [Armenian] independence."[27] These words referred to the Turkish-Armenian War along the border separating the two countries. *Hay Gin* and the AWA strongly supported the Armenian forces so that "the rivers of Armenia would not fill up with the blood of the innocent once again."[28] Indeed, Armenian women's associations, both in Constantinople and in other cities such as Cairo, Varna, and Batum, frequently sent money to Armenian soldiers and occasionally collected gifts from Armenian schools as well for Armenian soldiers at Christmas.[29]

After his departure from Istanbul in September 1920, Khadisian wrote a personal thank you note to the AWA in which he recognized the association's role in organizing a "Gold Fund." This handwritten letter was published on the cover page of *Hay Gin*, in place of the usual editorial. *Hay Gin* is silent after this point with regard to whether the "Gold Fund" day actually came to pass or not. The project was probably aborted because of dramatic political developments in Armenia.

On September 20, 1920, Turkish commander Kâzım Karabekir, one of the leading figures in the Turkish National Struggle or Turkish War of Independence (*Türk Kurtuluş Savaşı*) headed by Mustafa Kemal, invaded Armenia. The main impulse for this attack was to overturn the Treaty of Sèvres, signed on August 10, 1920, between the representatives of the Sublime Porte and the Allies, which awarded expansive Ottoman territory to Armenia, Greece, and potentially to Kurdistan, lands that these countries claimed to be their historical homeland. The war between Armenia and Turkey that began in September

1920 ended with an Armenian defeat in less than three months. On December 2, 1920, Kâzım Karabekir, the representative of the Turkish Grand National Assembly in Ankara, and Alexander Khadisian, the representative of Armenia, signed the Treaty of Alexandropol, which not only annulled the Treaty of Sèvres but also transferred almost half of Armenian territory to Turkey.

Meanwhile the Red Army had already advanced into Yerevan and negotiations were going on between Russian and Armenian political leaders. With the hope of negating the Treaty of Alexandropol, Prime Minister Simon Vratsian agreed to hand Armenia to the Soviet revolutionary committee a few hours before the signature of the treaty. On December 2, 1920, Armenia was formally declared a "Socialist Soviet Republic." The Soviets also demanded that Armenians give up any claims to the Greater Armenia of the Sèvres Treaty, whose borders had been drawn by US president Woodrow Wilson and was commonly referred to as "Wilsonian Armenia" (see Figure 2) (Wilson delivered his arbitral award on November 22, 1920.) The territory of Soviet Armenia was less than half of the independent republic.[30]

Hay Gin passed over these significant developments in silence, as if nothing had changed in Armenia. The discourse of help to Armenian soldiers metamorphosed into calls for humanitarian aid to Soviet Armenia, a country that was struggling with existential threats such as starvation. Moreover, the Armenia delegation continued its work in European capitals, seeking a piece of Anatolia as an independent or autonomous Armenian territory.

One year after Khadisian's visit, another messenger from the Caucasus came to Bolis with a similar plea. The famous poet Hovhannes Tumanian, head of the Armenian Aid Society (*Hay Oknutyan Miutiun*), embarked on a tour of Armenian diaspora communities to collect financial aid for Soviet Armenia.[31] Like Khadisian, in a meeting with Armenian women, Tumanian did not forget to emphasize women's unique role in the national survival and revival by saying that "[women's] capacity to safeguard the nation's values is more effective than military power."[32] Together with Anayis, Tumanian visited the *Hay Gin* office, which was in Mark's apartment. After revealing that he was a "true believer in feminism" and in the potential of Armenian women, he encouraged Mark to continue the publication of her journal for decades to come.[33] Like Khadisian, Tumanian believed that including Armenian women in the national struggle was crucial. *Hay Gin* shared this view wholeheartedly.

Hayganush Mark and Her *Hay Gin*

As mentioned on the cover page of its November 1919 inaugural issue, one of the goals of *Hay Gin* was to report on the AWA's activities.[34] The same issue also included the goals, plans, bylaws, and membership roster of the AWA, as well as pictures of some of its members (Figure 12). The involvement of the patriarchate was not mentioned, though the document detailing AWA-related information had the patriarch's stamp on it.[35] Anayis noted in her memoirs that *Hay Gin* was the official publication of the AWA.[36] Mark did not mention the connections between *Hay Gin* and the AWA in her autobiography published in 1954 in Istanbul. AWA's involvement with the Greater Armenia cause and its good relationship with the occupation forces formed part of a past that did not fit with post-1923 Turkish Armenians' purposes. A language of "pure" feminism independent from politics proper was more acceptable. Both in *Hay Gin* and later in her autobiography, Mark insisted that the journal remained "independent" during its thirteen years of publication. To the many organizations and political parties that wanted to co-opt *Hay Gin*, she would always respond that if there were one single banner under which *Hay Gin* could live, it was exclusively "the banner of womanhood" (*gnochagan trosh*).[37] AWA did carry the banner of womanhood, and the broader public saw organic links between the association and the journal, with Mark as a leading force behind both.

In 1921, around the same time that *Sargavakin Daretsuytse* published the image of the little soldier and the Red Cross nurse (Figure 3) that opened the preceding chapter, Yervant Odian, the most prominent Armenian satirist of the time, published a caricature of Mark in his almanac (Figure 11).[38] The drawing represented her in the garb of a French or British suffragette, holding the AWA banner in her right hand and the flag of *Hay Gin* in her left.

The image paid tribute to Mark's leadership position, but failed to point to a crucial aspect of her feminism, that it was "Armenian." With her outfit, overemphasized hat and neck coverage, and because of a lack of any Armenian references (except for the letters on the flags), Mark looked like a mere imitator of Western feminists. Because she did admire Western feminism and carried herself as a Western (yet Armenian) woman, she might not have necessarily seen this image as derogatory. Still, as the title of her journal suggests, Armenianness was an indispensable part of her feminist politics and her life.

Figure 12. Members of the Armenian Women's Association who were also writers for *Hay Gin*. Included are four of Mark's close friends and colleagues: *clockwise second from top right*, Arshaguhi Teotig; *seventh*, Zaruhi Kalemkearian; *eighth*, Anayis; *center right*, Zaruhi Bahri. *Center left* is Mari Stambulian, the vice president of the Armenian Red Cross in Constantinople. *Hay Gin* 1, no. 1 (November 1, 1919).

She was born Hayganush Topuzian in 1882 to a family of modest means. Although she herself was illiterate, her mother insisted that her only child receive a well-rounded education and that is why Hayganush tried three different institutions until she settled down at the Esayan Armenian School. She would later note gratefully that she took "feminism's first liberating steps" thanks to this hard-working woman who "did not know even the 'a' of the alphabet."[39] After high school, Hayganush began working as a teacher in Armenian schools and publishing literary pieces in periodicals. In 1905, she became engaged to Vahan Toshigian, a young and promising journalist. No less energetic, Mark began volunteering in various philanthropic, charitable, and educational institutions. Soon after their engagement, the couple began publishing a periodical, *Dzaghig* (Flower), as a women's journal. By this time the Armenian public had already warmed to the idea of women's press and activism. Since the publication of *Guitar* in 1862, Armenian feminists had used the press, novels, poetry, and philanthropic associations to pursue an activism both for the national(ist) project (whatever it might be) and for women's liberation.[40]

At the age of twenty, when Mark began publishing *Dzaghig*, she was already a passionate feminist (*gragod feminist*), keenly following the news of "English suffragettes' strong demands."[41] Impressed by Marguerite Durand's *La Fronde*, the French feminist daily run exclusively by and for women, she aspired to employ only women contributors to her journal.[42] But because there were not enough women, she allowed men to write in the journal on the condition that they used women's pseudonyms.[43] As for herself, like some of the European feminists she followed, she used neither a nickname nor a male's last name and in that she was a first among Armenian women writers. Still, though, she found a way to respect Armenian tradition, something that she did all her life, twisting that tradition without rejecting her heritage. She kept her first name and acquired a shorter version of her father's name, Markar, for a last name, Mark (see Figure 13). Most radically, she kept this name even after marriage.[44] This practice summarized the core principle of her feminism, that women were not derivatives of others but individuals in their own right. *Dzaghig* folded when the couple left for Smyrna to publish other papers.

It was only in 1919 and under the unprecedented conditions associated with the Ottoman defeat and the Allied occupation that Mark began publishing *Hay Gin*. The apparent need for women's involvement in the national agenda empowered Mark to begin a journal that urged women to partake in the National Revival *and* work for the women's cause (*gnoch tade*). Although she founded and edited *Hay Gin*, its initial finances came from Toshigian's income from his editorial responsibilities at the Armenian daily *Verchin Lur* (Latest News).

Mark's definition of feminism was a direct but unacknowledged translation from the famous French feminist Odette Laguerre's booklet published in 1905: "a thrust of justice that tends to equalize the rights and duties of man

Figure 13. Hayganush Mark in 1910. *Hayganush Mark, Gyankn U Kordze* (Istanbul: n.p., 1954), 417.

and woman. It is not only a thrust of justice but it is also a thrust of liberty that marks the end of man's reign."[45] Mark explicitly noted that her understanding of the women's cause was shaped by a variety of Western thinkers who were liberal or socialist feminists, such as Laguerre, John Stuart Mill, August Bebel, Marguerite Durand, and Leopold Lacour.[46] The "women's world" and feminism occupied *Hay Gin* continuously and in multiple ways. At the same time that the journal was publishing news about the Medz Yeghern's orphans, women and children sequestered in Muslim harems, and was trying to mobilize the masses to support Greater Armenia, it was reporting news of international conferences on women's rights, providing the history and definition of feminism in different cultures at various historical periods, profiling the lives of famous feminists worldwide, serializing the works of Western feminists, such as the Italian Gina Lombroso and the German Lily Braun, and debating controversial feminist demands such as women's right to paid employment, even prenuptial sexual freedom for both sexes.

Though Mark was the most vocal feminist, many other contributors to *Hay Gin*, such as Nevrig Sebuhian, Kohar Mazlemian, and Zaruhi Bahri, also self-identified as feminists. The many *Hay Gin* writers who signed opinion pieces directing attention to particular forms of discrimination against women or arguing for the expansion of women's spheres of activity represented a variety of viewpoints but they all came from a similar milieu.[47] They were middle- and upper-class, urban, well-educated women mostly from Bolis but also from all around the world who frequently worked as teachers, journalists, novelists, and translators. In one way or another, they all represented the "new woman" who had occupied the thoughts of the Armenian public since the late nineteenth century and sat at the very center of *Hay Gin*'s masthead (Figure 14).[48]

The image was created by Sarkis Khachadurian, the well-known artist, who was a friend of the AWA.[49] The two figures in the outer corners of the frame represent the "old woman" contrasted with the "new woman" in the center. Mark noted that the women in traditional dress were "shy Armenian peasants" while those in the center were "modern Armenian women interested in literature and fine arts," as indicated by the paper they read and the piano in the background.[50] Remarkably, nothing looked Armenian about the new women, whose faux Greco-Roman clothing and blonde hair made them modern in a very European way. But Armenian symbols engulfed

Figure 14. Cover page of *Hay Gin*, December 1, 1931. The women in the center symbolize the "new Armenian woman" while those in the two upper corners represent the "old Armenian woman." Armenian National Library, Yerevan.

them. While the frame is full of Armenian-looking emblems, the letters spelling out *Hay Gin*, Armenian Woman, are stylized in the "bird" calligraphy of medieval Armenian manuscripts, a novelty at the time. Moreover, the new women are in the same frame with the old. Indeed, it was *Hay Gin*'s claim from the first issue on that the "ideal woman" was a mixture of the new and the old, that the feminist demand for more rights did not translate into a rejection of traditionalism and domestic (therefore patriotic) motherhood.

Hay Gin's first editorial, on November 1, 1919, titled "Our Road," began by affirming that despite its tragedy, the war had given birth to some "rare benefits" and went on:[51]

> During those four hellish years, we, especially Armenian women, have demonstrated that beyond housework and child care we can bear with all sorts of hardships. We can also be trusted with jobs and markets; and we have proven to those who have spoken against our cause that it is best that they keep their mouths shut.
>
> If we consider what we have accomplished during the Great War, how we stepped in for our husbands, brothers, children, and what we also have achieved after the war, how we embraced our orphans, how we shed tears as they cried, and how we took our duties seriously, our fate is bound to change. [...]
>
> We will assume our duties, create our rights, and shape our roles. Our feminist instincts will not hinder our homemaking chores. Rather, *the rebirth of our sex will take us to the summit of our nation and to the summit of our fatherland*.[52]

Here, as well as in most of her other feminist writing in the years to come, Mark presented women's ability to perform public functions as the ultimate proof of their capability to be and do *more* than what society had hitherto thought they could. Their dual potential rendered women deserving of more rights. Mark always remained cautious not to downplay the social and psychological importance of the domestic and the maternal. She did not want masculine women; she emphasized countless times that nothing would be gained from making women into men. If anything, Mark thought, men would have to be more like women, not in a queer sense, but in the sense of being more homebound, paternal, and caring. Aware of how feminists had been stereotyped in the Armenian community and beyond, Mark consciously tried to neutralize feminism's challenge to conventional womanhood and to the Armenian cause. She subverted stereotypes by arguing not only that feminists made better mothers and cooks, but that unlike and in addition to conventional housewives, they worked for their nation in multiple capacities. This is why the editorial ended by cementing the National Revival to the "rebirth of our sex." That rebirth, feminists argued, could only be realized when and if women *too* acquired their much-deserved political rights.

Working for the Women's Cause

Mark penned her first editorial for political equality in the fourth issue of *Hay Gin*. The piece, "Women in the National Assembly," began by congratulating Dr. Armenag Parseghian, a member of the National Assembly, for his support of "women's social rights." Mark reported that Parseghian had recently submitted a written proposal to the assembly stating that it was time that "women's voices be heard in the National Assembly."[53] Mark specially emphasized that the independent Republic of Armenia included three female MPs in its National Parliament and that all political parties, both in Bolis and abroad, agreed that "women too should have their voices in the fatherland's legislation and political governance."[54] She did not mention it but Dr. Parseghian was a member of the Armenian Revolutionary Federation (ARF, *Tashnagtsutiun*), the party in power in Armenia.[55] Moreover, Parseghian was one of the four Bolsahay men who had gone to Paris (in January 1919) to support the Armenian National Delegation's claims at the peace conference.[56] One of the most prominent strategies of the delegation was to represent Armenia as a European, Christian, and civilized nation that had long suffered under the Ottoman yoke. One proof that the delegation presented to this end was Armenian women's advanced level of "progress," which stood in stark contrast to their backward, segregated, idle, Oriental counterparts behind veils.

The timing of Parseghian's proposal, in the first half of December 1919, might also point toward instrumentalism. It was on December 1, 1919, that the first woman was elected to the British House of Commons. Lady Nancy Astor's election made news in the Armenian newspapers. *Hay Gin* evangelized about the news with a lengthy article devoted to Lady Astor's life and activities, and the piece was published in the pages immediately following

Mark's editorial on Parseghian's proposal. Women's presence in the National Assembly, however minimal, boosted the claim of the Armenian delegation in Paris that Armenia was *like* the West and *unlike* the East.

Mark used this mindset to add urgency to Parseghian's proposal. She was aware that many would find such a move untimely because the nation was busy with much more pressing problems such as orphans, refuges, and territorial expansion. She explicitly rejected such arguments, and insisted that there was no point in postponing women's rights. To add weight to her words, she pointed to the Turks: "On this occasion, too, our [Turkish] neighbors are acting earlier than us and taking useful steps. The ten votes that Ms. Halide Edib has recently gained illustrate this point, don't they?"[57] Here, she referred to Halide Edib (Adıvar), a Turkish novelist and a feminist who, even though she had not run for office, received votes in the 1919 election because of her acclaimed and lengthy support of the Turkish nationalist cause, including volunteering during the Turkish War of Independence.[58] Turkish women would not gain political rights until 1930, but the case of Halide Edib worked for Mark's purposes in putting Armenians and Turks into competition on the subject of women's political participation.

The National Assembly did not accept Parseghian's proposal. Given that the patriarchate's archives are closed, it is difficult to guess if the issue was discussed and if so, how. Mark neither reported this nor expanded on the reasons for the decision. *Hay Gin* simply continued to support the Armenian cause as well as publish pro-suffrage opinion pieces penned by men and women, Armenians and non-Armenians alike.

In 1921, disturbed by the frequent injustices that she witnessed in Armenian courtrooms, Mark began criticizing the Judicial Commission of the National Assembly, a group of Armenian attorneys and judges responsible for civic matters such as marriage, divorce, and custody. Mark's disapproval of the Judicial Commission was based on three points. First, the commission was composed exclusively of males; second, clergy were interfering with the functioning of the commission, which should have been completely civilian; and third, judges' decisions were based on old laws, which they often misinterpreted against the interests of women. In her protest, Mark criticized divorce cases in which cheated or abused women were not given the right to divorce. Moreover, she wrote, "many such unfortunate women are asking for our help and it is one of our greatest responsibilities to be the translators of their stories and sincere protests."[59] This is another telling example of how the interest of the nation and the interest of its women conflicted. National Revival and its conservationist aspects demanded that Armenian families remain intact and multiply, while for some Armenian women this meant continuing a life of humiliation or even abuse.

Though *Hay Gin* did not elaborate on the social problems of "unfortunate women," in her autobiography Mark described in detail a visit to her home by a battered young woman and her mother. They requested help in obtaining a divorce.[60] Mark intervened immediately and instructed the young woman to get a medical report from a doctor. Subsequently, Mark wrote a letter on behalf of the young woman requesting a divorce from the patriarchate, and appended it to the medical report. The woman, thanks to Mark's intervention, was subsequently granted a divorce. After this incident became known in the community, many women appealed to *Hay Gin* for similar favors, which led Mark to further question the all-male composition of the Judicial Commission.[61] In April 1921, she wrote in *Hay Gin*, "Women have to intervene in this situation. Women have to have a representative in the Judicial Commission who would prevent unfair decisions against their sex."[62] In other words, women had to have a say in the making and application of the laws to which they were subject. As an ardent follower of French feminism and its history, Mark was familiar with the life and activism of Olympe de Gouges, and certainly knew her famous phrase, which would become the motto of nineteenth-century French feminism: "Woman has the right to mount the scaffold; she ought equally to have the right to mount to the tribute."[63]

The Judicial Commission rejected the inclusion of women as members. They based their decision on the fact that there was no woman with a law degree, a precondition for membership.[64] This logic and the rejection energized Mark, who now seemed to be more committed than ever to fighting back. She had developed new feminist strategies and sharpened the ones that she had been using. The tactic that came easiest to her was exposing the contradictions in how "the nation" related to its women. Her insistence on exposing double standards went hand in hand with her logic of reciprocity, that is, if something was expected of women and they delivered it, they ought to receive something in return, such as their citizenship rights. Mark most clearly formulated this claim when the newly elected National Assembly in 1921 did not reserve any seats for women. With reference to the phrasing of the National Constitution and bringing in the example that the patriarchate *did* collect taxes from *all* Armenians, she wrote in June 1921:

> It is an unbearable injustice that they consider us capable adults [*chapahas*] and extract taxes from us, but they find us incapable minors [*anchapahas*] and deny our national rights. The irrefutable rules of logic have to correct us: are we adults and "national individuals" or minors who are not national individuals [citizens]? If we are national individuals, we would happily continue our national duty [and pay taxes] but we also demand our rights. However, if we are minors, thus deprived of rights, please also cancel our [national] dues. Doing otherwise would be a double standard and make the law unlawful.[65]

Here Mark was referring to the new Fatherland Tax, which applied to both sexes. For women who did not have the right to vote and be elected to the assembly it seemed like a contradiction that they were expected to pay taxes. Mark even questioned if the National Constitution really endorsed women's exclusion from politics. The constitution stated that "all nationals above twenty-one who pay the national tax" were eligible candidates for the National Assembly and its various commissions.[66] The Armenian language is gender-neutral; the term "national" refers to both sexes. Mark would use this neutrality to its greatest extent in her advocacy of women's equality and discussed it even in her autobiography. Denying women political rights deprived them of their status as "national individuals" (*azkayin anhad*), and therefore their membership in the nation.

Mark tried to make sense of why men would reject women's political participation despite the *obvious* fact that many women fulfilled the two basic requirements of age and tax-paying status. She explained this as an expression of male fear: men saw political participation as a zero-sum game. Men of power felt they had to selfishly hold on to that power because women's gain would mean their loss of authority and masculinity. Throughout the thirteen years of its existence, *Hay Gin* battled against this assumption in multiple ways. Antifeminist Armenians' most common arguments relied on Rousseauian themes: that women's meddling in men's spheres (of employment and politics) would make them inattentive mothers and wives with questionable morality, and therefore individuals who were detrimental to the post-catastrophe nation in desperate need of mothers. The reporting of the New York–based Armenian newspaper *Gochnag* (Rattle) on the granting of suffrage to American women is telling in this regard. According to *Hay Gin*, *Gochnag* was terrified over this development because, according to its reporter, public duties could lead women into forgetting their domestic responsibilities. This, the unnamed reporter claimed, constituted even a bigger problem for Armenians for whom "the basis of national reconstitution has to be the reconstitution of the home." The paper did underline that it appreciated Armenian women's *azkanver* (patriotic) work but that for women "raising men for the nation should always be a bigger responsibility than assuming a public role." Moreover, should Armenian women devote themselves to the outer world, they should never overlook their familial and maternal responsibilities. Otherwise, the reporter added, "they would have committed a sin against their nation." Mark reported this essay in *Hay Gin* only to point out how strongly feminists disagreed with *Gochnag*. Feminists were very happy about American women's victory and accepted no arguments against the principle of equality between the sexes, even when the group in question was the Armenian nation.[67]

In another instance, Yenovk Armen used even sharper language, accusing "shortsighted feminists" of "killing the most sacred feeling, that is, Motherhood." In a *Hay Gin* essay, he asked, "Can a mother who devotes her mind to the wretched calculations of the market carry the same generous feelings of a true mother who is devoted only to her child?" He continued, castigating female doctors for caring for other people's sick children instead of breastfeeding their own infants, and accusing (hypothetically Armenian) female lawyers of frequenting dirty courtrooms and arguing aggressively in their clients' defense instead of attending to their families' needs.[68] Mark let Armen pen such words in her journal because she wanted to expose this common thinking and provide a platform where feminists could rebut such arguments. It is probably not a coincidence that in the next issue after Armen's comments, she allowed a man, Kegham Krikorian, to defend women's rights:

> Feminism is a doctrine that seeks to elevate women's *consciousness of their individuality* through a healthy education in ethics—it is not an *enemy of*

their sex's appeal, which is love and family. However, it does not approve of marriages without love and enjoyment. Also, instead of a *forced familial regulation*, it sees motherhood as a sweet responsibility and sacrifice. Therefore, feminism wants women to be in marriages conscientiously and embrace their rights, not by force or unconscientiously. We repeat: feminism is not a plan to debase men, but a demand to elevate existing social customs. Therefore, it needs to continue at least until men understand that women are their friends, with the same *rights* and with the same *responsibilities*, especially with the same *dignity*.[69]

Along the same lines, Mark ended one of her editorials devoted to women's suffrage with a sarcastic trope: "Based on our experience in our journal, we declare with complete confidence that the writer who handles feminism the most is the one who makes the best desserts."[70] This person was most probably Anayis, who would proudly note in her memoir that "[Armenian] bourgeois men and men of Asian/Eastern mentality" ridiculed the AWA's demands for political rights but their scorn was unsuccessful in intimidating the association's members.[71] *Hay Gin*'s simultaneous coverage of feminist issues alongside articles about orphans and adult survivors, as well as advice columns on food, cooking, child rearing, and homemaking must have been meant to signal the compatibility of feminism with National Revival, domesticity, preservation of Armenianness, and tradition.

There was some productive tension, if not inconsistency, however, in how Mark conceived the right to vote. She sometimes argued that it was an inalienable right that must be given automatically to women on the basis that they "compose half of humanity" and pay taxes. At other times, probably when she felt the need to make a bigger impact, she emphasized the performance aspect of the rights-responsibilities equation: women accomplished their national and motherly duties, *therefore* they had to be given the vote; or if women were given the vote, they would *not* stop performing their womanly responsibilities. This was the case when *Hay Gin* presented examples of women who functioned perfectly well in both public and private spheres. One such example was Harriet Beecher Stowe, who was profiled in *Hay Gin* in 1921 as an inspiring woman who raised her seven children herself while being politically active and writing *Uncle Tom's Cabin*.[72] When the Judicial

Commission denied women membership, she protested by highlighting the existence of many Armenian Beecher Stowes, deserving yet wronged.

Instead of writing an editorial for the June 1, 1921, issue, Mark published a photograph on the front page of *Hay Gin* of a woman surrounded by children (Figure 15). This was the late Takuhi Tavit Kalantar and her students. The note highlighted that she was an "honorable Armenian woman, mother and educator whose exemplary personality and true life as a woman deserve our admiration and respect."[73] The photo spoke volumes about women's national worth and political rights. Takuhi Kalantar sits among children of both sexes, who are described as her "harvest." She has a proud but modest expression on her face. It is obvious that she has spent a great deal of time and energy in the classroom. She is a well-educated woman herself, considering the number of books on her desk. Her work never ends—an open book or notebook is in front of her and there is a pen ready to be used by her experienced hands.

Figure 15. "The Late Takuhi Tavit Kalantar and Her Harvest of Students." *Hay Gin* presented mothers with patriotic careers as proof that Armenian women deserved equal rights. *Hay Gin* 2, no. 15 (June 1, 1921), cover page.

Although she sits still and looks at the camera, the composition of the desk, the books, and the pen radiates action; she is a busy and devoted woman. The children are dressed moderately well, appear well fed and confident; they are the future of Armenia. As the only adult in the picture, Kalantar receives full credit for educating these children in a number of scientific and literary subjects and instilling in them proper Armenianness.

Accompanying the photograph, this issue of *Hay Gin* featured an obituary by Zaruhi Bahri, a friend of Takuhi Kalantar. They had met during World War I when their families moved to Kınalıada, an island physically close to but politically distant from Constantinople.[74] After graduating from the Mezburian Armenian School in Istanbul, "following the dearest tradition of sharing one's [intellectual] belongings with her illiterate sisters," Takuhi Manisalian left for Trabzon as the appointed principal of the city's (Armenian) National School. There, she met her future husband, Tavit Kalantar, another intellectual and educator. A few years later, they opened their own educational institution, the Kalantarian School, in Bursa, which became the first co-ed Armenian school in the Ottoman Empire. Additionally, before the war, Takuhi Kalantar was president of Bursa's Armenian Red Cross and Cilician Society. All along, she wrote articles about education and women for *Piuzantion* (Byzantium), one of the most widely read Armenian newspapers of the time.

If half of Bahri's article was devoted to the public persona of Kalantar, the other half praised her role as mother and wife. As Takuhi Kalantar herself had written in *Hay Gin* a few issues earlier, she and her husband had a very harmonious and intellectually nurturing marriage.[75] They experienced together the great loss of their son in the early 1910s, when they relocated to Constantinople. Together with their daughter, Vartuhi Kalantar, they were imprisoned in 1915. The Ottoman authorities interpreted Vartuhi's 1912–1913 letters to her parents from Lausanne, where she was attending university, as Armenian revolutionary nationalist commentary.[76] Although the mother was released after three months, the father and daughter remained imprisoned for two and a half years. After her release, Vartuhi Kalantar serialized her prison memoirs in *Hay Gin*, under the title "The Women's Section of the Central Prison."[77] Takuhi Kalantar's health deteriorated when she carried food and clothing to her family in prison. She died in the summer of 1921 before completing her work. Both the mother and daughter had been members of the Armenian Women's Association.

Mark, Bahri, and probably many other feminist contributors to *Hay Gin* believed that Takuhi Kalantar was the ideal representation of an Armenian woman who deserved full national citizenship but died without recognition of her rights. She not only worked for her fellow (male and female) nationals all her life, but was a devoted mother, companionable wife, and good homemaker. As her daughter wrote in *Hay Gin* a couple of months after her death, Takuhi Kalantar's life was "the story of a woman with a multitude of interests and talents, a woman who rushed from the classroom to the kitchen, from the salon to the workshop, from the bedside of her sick child to the orphanage, easily and beautifully."[78]

It was infinitely harder to come up with a convincing argument against women's representation in the National Assembly's Education Commission, and Mark made this point multiple times. Not only were there plenty of female teachers and school principals, some with their own textbooks and institutions, but also many (male) members of the Education Commission themselves had been trained by those devoted, female teachers. By denying "capable women" the ability to be useful to their nation in their full capacity, members of the Education Commission were effectively committing treason and betraying the nation. But Mark was cautious not be seen as aggressive because this would defeat the whole purpose of domesticating feminism, or portraying it as nonthreatening. After noting that men individually supported feminism but were collectively against women's political rights, she assured the reader that, sooner or later, women would get the vote. Until then, *Hay Gin* would choose not to wage war. Especially now that "the nation needed unity more than ever before," feminists would not "engage in internal polemics since [as women] their role, at every time and in every place, is to serve unity and peace."[79] Even in making this seemingly submissive retraction, Mark was bolstering another fundamental aspect of her suffrage argument: because women were by nature more peaceful, they had to contribute to the whole of humanity. Even though antimilitarism did not frequently surface in *Hay Gin*'s campaign for political rights—perhaps because *Hay Gin* cheered for the military of Armenia in its resistance against Turkish Kemalist forces—qualities that came with motherhood, such as giving life, nurturing, and caring, were presented as better alternatives to the contemporary logic of war, death, and destruction.[80]

In October 1925, the Education Commission finally decided that the time had come to appoint two female members. Mark was one of the two women selected. The choice is remarkable because even though Mark had experience in teaching at Armenian schools (she received her diploma in 1898) and inspecting schools for Armenian language instruction, her public persona was built on her career in journalism, not education.[81] Mark's history of advocacy of women's rights must have convinced the National Assembly members that she deserved priority. Yet, the news did not fully satisfy her. In reporting the commission's decision in *Hay Gin*, Mark did not fail to add that women had to be represented on all commissions, especially the Judicial Commission.[82] The second woman who was offered membership on the Education Commission was Sibil (Zabel Asadur), an accomplished teacher, poet, playwright, and writer of Armenian language textbooks, and also one of Mark's high school teachers.[83]

Neither Mark nor Sibil served on the Education Commission because it soon became apparent that they had been asked to become "auxiliary members." Mark found it insulting and refused to participate. But it is important to understand that Mark was not categorically against women serving in the role of assistant. Only a few weeks before the Education Commission's offer, she herself had advocated such an initiative. A tour of the Armenian Surp Prgich National Hospital led Mark to advocate a women's auxiliary committee to improve conditions in the hospital. She contended that the hospital failed to meet hygienic requirements because it lacked "women's hands" to organize its various sections.[84] She asked the National Assembly to intervene. In contrast to some of her previous campaigns, Mark's appeal this time was neither radical nor political. Moreover, there was a history of women's auxiliary involvement in the hospital. No doubt, these factors mitigated the resistance of the National Assembly. It was not long before a women's auxiliary body to the hospital was formed. This shows that when Mark's demands were considered reasonable or within women's traditional spheres, they were heeded. Mark welcomed the positive resolution of this concern in another article, and concluded by putting the onus on women to deliver the service.[85] A group of women immediately volunteered, and *Hay Gin* congratulated them for improvements in the hospital's cleanliness and orderliness. There was also praise for the National Assembly and the patriarchal vicar who facilitated the women's group.[86]

Significantly, however, Mark herself did not take part in this group, a fact that indicates a fundamental paradox in her feminism—the place of domesticity—and is also part of the reason she did not accept the Education Commission's offer to become an auxiliary member. We will return to the unresolved question of domesticity in Mark's feminism in Chapter 5. Suffice it here to note that she simultaneously elevated and demeaned housework and domesticity. In terms of charity, even though Mark appreciated women's involvement in providing for the needy and organizing for the vulnerable, at the same time she denigrated that kind of labor, arguing that it did not require any training or intelligence because any man or woman "with an average brain" could do it. But there were also "competent women" (like herself) who had much more to offer to the nation and to the world, and it was a pity to see these women's energy confined to soup kitchens and charity balls. It is telling that before leaving the Education Commission's meeting in which she informed them that she could not be simply an *auxiliary* member she shamed the men at the meeting with the following words: "Gentlemen! If, by any chance Sibil had accepted the invitation and had honored this meeting with her presence at this moment, who among you would dare to occupy the seat of the presidency *only because he is a man?*"[87]

⁓

In trying to understand the history of Turkish Armenian feminism, especially its failures, it is imperative that we take the relationship of domination into account. The Turkish government had the power to decide on Armenians' fate but Armenians as a group did not have such power over Turks. This imbalanced power relationship had consequences for Armenian women in general and for Armenian feminists more specifically. This power dynamic prevents easy conclusions about the history of Armenian feminism in which antifeminist men refused to share power with their women. This certainly was true to an extent. Many Armenian men supported *Hay Gin* when its agenda paralleled the goals of the national project but remained silent or hesitant when it came to the question of women's emancipation.

Nonetheless, the failure of Armenian feminism in ensuring women's representation in the governing bodies of the nation cannot simply be explained by conservative men's resistance to progressive feminism.[88] Ultimately, the tragedy of Armenian feminism in Bolis was that the target of its demands gradually waned due to the Turkish state's interference. In 1923, the Kemalist government signed the Treaty of Lausanne with the Allies, transforming Armenians, along with other non-Muslims who remained in Turkey, into officially recognized "minorities." The treaty guaranteed that minorities would continue to exercise their traditional rights over their educational and charitable institutions and continue to use their religious and customary laws in regard to personal status law. These clauses ended up conflicting with the new state's nationalization, standardization, and secularization goals; Turkey breached most of the treaty's articles pertaining to "minority protection." In 1924 the Law for the Unification of Education disestablished the Ottoman educational system and brought all educational institutions, including minority schools, under the control of the Ministry of Education. Therefore, the Armenian patriarchate's Education Commission, which until then regulated the Armenian schools inside Turkish borders, lost its raison d'être and a few years later ceased to exist. In 1926 the government passed the new Turkish Civil Code, which was secular in nature. It replaced religious courts and sharia-based family law. Under pressure from the state, the spiritual heads of each minority community surrendered their Lausanne Treaty granted right to pursue their canonical law in personal matters; after 1926, like all other Turkish citizens, minorities too became subject to the Turkish Civil Code. Therefore, the Armenian patriarchate's Judicial Commission soon lost its relevance and ceased to exist.[89]

As the larger political context shifted above them, feminists had to refashion their political standpoint, discourse, and demands. Many of them left the country in panic in the fall of 1922 when, after their victory in Smyrna, Kemalists threatened to enter the last "Turkish" city occupied by the Allies. It is to this exodus and its immediate aftermath that we turn in the next chapter.

Figure 16. "The newly elected patriarchal locum tenens Bishop Kevork Aslanian in his home with grandchildren (Vahakn and Varuzhan) on his lap." *Hay Gin* 4, no. 2 (January 1, 1923), cover page.

《 CHAPTER 3 》

AN EXODUS AND ITS AFTERMATH

The Allies are leaving town. The Armenians are dusting off their *fez*es. Mornings in Istanbul are mysteriously hushed, nights noisy. Sluts puke their political convictions in the street. Newspaper editors are busy writing their last menacing headlines and making preparations to leave town. The Soviet Armenian Republic has stuck a *fez* on the summit of Mount Ararat. The Armenian patriarch is pacing his room feverishly and gnawing at his beads. In the street, puzzled, disoriented men gather in small groups and peer at the sky. Shopkeepers are selling everything at a loss. Inside houses, hearts thump against walls and nervous fingers bundle up the silverware and worn-out wads of currency. [...] At night, the howl of approaching Turkish mobs is heard and everyone waits for the coming massacre. We sit with our revolvers on the table and our ears, like amplifiers, magnify a rustle into ominous footsteps. Darkness itself is on the move. At daybreak the sun looks at ashen faces. Everyone is still alive for the time being.[1]

This is how the novelist Gosdan Zarian depicted Bolsahays' terror when news of the burning of Smyrna reached the Ottoman capital. The same news, that the Kemalists had won a bloody victory against the occupying Greeks in Izmir, caused great relief among the Muslims of the city who took to the streets to celebrate.[2] The massive demonstrations became violent at times: the mob broke windows, damaged Allied property, and injured a few citizens. Some Turkish newspapers provoked the masses. A *Vakit* (Times) commentator warned an anonymous Greek soldier (probably a symbol for all pro-Allied Christians) that he should prepare himself for the cruelest death.[3] The Armenian press repeatedly urged the Turkish press, politicians, and the occupation forces to intervene in order to keep everyone calm. One Armenian journalist begged Turkish journalists not to stir up the masses with incendiary editorials that, among other things, called on soldiers to drink "the blood of the enemy" instead of water.[4]

The situation looked increasingly out of control. Some Turkish journalists tried to find an appropriate language to calm down the mobs without hurting their feelings of pride and joy. Two days after the above-mentioned article, *Vakit* editor Ahmed Emin (Yalman) warned that even though it was "natural" for people to desire retribution, the Turk, as a member of a "graceful and noble nation," had to know how to conquer his own impulses. Ahmed Emin assured his readers that traitors and criminals who needed to be punished would soon be tried by the laws of the *Milli* (Kemalist) government and receive their just deserts.[5] On September 12, newspapers announced that even though he sympathized with the Turkish populations' joy over the Kemalist victory, General Harington, British commander of the occupation forces, banned demonstrations, which were meant to be peaceful but turned out to be violent.[6]

The news from Smyrna and the responses of the city's Muslim population engendered outright panic among the city's half million Christians. Should the British leave, would the Kemalists who would retake the city repeat the carnage that befell Smyrna earlier that month? As the British were organizing the defense of the city against a possible Turkish attack, they began sending wives and children back home. Even orphanages under the care of the Allies began moving out of the city. The atmosphere of alarm was bolstered by the miserable state of the incoming refugees fleeing from the Kemalist advance in western Anatolia.

Armenians from the Asian shores of the city began moving to Pera, where the Allied powers and non-Muslim populations were concentrated. As Anayis noted, people were afraid that "Turkish thugs would come overnight and plunder rich houses of the Armenians and Greeks."[7] Like many others, she tried to get a visa from the Greek embassy but it proved impossible to enter the building for "people were hanging out of the embassy windows like bunches of grapes."[8] The pages of the Armenian press were flooded with advertisements of ferry companies promising immediate departure from Istanbul to Piraeus, Palermo, or New York, in the safety of transatlantics flying the American or British flag.[9] Those who had already left for abroad seemed fortunate now. The prominent poet and member of the National Delegation Vahan Tekeyan wrote a letter to Zaven Surmelian, his sixteen-year-old protégé who had recently left for America, a place he found quite boring. Tekeyan told Zaven that Armenians in Bolis had no clue what the future would bring. He thus assured Zaven: "Under these conditions, however awful it might be, your Kansas should be considered a heaven."[10]

During this climate of terror from September to December 1922, fifty thousand Armenians and Greeks fled the city.[11] Neither the Turkish authorities nor the Allied representatives tried to stop this exodus. In fact, both Turkish officials and the "Turkish mob" encouraged it. As early as November 7, Patriarch Zaven had protested to the Allied high commissioners that Christians were being targeted and thus "forced to leave Turkey."[12]

Much to the relief of many who decided or had to stay, the Turkish reconquest of the city turned out to be a diplomatic rather than a military affair. Although there was little mass violence against non-Muslim residents, 1,500 Greeks and 500 Armenians and their dependents were soon expelled for collaborating with the British.[13] Early on, the British convinced the Kemalists not to penetrate the neutral zone, but to accept an armistice instead, which they signed on October 11, 1922.[14] Kemalist representatives entered the city the same month. In November, the Ankara government and the Allies came together in Lausanne to renegotiate a peace treaty.

Until the end of the Lausanne negotiations in the summer of 1923, the city remained under the "dual de facto regime" of the Allied military forces and the representatives of the Ankara government. The Allies began evacuating shortly after the signing of the treaty in July 1923. Despite official Turkish historiography's claim that the occupation soldiers left Istanbul in shame and humiliation, their departure was marked rather by mutual acknowledgment of amicability and respect, which took a variety of forms, including soccer games and garden parties. On October 2, 1923, the Allies officially departed in a ceremony with the full participation of Turkish forces. General Harington, the representative of a country that had only a few of years earlier vowed to punish the perpetrators of the Armenian massacres, left Turkey in quite a pro-Turkish mood, having delivered Armenians nothing, let alone justice.[15] In his memoir Harington would remember his last day as a "a wonderful 'send-off' from a so-called enemy country."[16]

On October 6, 1923, a day still celebrated in Turkey as Istanbul's Liberation Day, the Turkish military entered the city, with pashas on horseback, reminding everyone of the reversal of the situation created by the Allies only about four years earlier when the French general D'Esperey entered the city on a white horse that a Greek resident gave him as a gift. Thousands watched the Turkish entry with tears of pride on their cheeks. Among the people who came to welcome the Turkish troops were Greeks and Armenians, who, instead of their usual European-style hats, chose to cover their heads with the fez, a symbol of their submission to the new Turkish Muslim regime whose motto was "Turkey for the Turks."[17] With the Turkish takeover of the city, Constantinople became Istanbul once again.

The Void around the Remaining Bolsahays

Hayganush Mark and Vahan Toshigian took the risk of staying in Bolis even though *Hay Gin*'s involvement in the Armenian cause would make her an easy target for the Kemalists. Perhaps they thought that because hers was "simply" a woman's journal they would not be harmed. Vahan Toshigian had been working as a journalist but he worked mostly behind the scenes as an editorial secretary. Neither in *Hay Gin* nor in her autobiography did Mark elucidate as to why and how they decided against leaving, this despite the fact that the majority of their peers fled the country. In its thirteen years of publication, it was only in November and December of 1922 that *Hay Gin* failed to appear for three issues in a row. Unlike other times when Mark had to skip an issue, when *Hay Gin* reappeared in mid-December 1922 Mark did not provide any explanation for the previous months' silence. That no explanation was necessary for this brief interruption is itself indicative of the upheaval in which Bolsahays found themselves in those days.

By the end of December 1922, most people that populated the preceding two chapters of this book had left the city. Those who jumped ship with their families to escape to safety included many *Hay Gin* writers, including

Hayganush Mark's three feminist comrades who were also members of the AWA. Anayis, who had failed to enter the Greek embassy given the number of people who flooded the building, also failed to get a Bulgarian and a Romanian visa. Not many countries were admitting Armenian refugees. But Anayis came from an elite family with good connections. She was the sister-in-law of Gabriel Noradungian, an important member of the Armenian National Delegation at the Paris Peace Conference. Noradungian had been the Ottoman minister of foreign affairs until 1913. The patriarch intervened on Anayis's behalf after which she procured a Bulgarian visa for herself and her daughter. She first traveled to Bulgaria, then stayed in Romania, and finally settled in Paris, where she would pass away in 1950. She continued sending literary and opinion pieces to *Hay Gin* from wherever she went. She also continued working in various Armenian organizations in the diaspora. Most significantly, she presided over the *Throtsaser Hayuhyats Engerutiun* (Education-Loving Armenian Ladies' Association), which operated orphanages and schools. Anayis and Hayganush Mark continued their personal correspondence for decades to come.[18]

Zaruhi Kalemkearian left for New York, where her daughter resided. Like Anayis, she continued to send articles to *Hay Gin* and continued to correspond with Hayganush Mark until the very end. In their personal correspondence, they addressed each other as "dear sister."[19] Mark, who never had children of her own (but a cat or two), seems to have had a special relationship with Kalemkearian's daughter and her grandchildren. Kalemkearian continued her feminist activism in New York, volunteering in numerous organizations. She also gave talks in New York about Armenian women's activism in Bolis. In 1928 she became the first woman elected as a key member of the Central Committee of the Armenian Benevolent Union, a development that *Hay Gin* reported proudly.[20]

Zaruhi Bahri's story took a different turn than Anayis's and Kalemkearian's but is equally representative of a section of the Armenian elite intellectuals who left Bolis in late 1922. During the genocide, Bahri had lost one brother, Parsegh Shahbaz, to the April 24 arrests in the capital, and a sister, Adrine, to the massacres in the interior. During the postwar years, she accepted Patriarch Zaven's offer and became the manager of the neutral house. Because she had decided on the Armenianness of many children and young women whose "families" claimed they were Muslims, she had received many death threats from Muslim relatives of people who were taken forcibly from their homes by the *vorpahavak*. After the Kemalist victory in Smyrna, the British embassy told her that should the Kemalists take the city the British could not guarantee her safety. It was indeed apparent that the incoming Turkish forces had not forgotten about the "Armenianized" Muslim orphans. One of the first things Refet Pasha, the Ankara government's representative in Istanbul, did was to demand from the Armenian patriarchate the return of the Muslim orphans being kept by Armenians.[21] After a thorough search of orphanages, Turkish officials found fifteen children suspected of having Muslim background. The children were to remain in Istanbul until their examination by a special commission was concluded.

In the fall of 1922, not only individuals but the populations of entire orphanages were moving abroad. It is in this atmosphere that Zaruhi Bahri left the city, together with her husband and four children, Krikor, Zhirayr, Anahid, and Noyemi. Mr. Bahri was a quiet, well-to-do lawyer who supported his wife's activism. Because the Bahris thought they were leaving temporarily, he left his law office to be run under the supervision of an employee. They first settled in Romania because they wanted to stay close to Bolis in order to facilitate an easy return once things calmed down. They were never able to return home. Like the overwhelming majority of Armenians and Greeks who left at this time, they too were denied reentry based on various Turkish laws and regulations. Bahri noted in her memoir that her family left 100,000 lira worth of property in Istanbul. The property was considered "abandoned" (*emval-ı metruke*) by the Turkish state and was confiscated. They moved to Paris, but her husband was incapable of finding employment as a lawyer in their new home. Zaruhi Bahri stopped sending articles to *Hay Gin* because she had to start working as a seamstress to support her family. Her husband soon died.[22] Her older daughter, Noyemi Elmayan, began writing for *Hay Gin*.[23]

Like many others who fled in 1922, in the 1940s and 1950s Anayis, Kalemkearian, and Bahri published their memoirs in which they extensively talked about the war and occupation years in Constantinople. Unlike their peers who emigrated, those who remained in Bolis, such as Hayganush Mark, penned their memories but they kept silent about the war years, occupation years, and the exodus of 1922. Given their precarious existence in a country that clearly did not want its leftover Armenians, those years belonged to a past that the new Turkey's Armenians could do nothing but suppress. The Armenian patriarch's expulsion from office related directly to this concern.

In late November 1922, Refet Pasha sent word to the National Assembly that if the Armenians wanted to live peacefully with the Turks, it was advisable that Patriarch Zaven be removed from office. After several emergency meetings, the assembly decided that "in view of the dominant mentality and conditions around [us]," the best thing for the patriarch would be "to remain silent and retire."[24] The assembly, whose numbers had already dwindled because of the recent departure of many of its members, decided that it had to sacrifice the patriarch in order to increase the chances of Armenians' safety and security in the Kemalist state. As an expression of goodwill, Turkish Armenians thus expelled the last Ottoman Armenian patriarch from office. By doing so they hoped to signal that the Armenian community's occupation-era "anti-Turkish" policies had come to an end and that the remaining Armenians would be obedient, loyal citizens of the new Turkey willing to do whatever their state asked them to do; an asset at best, a benign problem at worst.

In the early morning hours of October 10, 1922, the last Armenian patriarch of the Ottoman Empire left Constantinople secretly aboard a British cruiser. He thus shared the fate of the last Ottoman sultan, Vahdettin, who, only a few weeks earlier had exited the palace literally from the back door to leave the city aboard a British battleship. Soon, another man of similar stature would share their fate. The departure of the Greek patriarch Meletios Metaxakis, however, involved more drama, including having the anti-Metaxakis section of the community invade the private chambers of the resisting patriarch and drag him down the stairs of the patriarchate until Allied police forces dispersed the protestors. Metaxakis, too, would leave Turkey aboard a British steamship.[25] As these men were disappearing over the horizon, a new chapter was opening up in Armenian, Greek, and Turkish history.

The editorial of the first *Hay Gin* after the journal's brief silence was titled "The Woman and the Church."[26] Even though Mark had not been anticlerical before, she wasn't known for her proximity to the church. Therefore, it is striking that she would pen such a forceful pro-church article in which she first explained the importance of religion and the church for Armenians and then urged mothers to take their children to church instead of movie theaters. As someone who had previously criticized the religious establishment, and specifically the Armenian Church for its discriminatory practices against women (see Chapter 5), Mark was aware that her words would sound unprogressive to many ears. But, she wrote, "asking for a return to the church does not mean advocating backwardness. If it were, all those [Western] countries that we look up to as exemplars of civilization would have been backward."[27] That at this moment of turmoil Mark turned to the church for a sense of normalcy, ritual, and perhaps even survival is representative of not just her own post-1923 trajectory but also that of the Bolsahay elites and intellectuals who decided to stay home, literally and metaphorically. As a feminist, Mark felt the urge to defend her conservative instincts with various textual strategies. In this instance, Mark picked the Western example to convey the belief that tradition and progress do not exclude each other.

The next *Hay Gin* issue appeared on January 1, 1923. Instead of Mark's editorial, the cover page featured a picture. The newly elected patriarchal *locum tenens* Bishop Kevork Aslanian posed for the camera with his two grandchildren (Figure 16).[28] This ordinary picture conveyed many layers of meaning. Was it a coincidence that, out of all the photos of Bishop Aslanian, Mark chose this particular one? Armenian priests have to be celibate in order to be ordained as a bishop. That he had grandchildren meant that Kevork Aslanian was married before he decided to pursue a career in the church. Why, at some point, did Aslanian choose to provide this photo to the press, one posed at his home, as indicated in the caption, with his well-dressed, well-kept grandsons? These children, whom the bishop held with a proud, solemn look, represented a kind of continuity between the previous era marked by Patriarch Zaven's activism, outspokenness, and quest for justice, and the new one under Aslanian's leadership, which would be marked by quiescence, domestication, and conservatism. Children could be used for both purposes. In the picture, these domesticated children (contrast them with the little soldier and the Red Cross nurse published in 1921) served as real-life proof that Armenianness could and would survive even after this latest Turkish victory.

For those who knew Aslanian's personal history, the picture communicated even more meanings. Born in 1856, Aslanian turned to the service of God only after losing his wife to the Hamidian massacres of 1894–1896 during which "Turks burnt her alive."[29] Aslanian survived these massacres and the later genocide. He found his way to Constantinople after 1918 and began serving in the patriarchate. He remained the *locum tenens* until the 1927 election of the new patriarch, Mesrob Naroyan. In 1926 out of his personal income he donated a significant amount to the Armenian National Hospital in Yedikule for the expansion and renovation of its maternity ward. To honor Aslanian's deceased wife, Nazeni, the board of the hospital named the new ward Nazenian. In 1925, when *Hay Gin* reported this new development, the journal referred to Aslanian's deceased wife as a "martyr," but did not explain why and how she had been martyred.[30] This allusive reference serves as a small but illustrative example of how Armenians would watch their language when they talked about the past without giving up on their understanding of what had really happened. It is also worth noting that in the mid-1920s the Armenian National Hospital unofficially renamed itself *Azkin Dune*, that is, the Nation's Home. Both the picture and all the instances from this clergyman's life and visual representation suggest how a strong, persistent, and deeply linked imagery of home and family enabled Armenians to process the multiple traumas they experienced at this time.

As for Hayganush Mark, it was not until one full year after the exodus of the Bolsahay population that she seemed to have found the right words to talk about the subject and explain her reasons as to why and how she decided to continue *Hay Gin*. In the January 1, 1924, issue, taking the beginning of the new year as a good opportunity, she evaluated the previous year:

> Looking back to our past means looking back at a void. A void in our surroundings and everywhere. [. . .] It is not a secret that this emptiness, which impacts us so much, is a result of voluntary migrations. Many of our [female] readers left without anything, others in better shape. But it is exciting to be able say that we still have masses of readers who want to see this journal continue publication at all cost. It is this feeling that encourages us to continue. As an idealist institution devoted to the Armenian woman's moral, intellectual, and physical well-being it is our role to try to always exist, whatever conditions life may bring our way. Out of those conditions we will create possibilities to live and to progress. We will build ladders atop those conditions so that we can all rise up and up. As in the past, we will try to elevate the conditions of our sex.[31]

Those "conditions" under which Mark had to build a new feminism were complex and intricate, and their roots go back to the Lausanne Conference where the Ankara government's representative and the Allies renegotiated a treaty that would finally bring much-sought peace to the Near East. At the expense of Armenians' dreams for justice.

The Birth of a Minority

The peace conference convened in Lausanne from November 1922 to July 1923. The ensuing treaty replaced the Sèvres Treaty that the Ottoman government signed in August 1920 and had authorized the partition of Anatolia.[32] This treaty had galvanized the Kemalist resistance movement. The Armenian delegation was a signatory to the Sèvres Treaty because at the time Armenia was an independent republic and the treaty assigned territory to Armenians.[33] At Lausanne, Armenians lacked a representative government because Armenia had already been Sovietized. Nonetheless, an Armenian delegation, a continuation of the former delegation that had been working in Paris and other European cities since the beginning of the Paris Peace Conference, went to Lausanne in order to lobby among the Allies' representatives and get a hearing. Despite the Turkish delegation's protests, they received a hearing at a Minorities Sub-Committee meeting that lasted for an hour and ten minutes.[34]

An important issue that occupied the Lausanne conference pertained to non-Muslim residents of Turkey. Because Armenians did not have a state that represented their interests, the question of who represented the interests of Armenians in Turkey became a contested issue. The members of the Armenian delegation argued that they represented "the sentiment and the mind of the entire Armenian people, regardless of party, origin, or location."[35] The Turkish delegation, however, disagreed on this point and argued that because Turkish Armenians were subjects of Turkey it was the Turkish delegation that represented their interests.

Back in Istanbul, the Kemalist representatives pressured the National Assembly to disown the Armenian delegation in Lausanne and telegraph the Allies accordingly. It was Patriarch Zaven's refusal to fulfill this demand that cost him his post. Refet Pasha had told the National Assembly that Zaven had to go, a new patriarch had to be elected, and he had to publicly renounce the Armenian delegation. Even though the Armenian National Assembly had advised the patriarch to do as Refet Pasha ordered, the patriarch left the country without officially resigning. By doing so, he prevented the election of a new patriarch who would have to abide by the orders of Refet Pasha. The patriarchal *locum tenens* did not have the formal authority to reject the representative power of the Armenian delegation in Lausanne.[36]

It was at this time that there was a serious splintering among the Bolsahay elite. Many who had not been too vocal about their opposition to the patriarchate's support of the Armenian cause over the preceding three years began to raise their voices and get organized. These loyalists were especially agitated by the fact that Patriarch Zaven left without resigning, which disabled the remaining Armenians from formally disassociating Armenians in Turkey from Armenians abroad who still pursued some form of a territorialist agenda at Lausanne. There were also others who had in the past supported Patriarch Zaven's secessionist efforts but changed their minds about the viability of this project after the Kemalist victory in Smyrna. They lost faith in any European powers' sincerity in helping Armenians, and therefore they had no faith in the possible effectiveness of the Armenian delegation in Lausanne. They thought that by not distancing themselves from diaspora Armenians' "anti-Turkish policies," Turkish Armenians were further jeopardizing their already suspect existence among the victorious Turks.[37]

At the Lausanne Conference, the main aim of the Armenian delegation was to convince the Allied representatives to persuade Turkey to designate an "Armenian National Home" inside Turkey. This was to be a "home" where Armenian refugees from all around the world would congregate, a place where they would continue Armenian traditions and live in safety. They argued that Soviet Armenia was too small and weak to host the more than half million refugees dispersed across the globe as a consequence of the aggressive Ottoman policies toward Armenians during and after the war. The Armenian side was ready to accept an autonomous status or being a colony of Turkey, and having a constitution similar to that of the British dominions.

At the Lausanne Conference, the main aim of the Turkish delegation regarding Armenians was to exchange them with Turkish Muslims in Soviet Armenia.[38] This was part and parcel of their overall policy aiming at getting the Lausanne Conference to authorize the exchange of all non-Muslims in Turkey with Muslims/Turks in other countries.[39] The ultimate goal was ensuring the religious homogeneity of the new country. At the parliamentary deliberations, MP Mehmed Şükrü (Koçoğlu) summarized the general feeling by stating that the religious minorities were "deceitful people [who have] tried every possible crime to ruin this state and devastate this nation [*millet*]," therefore "they have no place in this country anymore. There is only one thing that can be done with them: an exchange of populations."[40]

It became apparent very early on during the negotiations that the Turkish side would not grant Armenians any national home anywhere. The head of the Turkish delegation, İsmet Pasha (later, İnönü) summarized their position with the following words: "Just as it is unthinkable that the Greeks settled in Marseilles establish an independent Greek State or annex it to their motherland, in the same way Turkey's Greeks or Armenians do not have the right to propose similar suggestions."[41] Indeed, the prevention of such states was one of the main reasons the Kemalists fought a resistance movement. The Allied powers knew this all too well and after a few sessions of insisting on an Armenian national home (partially in order to appease their largely pro-Armenian public opinion) they deferred to the Turkish side.

For the Turkish side, what they recognized early on was that it would not be possible to exchange the remaining Armenians with anyone. İsmet Pasha did not even bring this subject to the negotiating table because he could not find an appropriate party with whom to discuss the topic without jeopardizing the Turkish delegation's position on other matters. Most importantly, Ankara did not want to involve Moscow in these negotiations. Therefore, the foreign minister concluded early on that he did not see "any other option but to accept that Armenians will stay in our county." For Armenians who were going to stay inside Turkey, the foreign minister said that he wanted, "if possible, to make them reject minority rights" and added: "my idea is to make them look like citizens" (*Benim fikrim onlara vatandaş yüzü göstermektir*).[42]

The "minority rights" that İsmet Pasha did not want Armenians to have were the minority protections that the Allied powers insisted that newly formed, expanded, or defeated states should guarantee to their populations that culturally, racially, linguistically, ethnically, and religiously differed from the majority. Since the Polish Treaty that the Allies signed with Poland in June 1919, issues pertaining to minority protection had been central in the peace treaty negotiations. The Great Powers argued that to ensure a durable world peace, every nation should be sheltered in a state, and each state should be governed by consent.[43] Yet "national self-determination" was clearly impossible to attain everywhere, for everyone. To accommodate the near unattainability of one state for one nation, the concept of "minorities" was engraved in the national and international legal order. According to this mentality, if minorities were protected and given room to express their differences they would not forge extraterritorial alliances and act as a fifth column. Instead, these protections would help them gradually assimilate to the majority's values and culture. The Allies wanted to create "tolerant majorities and loyal minorities" and their thinking rested on US president Woodrow Wilson's understanding of multicultural liberalism.[44] They therefore insisted that Turkey designate all populations in Turkey that were non-Muslim, non-Turkish, and non-Turkish-speaking as "minority" and guarantee to respect their cultural, religious, and linguistic differences without any discrimination.

Turkish politicians' thinking regarding ethnic and religious difference fundamentally contradicted the Allies' logic. From their Ottoman predecessors' experience with multiethnicity, which they interpreted as having been marked with the toleration of people's difference, they inferred that giving rights to non-titular groups would not make them loyal. The cultural rights that the Allies argued minorities should have—such as over schools, courts, language, and charitable institutions—eerily resembled the entitlements that as dhimmis Ottoman non-Muslims had enjoyed for about half a millennium.[45] Although this *millet* system worked more or less successfully, problems arose in the early nineteenth century. The rising economic and military success of the West was accompanied by the increasing consciousness of religious and national differences among Christian Balkan subjects, who then demanded and—with the help of the European powers—achieved their independence. The Ottoman center had tried various integrationist strategies to create a common Ottomanist identity in order to preempt centrifugal forces and delegitimize European meddling in its domestic affairs on behalf of Ottoman Christians, but nothing worked to reverse the tide of disintegration.

By the time the Turkish delegation sat at the negotiating table in Lausanne, its members were confident they knew why all these efforts had failed. There were three chief culprits: the Great Powers themselves, which did not respect Ottoman sovereignty; Ottoman Christians, who let themselves be used as pawns of a Europe that had pretended to care for them but was in fact pursuing its own economic interests; and the dysfunctional Istanbul government, which by allowing room for the expression of diversity prepared the ground for intrusion from outside. In short, the majority's tolerance did not lead to minorities' loyalty. Because the Turkish delegation was acutely aware of the Great Powers' historical role in this outcome, they interpreted the insistence on minority rights as not only humiliating but also an excuse for future infringements on Turkish sovereignty. Minority rights threatened the new Turkey because they signaled the potential repetition of the past.[46]

Not wanting a repetition of the past and assured of non-Muslims', especially Armenians' and Greeks', proclivity for treason given their activities during the occupation years, the Turkish delegation asserted that because all Turkish citizens would be equal before the law in the new Turkey, no one would need extra protection of their rights. Moreover, signaling early on what kind of liability "minority protection" would be for the minorities, İsmet Pasha told the Allies' representatives that "in Turkey, for an average citizen, the best way to benefit from all the rights is not to have any suspicious ties with outside actors."[47] He equated "minority protection" with "outside intervention," and invoked Turkish Jewry as an example of a model minority that had not been bothered because they had not been collaborating with "outside forces."[48]

In the end, the Turkish side reluctantly agreed to the Allies' insistence on minority protection but granted this status only to non-Muslims and not to Muslims who were of non-Turkish ethnic backgrounds, such as Kurds. The Treaty of Lausanne guaranteed "non-Moslem nationals" of Turkey control over their own family laws, schools, and charitable institutions. They could practice their religion and use their languages freely, with no discrimination. They could maintain their patriarchates but these institutions would act merely as spiritual centers devoid of any of the political and administrative authority they had previously enjoyed.

Given the conditions attending their birth and the deep past that colored the relationship between the Allies and the Turks, these minority protection guarantees came to life with inherent defects. That they were forced on the Turkish state might not have been a problem had the Allies themselves been subject to the same regime. Yet the obligation to protect minorities did not apply to the Great Powers themselves.⁴⁹ The Great Powers argued that their superior Western European civilization had already evolved procedures to facilitate the peaceful assimilation of minorities. These procedures, they noted, did not yet exist in "immature states."⁵⁰ Therefore, like all other states (such as Poland, Czechoslovakia, Romania, Albania, Austria, and Hungary, among others) on whom minority protections were forced, Turkey resented them as the final expression of a long and unequal power relationship between the Great Powers and their "juniors."

That the newly formed League of Nations would supervise these states to see if they abided by minority protections further bolstered this perception. Because the Ottomans had a history of Great Powers using the suffering of their Christian counterparts inside the Ottoman Empire as a pretext to intervene in Ottoman domestic affairs (at least this is how the state actors interpreted the process), minority protections were not just bothersome but alarming for the Turkish Republic's political elite. This situation had its worst effects on people whom the protection clauses aimed to protect in the first place: minorities. The fact that minorities, especially Armenians and Greeks, were given "privileges" (this is how the state actors and the majority interpreted minority rights) by the Lausanne Treaty tainted the already fraught relationship between the majority and the minorities.

For Turkish Armenians it was also important that the Lausanne Treaty amnestied all war-related crimes committed between August 1, 1914, and November 20, 1922. The amnesty statement declared that the powers that signed the treaty were "desirous to cause the events which have troubled the peace in the East to be forgotten."⁵¹ Effectively, the Allies pardoned the perpetrators of the Armenian genocide. This was a major blow to all Armenians but particularly those who would stay inside Turkey. Many perpetrators and usurpers of the properties of deported or murdered Armenians became ministers, parliamentarians, and powerful state actors in the Republic of Turkey. For example, Dr. Tevfik Rüştü Aras. During the Armenian deportations, he was an influential officer of the Supreme Hygiene Council, whose task was to destroy the bodies of Armenian victims. Rüştü was sent, with thousands of kilograms of lime, to the provinces where massacres had taken place. The bodies were dumped in wells that were then filled with lime and sealed with earth. Tevfik Rüştü was given six months to complete his task, after which he returned to Istanbul. Rüştü became a long-serving foreign minister (1925–1938) under successive republican governments.[52] In the words of Erik Zürcher, "Many of the people in central positions of power (such as Şükrü Kaya, Kazım Özalp, Kılıç Ali) had been personally involved in the massacres, but besides that, the ruling elite as a whole depended on a coalition with provincial notables, landlords, and tribal chiefs, who had profited immensely from the departure of the Armenians and Greeks."[53]

Moreover, Turkish state officials willingly and purposefully embraced their predecessors who had ordered the Armenian deportations and massacres. Between 1921 and 1922, in a covert operation called "Nemesis," Armenians killed several masterminds of the Medz Yeghern, including Talat Pasha. In 1926, the Turkish assembly passed a law granting property to the family of Talat Pasha and all other Turkish leaders assassinated by the Armenians. Their families would be given property that once belonged to the Armenians. MP Recep Zühtü Bey (Soyak), a close confidant and the private secretary of Mustafa Kemal, said in Parliament: "This is a strong warning message to assassins: you may execute a Turk through an assassination! But we will raise his offspring with your money so that tomorrow, he will gouge out your eye and break your head."[54]

Although, in an official ceremony in 1943, Turkey received the remains of Talat Pasha from Berlin where he had been assassinated in 1921, it did not allow reentry to Armenians who had fled the country in 1922. The Lausanne Treaty's declaration of amnesty did not extend to Armenians. Despite the Great Powers' insistence, Turkey successfully rejected accepting the mass return home of Turkish Armenians. The delegation repeatedly maintained that Armenians who had never betrayed Turkey would be allowed to return, and that their applictions would be evaluated on a case-by-case basis. But the return of "revolutionaries, assassins, and bad elements" posed a "security threat," and therefore was unacceptable.[55] Even though İsmet Pasha noted in his memoir that only *muzır* (deceitful) Armenians were to be denied entry, in practice, Turkey assumed that almost all Armenians were *muzır*, and forbade their repatriation. Anayis, Zaruhi Kalemkearian, and Zaruhi Bahri, like hundreds of others who fled Istanbul in 1922 or were deported before, never returned home. One of the main reasons for this policy was that it paved the way to declaring their properties "abandoned." As maintained by the Turkish minister of finance in a closed parliamentary session, Armenians' properties were to be confiscated in order to close the new state's budget deficit.[56]

The Treaty of Lausanne ended up not mentioning Armenia and Armenians even once. The Armenian delegation responded by penning a letter of protest addressed to the Allies. As the representatives of a nation "who has known all the forms and all the consequences of abandonment," a nation whose scattered remnants were "tolerated rather than welcomed in most places," the delegation declared the "peace of Lausanne a fiction."[57] Some more sympathetic representatives of the Allies assured Armenians that their case would not be buried and that the League of Nations could settle these issues. However, the League of Nations' involvement with Armenians remained strictly in the sphere of refugee care.

While it was an absolute devastation for the Armenian delegation, the Treaty of Lausanne was a diplomatic victory for the Kemalists that crowned their earlier military victories. Even so, upon their return to Ankara, the Turkish delegation met with fierce criticism in the parliament. Many MPs expressed their dissatisfaction with the minority protection clauses, and especially the fact that the League of Nations would supervise Turkey in this regard. Dr. Rıza Nur, assistant to the head of the Turkish delegation and the main person who participated to the Lausanne's minority commissions, tried to calm down his concerned colleagues by pointing to the ineffectiveness of the league. He told the floor that "even though Bulgaria and Romania had similarly agreed on minority protection and League of Nations' supervision, they recently bothered their Jews badly [*fena halde zedelediler*], and the league did nothing about it." He assured his colleagues that "That's why all these supervisions are only in words" (*Yani bunlar laftadır*).[58] The MPs also complained about the fact that the Greek and Armenian patriarchates, which had proven so disloyal in the recent past, would be allowed to remain in Turkey. Rıza Nur defended this policy by saying that the patriarchates were to be deprived of all political, administrative, and judicial power and would only deal with religious matters. He said that it was in fact better to keep the patriarchs as "simple priests under our claws" and that "it was better to keep the [Greek] patriarch inside the country rather than send him to Mount Athos [in Greece] where he would certainly act against our government."[59] Finally, when he was pressured to address the question of emigration and immigration of minorities, he declared that their entry into Turkey would be very restricted but their exit would be facilitated. He added, "We are especially open to their migration. Let them go. Their departure is exactly what we want. That is why we passed [all these laws]."[60]

Even though thousands of non-Muslims left Turkey before, during, and after the Conference of Lausanne, minorities constituted approximately 3 percent of Turkey's population, or about 300,000 people, in the 1920s and 1930s.[61] Of those, about 80,000 were Turkish Armenians. The signing of the Lausanne Treaty marked a turning point in their long history under Turkish rule but they were equipped to take it. As had always happened in the past when they endeavored to remake their community, Armenians relied on gendered imagery and familial social and political organization.

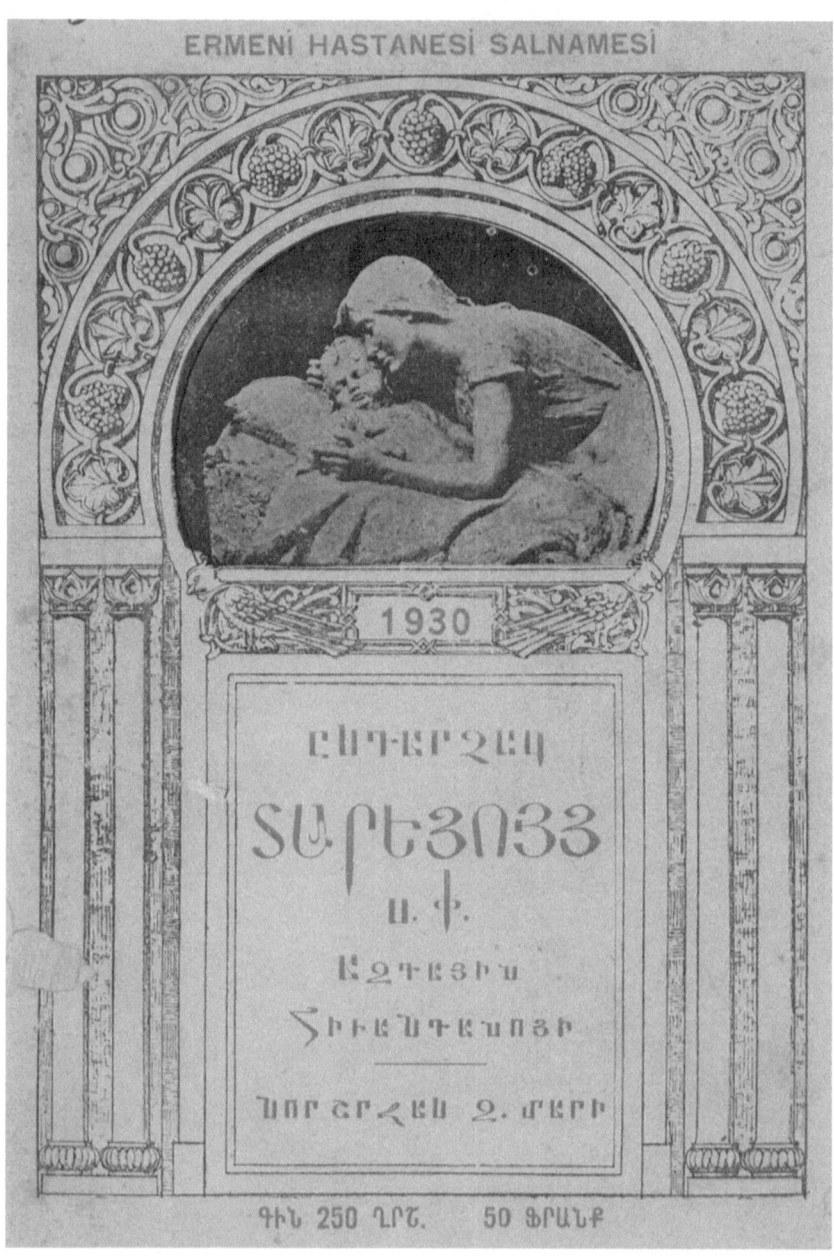

Figure 17. Cover page of the Armenian National Hospital's 1930 almanac. A Mary-like mother is passing the Armenian identity to her child. *Entartsag Daretsuyts Surp Prgich Azkayin Hivantanotsi* 6 (1930).

{ CHAPTER 4 }

A TAMED MINORITY

One could almost hear the gloom in Hayganush Mark's voice in her editorial "We and Our Church," a piece about the first Armenian Christmas in Istanbul after Turkey's ratification of the Treaty of Lausanne. She began by noting that on this January 6 the congregation had filled the churches of the city to capacity. "Everyone who went to church that day felt a different sense of belonging and unity," she wrote, and continued:

> Honestly, the church is a different thing for us. For other nations it is a prayer room where people practice their faith. For us, however, it is more than that; it is a mother with open arms. For the vagabond wrecks of our nation, in every country, it is an affectionate mother who attracts her wandering children. And she provides their souls with consolation through prayer, endless compassion, and weeping. [...]
>
> For us, a nation dispersed all across the world, against the threat of dissolution [*koyaludzum*] and assimilation [*tsulum*], the church is the most important place of refuge for self-preservation. [...]
>
> For a nation like us that has such a bad fate, the highest happiness is to respect [our] religion and mother tongue. Among the ups and downs of daily life, under the circumstances of this leaderless existence, and in the whirl of painful everyday life, for our nation there are only two channels to salvation: religion and the mother tongue.[1]

Mark was gloomy but not hopeless. She acknowledged the pain of everyday life after the departure of many people and the political developments that left those remaining without a substantial number of political, intellectual, or religious leaders. Yet she was able to suggest antidotes to this "bad fate": respect religion and the mother tongue. Those two "channels of salvation" would bring the "highest happiness" to Armenians worldwide. Equating happiness with "self-preservation," she contrasted them with "dissolution" and "assimilation," potential problems she diagnosed both in the dispersed and in the remaining.

Mark did not explain why Armenians needed to be consoled. Everyone already knew the reasons and she had not yet crafted a safe terminology to talk about the recent past. She emphasized, however, that consoling was to be done by a mother-like figure. Like *mother tongue*, but on a more metaphorical level, she feminized religion, thus idealizing both the actual mother and the image of motherhood in the preservation of Armenianness. "Among the ups and downs of daily life," in every corner of the world, Mark urged Armenians to know that there was a church they could return to, and it was the mother-like, compassionate figure that would unconditionally care and, most critically, weep for them.

Mark anticipated that immigrant communities would face challenges similar to those faced by Armenians who had stayed behind. She thus suggested the same cure for all of them. She put emphasis on the church as one marker (and site) of difference that Armenians worldwide shared, one thing that rendered them Armenian and united them as one. Churchgoing was thus a "diasporic moment" shared by Armenians irrespective of the state that hosted them.[2] In addition, churchgoing had proven to be time resistant. Religion was something that present Armenians shared with those of the past. Therefore, religious traditions, ceremonies, and architecture had helped Armenians imagine a temporal continuity. This continuity, in Mark's otherwise secular-leaning political imagination, could render present Armenian dispersion irrelevant precisely because Armenian-speaking communities had long been scattered throughout the world and still survived as Armenian. Last but not least, religious liberty, along with the right to continue one's native tongue and operate schools, were rights that the new Turkey promised to its minorities with the Treaty of Lausanne. All these continuities helped Mark and others in her milieu imagine a continued presence for their community in the Republic of Turkey, a Turkey that claimed to be new but looked only partially fresh to Armenians.

Can an Armenian Be a Turk?

The people of Turkey experienced profound transformations in the first two decades after the Lausanne Treaty. On October 13, 1923, Ankara became the new capital; on October 29 the country was declared a republic. Within nine months the country ratified the founding constitution of the land. Until his death in 1938, Mustafa Kemal Atatürk remained the president of the republic. During this time Turkey was a single-party regime governed by the Republican People's Party, a place that equated dissent with opposition and punished anyone who dared to disagree, even mildly, with the government's policies.

Article 88 of the new Turkey's first constitution defined who a Turk was. When the draft article was first introduced to the Grand National Assembly, it replicated the first Ottoman constitution of 1876 except that it replaced "Ottoman" with "Turk": "The people of Turkey [*Türkiye*], regardless of their religion and race, shall be called 'Turk' [*Türk*]."[3] The floor immediately raised objections: Did "Turkness" (*Türklük*) mean nationality (*milliyet*) or subjecthood (*tabiyet*)? asked one member of parliament.[4] "But republics can't have 'subjects,'" another declared. MP Celal Nuri (İleri) defended the wording of the article by saying that it did not aim to provide an ethnographic definition of "nation." He went on to counter another MP's suggestion that they add an explicit condition for Turkness, such as "possessing Turkish culture."[5] Celal Nuri warned that this would contradict Article 39 of the Treaty of Lausanne, which had established that "Turkish nationals belonging to non-Moslem minorities will enjoy the same civil and political rights as Moslems" and that "all the inhabitants of Turkey, without distinction of religion, shall be equal before the law." Moreover, Article 37 mandated that Turkey not pass any laws that contradicted the minority clauses of the treaty.[6] As the anxious deputies continued to debate these questions, Hamdullah Suphi (Tanrıöver), MP from Istanbul, came up with a solution.

Hamdullah Suphi started his long tirade against the draft article's inclusiveness with an emphasis on the recent "national resistance" and the delicate situation. "We have just come out of a very difficult struggle and none of us is of the view that it is over," he declared. "That's why legally erasing the division between non-Turks and Turks that exists in *reality* would be dangerous."[7] He emphasized that, in theory, it was not impossible for non-Turks to become Turks, but they would have to meet some conditions to make the move. Hamdullah Suphi gave the example of Jews in France: they were fully assimilated; therefore, they were French. The evidence of their assimilation was that "they had forgotten their language, and do not have separate schools." Yes, they remembered their descent and ancestry as Jewish but they were "culturally" French and carried French sensibilities. Then he gave the example of his former classmate, a Turkish Jew, who had recently asked Hamdullah Suphi what he could do to become a Turk. Hamdullah Suphi assured his friend that once Turkish Jews embraced the language of the land instead of using the language (Judeo-Spanish) of the people who had expelled them, and considered Turkish schools as their own schools, they could become Turks, much like French Jews had become French and English Jews had become English. But, given that Turkish Jews had not been doing these things, "can we expect the law to render them non-Jewish?" "No!" the floor yelled. So Hamdullah Suphi returned to the question of Armenians, whom he said had been living peacefully with Turks. Then, "propaganda and factions" had made them believe they were different from Turks, and they had asked for a separate state. Hamdullah Suphi addressed an imaginary Armenian—no Armenian was present in the room—and said, "Close down your schools, renounce Armenianness, and accept the Turkish culture and then we will call you 'Turk!'"[8]

Hamdullah Suphi saw Turkness and Armenianness (or Jewishness) as mutually exclusive, in the present and the future. It is remarkable that the ultimate evidence he provided for the "difference" between Turks and non-Turks was not religion, race, or ethnicity but the language they spoke and the fact that they operated separate schools. These were exactly the kind of freedoms that *dhimma* possessed under Ottoman rule, something that did not change even after the modernization and centralization reforms of the mid-nineteenth-century (Tanzimat). These were also rights that Turkey accepted to legally guarantee its minorities by the Treaty of Lausanne. Here, then, Hamdullah Suphi was accusing Jews and Armenians of perpetuating their groupness by practicing their *millet*-system entitlements and/or Lausanne-granted minority rights. This is an early sign of how the Turkish political elite and mainstream nationalism would, in the coming years, continue to talk about Lausanne's minority rights as "privileges," some of which minorities had to "relinquish" in 1926.

As Hamdullah Suphi's discussion of French Jewry as a model minority and, by extension, of France as a model host illustrates, the new Turkey aspired to the anti-*communautarisme* of French Republican citizenship and not the liberal Wilsonian version that contemporary scholars refer to as "multicultural citizenship" or "group-differentiated citizenship."[9] After the French Revolution eliminated hierarchically organized society, Jews gained equal citizenship rights on the condition that they surrender their special privileges of communal autonomy and rabbinic jurisdiction in civil affairs.[10] In this type of political theory, equality is achieved by making one's social, religious, ethnic, and other origins irrelevant in the public sphere.[11] The long Ottoman experimentation with creating loyal citizens informed the Turkish conclusion, summarized in Suphi's words, that people should be rewarded with equality when and if they shed their particularistic identities. In other words, literal sameness was necessary in order to reach the abstract universalism of sameness before the law. In light of this thinking, it is easy to see why the MPs found the notion of minority rights and equality of citizenry conflicting and inherently detrimental for the well-being of the state.

To further push for a change in the wording of the draft article, Hamdullah Suphi invoked the example of a recent planned decree that would compel foreign-owned private companies to lay off their Armenian and Greek employees. If the draft article passed as it was, he warned, these companies could have legal grounds to refuse to lay off Armenians and Greeks on the basis that the constitution of the land defined them as Turks.[12] Alarmed, the MPs unanimously agreed on Hamdullah Suphi's proposition to add the clause "in terms of citizenship" to the sentence under discussion in Article 88. As a result, Article 88 of the 1924 constitution read: "The people of Turkey, regardless of their religion and race shall, *in terms of citizenship*, be called 'Turk.'"[13] Thus it established two separate ideas of Turkness: real or authentic Turks and citizen-Turks. The MPs left the definitions of Turkness and Turkish citizenship intentionally vague in order to be able to differentiate *real* Turks from Turks-by-citizenship.[14]

During the discussions, MP Celal Nuri defined "our native/real/main citizens" (*öz vatandaşlar*) as "those who are Muslims of the Hanafi sect and speak Turkish."[15] In the decades to come, Turkey relegated its citizens of non-Muslim faiths, of non-Hanafi Muslim sects, and with non-Turkish mother tongues to the status of what I have elsewhere called *üvey vatandaşlar* (step-citizens).[16] As the unfolding policies would disclose, however, even though sect, linguistic, and ethnic differences would remain relatively bridgeable, religious difference remained fixed.

Secular Dhimmis of the Republic

The anti-minority attitude of the parliament constituted part of the broader state agenda for homogenization, standardization, and nationalization. To that end, immediately after the promulgation of the republic, the state began implementing various Westernization and secularization reforms. The stated goal of these reforms was the upgrading of Turkey to the level of "advanced [Western] civilization," which required the decoupling of the Turkish present from its Ottoman, Islamic, multiethnic, and "backward" past. The reforms included: the abolition of the caliphate (1924), the prohibition of the fez and requirement that all men wear panama hats with brims (1925), the abolishment of sharia and its replacement with secular civil law (modeled after its Swiss version) (1926), the removal of the constitutional provision establishing Islam as the official religion of the country (1928), changing the Turkish alphabet from the Arabic to the Latin script (1928), and granting suffrage rights to women (1934).[17] Opposition was strictly suppressed during the passing and implementation of these reforms.

Despite all these secularization reforms, however, and in a single-party regime dominated by men like Mustafa Kemal Atatürk, who were known for anything but their religiosity, religion remained the dividing line between "us" and "them" in the new Turkey. The state saw Muslims as Turks (or future Turks) but did not consider and treat non-Muslim Turkish citizens as true Turks, and did not trust that one day they could become fully Turkifiable. Secularism in Turkey never meant state neutrality toward religion, or its full relegation to the private sphere even though this was what the political elite claimed *laiklik* (laïcité) meant. Instead, in practice the state established Sunni Islam as its implicit "public theology" even when it initiated radically Westernizing reforms.[18] Initial institutionalization of secularism coincided with the marginalization of non-Muslims in political and public life.

The primacy of religion in the construction of citizenship in the new Turkey was certainly a legacy of centuries-old Ottoman rule in which religion determined a subject's legal status and his or her rights and obligations. In principle and according to the terms of sharia, Islam had to remain superior to all other religions practiced inside the Ottoman Empire, mainly Judaism and Christianity, the two Abrahamic religions that the Quran recognizes. A second and related reason for the prevalence of religion in Turkish citizenship practices relates to the fact that since the early nineteenth century religion had become the main language in various events and processes that eventually led to the demise of the Ottoman house. For instance, Balkan people's movements for independence from Ottoman rule used Christianity as their cause. Similarly, when the Great Powers undertook the protection of suffering Ottoman subjects they used a language of Christianity in order to justify their actions which quite often had imperialist undertones, leading the Sublime Porte to view such gestures as uncalled for intervention in its domestic affairs. All these historical processes and the devastating experience of World War I, genocide, and the divided loyalties that emerged during the occupation years made it almost impossible for the peoples of the new Turkey to detach religious identity from national identity. The Lausanne Treaty's minority clauses reinforced the acceptability of this separation by reserving minority status only for non-Muslims, therefore maintaining the relevance of religion for citizenship and belonging.

As a result of this entangled history and the inherent conflicts in its various agendas, the Turkish state treated minorities not consistently but paradoxically. On the one hand, Turkish laws and regulations excluded minorities from the emergent category of the "Turk." For instance, minorities were banned from careers in the military and civil bureaucracy and from traveling freely inside the country. Many such restrictions resembled the dhimmi laws of the pre-Tanzimat (1839) Ottoman Empire during which Ottoman non-Muslims had been forbidden from engaging in certain occupations including politics, the military, and the state bureaucracy. As dhimmis, Ottoman Christians and Jews had to endure these kinds of deprivations in return for their physical security and a certain level of religious freedom.[19]

On the other hand, unlike their imperial ancestors, the lawmakers of the new Turkish nation-state saw difference as a mortal threat and wanted to eliminate it. Therefore when the Turkish state embarked on nationalizing projects such as administrative standardization, institutional modernization, and wholesale secularization, its laws invited, sometimes even forced, minorities to be Turks or be *like* Turks. For instance, in 1926 minorities had to stop using their canonical laws for family matters; instead they were to be subject to the newly passed, secular Turkish Civil Code. Similarly, in 1935, like all other Turkish citizens minorities had to acquire Turkish-language last names and forgo their original last names, which used to denote their group belonging.[20] Most Armenian last names that had ended with *-ian* were thus changed into Turkish last names, many of them ending with *-oğlu*.[21]

One example illustrates this paradox perfectly. In 1933, when the Ministry of Education passed new legislation obligating primary school students to recite the "Student's Pledge" (*Andımız*) every morning, it did not exempt minority schools. The Student's Pledge read in full as follows:

> I am a Turk, I am righteous, I am hardworking. My principle is to protect my juniors, to respect my elders, and to love my country and my nation more than my own self. My motto is to rise, progress, and go forward. I commit my being to the existence of the Turks.[22]

Effectively, then, Turkey had forced *all* Turkish-citizen children to affirm their Turkness every day while denying *some* of these children their fundamental citizenship rights on the basis of their non-Turkness. (The pledge remained in effect until October 2013.) Given how much the terms of this paradox borrowed from the Ottoman past but belonged to the world of a nation-state that endorsed laïcité, I refer to the state-minority relationship in the early Turkish Republic as "secular dhimmitude."

"Secular dhimmitude" captures the intricacies of non-Muslims' assimilability paradox because it is an oxymoron that self-consciously places an Islamic legal category, dhimmi, in the framework of a secular, majority Muslim state. Moreover, the term enables us to conceive of the relationship in contractual and bidirectional terms. "Secular" was the project of the state and "dhimmi" referred to minorities. When we look at the roots of the term, we see that *dhimma* (plural) means "people of the contract" in Arabic, the contract between the Muslim ruler and his non-Muslim subjects. According to Islamic law, in exchange for not being persecuted or forced to convert, conquered Christians and Jews pay literal and symbolic tribute to Islam and its followers.[23] They agree not to imitate Muslims, to defer to them at all times, to pay a poll tax, and to remain loyal. They are then entitled to Muslims' protection, security, religious freedom, and the organization of their everyday lives according to the tenets of their faith (as long as they do not dominate the public sphere or try to proselytize). This system promises justice, not equality, to everyone. The Muslim ruler can terminate the contract unilaterally if he observes that the *dhimma* have trespassed their rights, for instance if they behave disloyally and help the enemies of Islam. In that case, these non-Muslims would cease to be dhimmis and could no longer enjoy the protection of the ruler. Instead, the rules of war would apply to them.

Bolsahay opinion makers who had lived through the last decades of the empire projected the republic as yet another Turkish state with which they had no choice but to cooperate, and they felt they knew how to do so. They reenacted dhimmitude because this was the repertoire that came easiest to them given how accustomed they were to its terms. Far from getting confused about the dizzying simultaneity of estrangement and invitations to belong, therefore, Armenian public figures who remained in Turkey worked along and worked with the paradox, thus helping reproduce a reactivated form of imperial subjecthood.

Dhimmitude had always worked as a legal instrument for political marginalization *and* inclusion; it looked like its secular version would continue in the same vein. If they employed the right rhetoric and disciplined their community into correct practices, Bolsahay leaders reasoned, "Turkish Armenians" as a group could avoid hostility and even receive a half-hearted pass as a benign problem and thus continue their everyday lives in a more or less "normal" manner. Security was not supposed to be a citizenship right but a favor delivered to them in return for their good behavior.

Loyalty to the new rulers and dis-identification with the past composed the two main pillars of neo-dhimmitude. Only two weeks after Patriarch Zaven's departure, a group of Turkophile Armenians (*Türkofil Ermeniler*, as they referred to themselves) along with several Turkish professionals established an organization called the Society for the Elevation of Turks and Armenians (Tr., *Türk-Ermeni Teâli Cemiyeti*; Arm., *Turkyevhay Partsratsman Miutiun*, hereafter SETA).[24] Although we lack information on the background of most of the Turkish members of SETA, the Armenian members were teachers (including at least two well-known instructors of Turkish language), writers, doctors, pharmacists, and lawyers. Some members also served in the Armenian National Assembly, signaling some overlap between SETA and the patriarchate, at least in its initial years. Some Turkish and Armenian newspapers claimed that in the beginning SETA was financially supported by the patriarchate. The honorary president of SETA was Berch Keresteciyan, who was known for his close relationship with Kemalists (he would later serve as one of the four non-Muslims in the Turkish parliament in the 1930s and 1940s and was given the last name "Türker" by Mustafa Kemal).

SETA's stated goal was to function as a "scientific, technological, social, economic, and literary club" that hoped to bring Turks and Armenians together "in order to create serious and honest rapprochement [*muhadenet*]." With the ultimate goal of "shaping a new generation that would benefit the Turkish Grand National Assembly," SETA embarked on a program to extend scholarships to Turkish and Armenian students, establish hospitals and dormitories, and help the poor.[25] Rather than staying busy with such charitable goals, however, SETA involved itself more with politics. One of its first organized efforts was to send telegrams to the Lausanne Conference's Turkish delegation stating that Turkish Armenians wanted to be represented by no one other than İsmet Pasha, the head of the delegation. By doing so, these "loyalist" Armenians hoped to disassociate themselves from the separatist and territorialist policies pursued by outgoing Patriarch Zaven Der Yeghiayan, whom the Kemalists loathed. Even though SETA did not have any authority to represent Turkish Armenians, this symbolic gesture was meant to signal to the Turkish public that at least some Armenians were not willing to be associated with the larger Armenian leadership (and the Armenian delegation at Lausanne) but with the Kemalists and their delegation.

For the same purposes, SETA published a Turkish language pamphlet titled *Türkiye Ermenileri* (Turkish Armenians) and expressed loyalist Armenians' take on the past, present, and future of Turkish and Armenian coexistence.[26] The undeniable enmity of the past, the text asserted, was only a matter of the past quarter century, and in any case it was not a conflict between the two nations but between some of their members, and it was a conflict stirred up by foreigners. The text refers to Armenians who worked for a Greater Armenia as *komiteci*s, that is, committee people, the main and pejorative term that the Ottoman government and the Kemalists applied to members of Armenian political parties in reference to the many "committees" that they established. SETA's text calls *komiteci*s idiots, wrenched fools, anarchists, and propagandists while it accuses the Western powers that engendered hope among those idiots of first inciting violence, and then using the pretext of "cleaning blood" to meddle in others' affairs and even settle in other people's lands.

By using such forceful language and othering Armenian nationalists and "Western imperial powers," SETA explicitly stated that under these conditions the Ottoman government understandably decided to get rid of the Armenians. The subtitle of the section where this topic was discussed explained it all: "Those who trespass their limits [*had*] deserve[d] the sword," a line from the late seventeenth-century Ottoman poet Nâbi.[27] The wholesale deportation was legitimate, the text argued, not only because it was self-defense (which legitimizes even murder, according to the text) but also because any government would respond to such treachery similarly. The pamphlet included the examples of the French in Africa and the British in India as proof that violence was a commonly employed tool in politics. All this discourse was meant to emphasize that Armenians who would remain in Turkey would not accuse Turks of any wrongdoing, that they would not seek revenge, and that they regretted the actions not of the Turks but of their Armenian counterparts (dead, deported, or fleeing).

By putting the blame for the deportations/genocide on Armenians themselves the text constructed "Turk Armenians" (*Türk Ermenisi*) as the diametric opposite of the *komiteci*, who were twice referred to in the text as "enemies." Other than their loyalty, the second most important quality of "Turk Armenians" was that they had been well integrated with the Turks. "They were born in Turkey, raised among Turks, have spoken Turkish, and sang Turkish songs." They were conscientious, faithful, wise, and foresighted. What ultimately differentiated them from *komiteci*s was that they "don't know where 'Armenia' is geographically" and they "don't know what independence is and are afraid of revolution as much as their death." These Armenians were, and would in the future be, useful to the Turks. The writers of the pamphlet were clearly aware of how non-Muslims had been branded as dangerous parasites. The pamphlet emphasized that SETA's goal was to blend together with the new government and work against deceitful people because they "look at the world from the eyes of a Turk and see the *komiteci*s the same way a Turk does." All SETA wanted, in return, was to secure the new government's backing and approval. With this pamphlet the SETA members not only communicated their goodwill to the incoming Kemalist forces but also hoped to give them a new language in which to think about leftover Armenians and decide what to do with them.

A few days before the signing of the Treaty of Lausanne, SETA hosted a tea party at the luxurious Tokatliyan Hotel in honor of Istanbul's recently elected parliamentarians. MPs went to the party to express their support for Turkish and Armenian reconciliation as well as to thank SETA and its constituency, which had supported their campaigns for election.[28] Hamdullah Suphi was among the attendees as was Harutiun Mosdichian, chair of the Armenian National Assembly, who had been influential in Patriarch Zaven's resignation. In the near future, Mosdichian would act as SETA's vice president.[29] During the tea party, Turks and Armenians exchanged expressions of goodwill and their commitment to a better future. Hamdullah Suphi did not forget to note that Turks were cautious about believing the sincerity of Armenians' expressions of loyalty because many Armenians still worked against Turkey from Britain or Germany. Mosdichian responded with the most basic Armenian loyalist argument: many Armenians have always been loyal and they should not be punished for the crimes of others. The tea party concluded with applause and cries of "Long live the Turkish nation, long live Mustafa Kemal."[30]

While SETA's activities and discourse provided an early sign of how at least some Armenians were ready to internalize dhimmitude, they were by no means isolated or exceptional. SETA's language would soon become the dominant Armenian discourse, especially after 1925 when the state's authoritarianism intensified after the Kurdish Sheikh Said Rebellion. For instance, in 1927 Mustafa Kemal's first visit to Istanbul after the Kemalist victory gave the Armenian press many opportunities to express their admiration of the new regime. *Hay Gin*'s coverage of his visit is illustrative of the overall transformation in Armenian discourses. In January 1922 the journal published on its cover page a painting of Mount Ararat, the epicenter of the Armenian historical homeland, which was an Ottoman territory that Armenians claimed was their own.[31] This move could be seen as an expression of the journal's support of Armenian territorial aggrandizement. In July 1927 the same *Hay Gin*, under the directorship of the same editor, featured Mustafa Kemal (the person whose movement put an end to Armenian dreams) on its cover page with welcoming words.³²

Not every Armenian institution and periodical assumed the same exact stance vis-à-vis the state. Some newspapers were more vocal about loyalism and others were less so. But the important point is that *none* that did not proclaim their loyalty could continue publication in a Turkey in which censorship was becoming increasingly strict, especially during the period beginning in the 1930s to which the historiography refers as "High Kemalism." Along with the intensification of authoritarianism, the Armenian discourse of obedience and submissiveness also intensified, and voices that remained neutral were muted. The *Nor Huys* (New Hope) weekly, which began publication in 1935, was among the newspapers that took the mission of loyalty most seriously.³³ Its first issue (April 13, 1935) featured a front-page article titled "How Can We Become Authentic Turkish Citizens [*hayrenagits, vatandaş*]?" A writer with the pseudonym M. Vankaya explored this question in an editorial in the next issue.³⁴ In order to demonstrate Armenians' loyalty to Turkish-speaking readers, his pieces were translated into Turkish and printed on the front page. Vankaya asserted that "we will live in this country as Armenian in religion and Turkish in nationality."³⁵ He encouraged Armenians to use the Turkish language, and emphasized that "we" embrace "laicism and populism" and support Atatürk's Republican People's Party. Vankaya insisted that Armenians were far more satisfied with the Turkish secular rule than with the ramshackle Ottoman rule. Kemal's efforts were praiseworthy, for they "brought together all Turkish citizens [even non-Muslims] with bonds of Turkification." In the same year that the surname law obligating everyone in Turkey to assume a Turkish last name was enacted, Vankaya wrote:

> We, with our fullest existence, desire to acquire Turkish last names like the civilized Turks. We will use these last names proudly (how happy one is who says he is a Turk). We have to accomplish this task without wasting time; otherwise we will lose a great deal. For example, a sign on our shops with a Turkish last name would attract a decent Turk. Otherwise, a Turk would not come near our shops unless he has to. The Turk has the right to impose these kinds of conditions [on you] in order to share the rights of his country, which he has acquired with his blood.³⁶

The same year, Ankara uncovered two Syrian-based Armenian assassination plots against Atatürk. After this news reached Istanbul, *Nor Huys* published a full page in Turkish. This cover page included a large photo of Atatürk, with these words written in Armenian above it: "A criminal attempt against the person of our beloved Atatürk is a blow against the heart of our republic." Underneath, written in Turkish, was this caption: "The Republic of Turkey Is Immortal" (Figure 18).[37]

In the decades to come Turkish Armenians either ignored or actively distanced themselves from Armenians in the diaspora who worked for pro-Armenian causes, such as refugee care, assassination of genocide perpetrators, lobbying among Western powers, and petitioning the League of Nations about anti-Armenian activities in Turkey, especially illegal land grabs. On the contrary, the Turkish Armenian press did not miss any opportunity to highlight each and every instance when Armenians in the diaspora did or said anything good about the new Turkey. For instance, the volume prepared for the fifteenth anniversary of the republic in 1938 had a special section called "The Armenian Press Abroad and in Turkey" wherein laudatory remarks of Armenian periodicals in Paris, Venice, and New York were given space.[38] The underlying idea was that not all Armenians abroad bore resentment or enmity toward Turkey.

Bolsahays tried to control their community's public image. Intellectuals occasionally sought the limelight with actions and stories that enhanced their reputation as useful citizens. For example, the headline in the first issue of the weekly *Sharzhum* (Movement) in 1930 read "Turkish Writers Exalt the Armenian Mind."[39] The Turkish Writers' Union had paid a visit to the grave of Kevork Terzibashian and left a wreath in appreciation of his superb study of the medieval Azerbaijani poet Fuzûlî.[40] *Sharzhum* was thrilled by this gesture of gratitude to an Armenian intellectual. In the following days, interviews were conducted with several Turkish public figures, including parliamentarians, writers, and historians, to ask them about their views not only on Terzibashian's book but also on Armenian literature and the intellectual relationships between Turks and Armenians. These interviews were published under the title "We and the Turks," which in and of itself suggests that the two categories had not and were not to merge. The newspaper italicized the comments of the interviewees when they alluded to the need for better relations between Turkish and Armenian intellectuals

Figure 18. "The Republic of Turkey Is Immortal." *Nor Huys* (New Hope) weekly, October 26, 1935. This Armenian language weekly published its most pro-Kemalist pieces, such as the one depicted here, in Turkish.

or acknowledged the contributions of Armenians to Turkish literature or theater. The interview titles included "An Intellectual Bridge Is Necessary [between Armenians and Turks] Says Celal Nuri Bey [MP from Gelibolu]," and "There Are Strong Links between Armenian and Turkish Literature, I Believe That the Closing of the Intellectual Gap between the Two Nations will be Beneficial, Says Köprülüzade Fuad Bey."[41] The press was selective. Cordial interactions between Turks and Armenians made the news, but hostility and discrimination, past and present, went underreported.

Like Jews living in Nazi Germany, Armenians had to master selectivity in order to be able to sustain normalcy in their everyday lives.[42] Armenians' responses to the "Citizen, Speak Turkish!" campaigns are telling in this regard. These state-sponsored campaigns started in the late 1920s and were occasionally re-invoked until the 1960s.[43] They aimed to make it illegal to speak any language other than Turkish in public. Signs in theaters, restaurants, hotels, and ferries urged everyone to speak Turkish. Despite the financial and moral support of the Turkish authorities, at least in Istanbul the campaign was not translated into law. But scores of non-Muslims were harassed for speaking another language in public. Many of them were criminalized simply because not speaking Turkish was frequently considered "insulting Turkishness," a punishable act.[44] In his memoirs Agop Hacikyan, who was about ten years old at the time, recalls:

> It was a treat to go shopping with Mother in Pera. To get on a street car, to read out loud the store and street signs and look around to see if people were impressed and hear my mother's bravos. Then I would speak to her in Armenian to demonstrate my bilingual proficiency. She'd at once get upset and tell me to shut up. I'd read the store and street signs but turn a blind eye to the signs stuck in the streetcars, buses and shops to remind us, the country's minorities, to speak Turkish.[45]

If one way of adapting to Turkey was turning a blind eye to a bothering reality another was choosing silence over expression, which is similarly summarized in Agop Hacikyan's words when he observed his mother shopping: "In the stores, my mother embarrassed me; she spoke Turkish with a pronounced Armenian accent. It didn't only embarrass me but I felt terribly uneasy for she was manifesting our ethnicity, our otherness."[46] Agop's personal and perhaps childish tendency to cover up his visible and audible difference was in fact a communal reflex that the Bolsahay elites largely shared and it was an indispensable base for the correct performance of dhimmitude. A telling example is Turkish Armenians' response, in 1935, to Metro Goldwyn Mayer's announcement that it would produce a film based on Franz Werfel's 1933 novel *The Forty Days of Musa Dagh*, which was derived from the real experiences of a group of Armenians in southern Turkey during the genocide who successfully rebelled against deportation and probable death.[47] The Turkish government reacted harshly to this announcement, threatening that Turkey would not only ban the film but also all the company's productions. Ankara used diplomatic means to facilitate Washington's intervention in the matter. In an attempt to challenge the credibility of the novel, Turkish newspapers announced that Werfel, like Henry Morgenthau, the US ambassador to the Ottoman Empire during World War I and an influential witness to the Armenian massacres, was Jewish. Turkish Armenians joined this campaign. They condemned the action of the Jews in "exploiting regrettable incidents of the past" to harm "the brotherly feelings between Armenians and Turks."[48] Moreover, some Armenians held a meeting in the Pangaltı Armenian Church, and "an effigy of the offending author was solemnly burned, together with a copy of his book."[49] Ultimately, the film was not produced. Armenians continued to burn, bury, or hide Werfel's and other similarly "dangerous" books.[50]

Bonds of Modernity

Did post-1923 Armenians perform loyalty only to strategically preempt aggression? Did they sincerely believe that the new Turkish state was different from its oppressive predecessor? If so, was this wishful thinking or insidious camouflage? Notwithstanding the impossibility of measuring "sincerity," I contend that Kemalism held out a promise for Armenians, and this was an important reason why at least some of them could have *really* liked the new Turkey. In the oral history interviews that I conducted with elderly Bolsahays now living in the United States and Canada, many of them expressed their content with Kemalist modernization measures. Many of these interviewees cried the day Mustafa Kemal died; one of them, Shakhe Shelemian, then a middle-school student at an Armenian school in Istanbul, cried so intensely that in the end she fainted.[51]

In the early Turkish Republic, even though Islam remained the unmentioned public theology and the formal factor that disqualified Armenians from full membership in Turk-hood, Armenians did not necessarily see secularization as a tool for exclusion. On the contrary, secularization made their inclusion possible in a variety of ways. The lessening of Islam's prominence—however superficially—downplayed their fundamental difference, their Christianity, at least ostensibly. This was important because in the early Turkish Republic, sameness was equated with belonging and difference with foreignness. Armenian representatives of all political backgrounds and ideological proclivities appreciated the men's hat reform as well as Muslim women's increased unveiling, a practice strongly encouraged by the state. The Panama hat brought unanimity and thus anonymity. Ironically, the uncovering of Muslim women—at least in Istanbul—enabled non-Muslim women to cover their difference. In short, Kemalism promised an easier way "to pass" as Turkish without necessarily turning into one, an ideal solution for Armenians who themselves did not aspire to become Turks anyway.

Although it frequently contrasted with their real-life policies, the Turkish ruling cadres employed a rhetoric of unity and sameness among all sectors of the population regardless of religion, ethnicity, and class. Even though this rhetoric was geared for homogenization and not for equality and peaceful coexistence among a diverse people, it still appealed to Armenians precisely because it contrasted with the former Ottoman ways of organizing society in which non-Muslims were inferiors to Muslims, a legally endorsed social organization that did not fully change even after the mid-nineteenth-century Tanzimat reforms. Although this principle had ensured relatively violence-free centuries, in the early Turkish Republic, Armenian spokespeople "read" this past as one in which they had been the constant victims of the Muslim sultan's whims. This, of course, was a teleological reading. Armenians were simply aligning themselves with the Kemalist narrative with regard to the Ottoman past, and thus othering it.

Armenians welcomed Kemalism for other reasons that added to its appeal as a breathing space conducive to camouflage. Modernization reforms signaled Armenians that the new Turkey, led by an avid Westernizer—a blue-eyed blond man in a tuxedo who loved drinking and dancing the Charleston with women who sported bobbed hair, short skirts, and high heels—was *really* changing (see Figure 19). And it was changing in the direction that Armenians would want: from East to West. Since at least the early nineteenth century, large sections of the Armenian intelligentsia worldwide had identified their nation with a superior Western "civilization" to which they argued Armenians belonged thanks to their religion, history, language, and lifestyles, including how their women occupied a cherished place in society. Bolsahay elites were now observing that the Turks too were finally understanding that the Western—thus, civilized—ways were better than

Figure 19. Atatürk dancing with his adopted daughter at her wedding in 1925. Armenians took heart in seeing Turkey's modern, Westernized, "civilized" new leaders. Getty Images.

Eastern—thus, backward—ways (which they reasoned had led to the prior massacres). As an added benefit, Westernization reforms made Armenian lives easier. It is not difficult to imagine Armenians' gratification when, in 1935, the state changed the official day of rest from Friday to Sunday. This change is a good summary of the puzzle of Turkish secularist modernity: the same state the high-ranking echelons of which had actively contributed to the massacring of Ottoman Christians was now adapting Western *and* Christian models and tastes in the name of laïcité and higher civilization.[52]

Moreover, some dimensions of the modernization project happened thanks to Christian, specifically Armenian, absence. An integral part of the genocide was the transfer of wealth, including personal property, real estate, and businesses, from Ottoman Armenians to Ottoman Muslims. One example will elucidate how these processes were connected. From early on the leadership of the Turkish War of Independence chose Ankara as their center and Atatürk acquired a residence there. Çankaya Köşkü, the residential palace (the Turkish White House) of President Atatürk, originally belonged to an Armenian (though this had not been public knowledge until the 2000s).[53] The property was confiscated, without any compensation, from the Kasapian family, which had been ordered deported but thanks to influential connections managed to go to Istanbul instead of the Syrian deserts. Similarly, the founding fathers of the new Turkey settled in "abandoned" vineyards in Ankara once belonging to wealthy Armenians. The houses there, built in the latest fashionable styles, also had the "symbolic function of showcasing the modern way of life the republican leadership sought to install in Turkish society."[54] The Kasapians survived and stayed in Istanbul after the republic but were never compensated for their losses.

Kemalist modernization projects did not shy away from employing qualified Armenians. This was also a similarity between the Ottoman Empire, which had multiple non-Muslims in the service of the court (from physicians to cooks, from lawyers to musicians), and the new Turkey, which was willing to ignore individual Armenians' Armenianness when there was need for their talents or specialization. One of the most prominent such figures was the linguist Hagop Martayan, a specialist in the Turkish language.[55] In 1932, during his language reforms, Mustafa Kemal extended an invitation to Martayan (who was living in Sofia at the time) to help the newly established

Turkish Language Association cleanse modern Turkish of the Ottoman language's Persian and Arabic influences. In appreciation of Martayan's help, he was, at Atatürk's request, rewarded with the last name "Dilaçar," that is, the unlocker of language, or "tongue opener." Dilaçar soon became the leading expert in the Language Association and taught at Turkish universities in the 1940s and 1950s. He was one of the many professors who continued to work as state functionaries despite the theoretical (though ambiguous) ban against non-Turks' becoming civil servants.[56]

Given the repressive measures of the government, Bolsahays did not write about how the "Turks" did away with Armenians but appropriated their tastes, homes, jobs, and frequently, women and children. Instead, they dutifully performed as loyal, silent, invisible, accommodating, and useful members of society, grateful for the sponsorship of their overlords. In return, they expected safety, security, and relative autonomy in how they handled their community's "private life." These were the basic terms of the non-verbalized but assumed relationship between the secular state and its neo-dhimmis.

Domesticated Survival

The family and the household were the sites in which Armenians exercised the most control and as such they were the nuclei of the community's "private life," a life the state was expected to stay away from. This was especially the case because, like its Ottoman predecessors, the modern Turkish state halted its regulatory energies at the threshold of the residential household. The state did intervene in the private sphere to organize gender relationships but not the ways of life driven by a particular religion, sect, or ethnicity since these were practices inside the household. The state's laws and regulations regarding family (who the breadwinner is, how can one seek divorce, etc.) applied to *all* Turkish citizens regardless of religion. That the state did not target minorities' family structure as such made the family, marriageability rules, and kinship networks especially important beacons of continuity for the free and legal performance of Armenianness. The family thus continued to be the *in*-side of the Armenian community.

There were also a number of sites that had traditionally belonged to the Armenian *millet* but under the new Turkish rule had to be regulated by the state's laws. In the management of their churches, schools, hospitals, orphanages, charitable organizations, endowments, and cemeteries Armenians now had to share power with the Turkish state, the reason why I call them *mid*-sides of the community. In these mid-sides Armenians mainly interacted with other Armenians and were able to maintain their traditions as long as they abided by Turkey's laws. In this spherical imagination in which concentric circles open up to the *out*-side of the community, Armenians related to *aylazk*s (people of other nations, usually in reference to "Turks") in the non-family, non-kinship, non-school, non-church, non-cemetery sites that belonged to the *Turkish* public sphere. In this enclave-like existence where Armenians closed in on themselves there also was an *Armenian* public sphere. In the Armenian press, theater groups, and choirs, an Armenian readership and audience exchanged ideas and tastes, thus reproducing their very own Armenianness. The whole Armenian organization and reorganization implicated women and men differently in the sustenance of identity and community and therefore had gendered consequences.

After 1922, the Turkish state expected passivity and invisibility from all Armenians, regardless of their sex. They were expected to recoil from the public sphere all at once. Even though both Armenian men's *and* women's public activism for nationalist goals came to a halt with the Kemalist victories in 1922, Armenian men continued to hold public roles in the mid-side of the Armenian community and act as liaisons between this mid-side and the state (i.e., the outside). Women, on the other hand, as the heart of their families, were expected to retreat to the domestic and spend their uniquely female energies conserving that which made Armenians different. This "conservation duty" did not necessarily chain women to the home because teaching at Armenian schools or volunteering at charitable organizations (mid-side) remained respectable and desirable.

The cessation of activism for the Armenian cause was palpable in *Hay Gin*. As the militant and propagandist tone of the former era waned, articles encouraging women's domesticity crowded the pages of the journal. The women's "patriotic ideal" (*azkanver ideal*) that had been the staple of the 1918–1922 era gave way to a language of women as "savior" (*prgarar*). In the pre-1922 period, Mark had asked women to give their money to the Armenian cause instead of to expensive tailors or manicurists, but after 1922, the same money was to be devoted to their children's food.[57] *Hay Gin* still urged women to volunteer in community institutions such as hospitals and orphanages, but the sense of urgency had disappeared. In general, women—within the home or without—were asked to work for the maintenance of the status quo.

In the face of dispersion and looming threats of assimilation, mothers were expected to make Armenianness a home for the new generations, albeit metaphorically. Language, religion, religious and nonreligious holidays, stories, songs, and lullabies would all engender the reproduction of an Armenian self both in hostile Turkey and in lands far away from a homeland to which many were unable to return. In early 1924, Vartan Parunagian wrote to *Hay Gin* from New York applauding his mother, who had insisted on celebrating January 6 as Christmas even though in America "everyone" celebrated it on December 25. Parunagian's mother might simply have been used to celebrating a different day for the holiday because she came from a place where it was the norm for different groups to have their own sacred days—a point Parunagian did not make. What he instead emphasized was that "the Armenian woman is devoted to her customs and traditions more than anyone else," and that he was grateful to his mother "for not forgetting her 'essence' even in this foreign country."[58]

Along with Armenian women, children were also domesticated, which should be seen as an expression of Armenians turning inward. "The yesterday of the orphans is a past that must be forgotten, but what will be their future?" asked Mark in her May 1924 editorial.[59] This striking quote summarized in a few words how the representation of orphans and children, *and* the discourse of the recent past, had changed in the journal. In the pre-1922 years, children had been seen as the ultimate symbols of Armenian suffering as well as Armenians' hope for a bright future, emblemized in Greater Armenia. Not only the events that had orphaned children, but also orphans' memories of those events had mattered to the Armenian cause before 1922 because remembering and vengeance would bring together the wrecks of this victimized nation. After 1922, as indicated by Mark's question, the causes of their orphanhood had to be forgotten, along with feelings of revenge. In 1924, after congratulatory remarks on continuing orphan-care efforts by Near East Relief in the United States, Matilda Jelal wrote that Armenian orphans' upbringing required *"love and forgiveness* even against those who did not treat them nicely." Then she added, "and there should not be any space for vengeful feelings in their tiny hearts."⁶⁰ The issue of orphans and orphanages slowly faded into the background of the journal. After the mid-1920s, when *Hay Gin* mentioned children it was usually in the context of pedagogy experts writing about modern schooling, parenting, and disciplining methods.

Many *Hay Gin* writers, as well as most other Bolsahays, considered schools—especially primary schools—an extension of the household. Since the early nineteenth century Armenian schools acquired a cherished place in the consciousness of Armenian lay and clerical public figures. It is telling that in October 1924 the new publication of the Armenian Apostolic Church, *Hay Khosnag* (Armenian Spokesperson), put equal emphasis on church and the schools as special sites in which Armenians could exercise self-determination:

> For a race/nation [*tsegh*] like ours, who had, during the course of long centuries, lost its condition of living freely and independently, and therefore is deprived of normative citizenship, the Church and schools remain uniquely indispensable factors of existence and self-determination [*inknoroshum*] [. . .]. We should candidly admit that the Bolsahays still possess these two agents that symbolize their race/nation. [They] protect them and they need to protect them at the cost of every sacrifice.⁶¹

Like the church, schools had to be preserved "at the cost of every sacrifice" because it was a legal and traditionally accepted way of maintaining identity and recovering Armenianness. Until 1924, Armenian schools were under the auspices of the patriarchate, which helped with their funding, appointed teachers and inspectors, and provided textbooks. After the 1924 Unification of Education Act, like all other educational institutions, Armenian minority schools too were put under the control of the Ministry of Education. Minority schools were soon required to hire a certain percentage of Turk teachers who did not belong to minorities. These were all breaches of the Treaty of Lausanne's minority protection clauses. Turkish literature, geography, and history had to be taught by Turk teachers, and the vice principals had to be Turks.⁶² These teachers and administrators had to be appointed by the Ministry of Education from among teachers who possessed "national consciousness" and "national sentiments."⁶³ As testimony to the importance Turkish leaders attached to the remembrance and the study of the past, minority schools were not permitted to teach the history of their separate communities but only the history of the Turks—and only through standard textbooks distributed by the Ministry of Education in which all minorities, but especially Armenians and Greeks, were depicted as enemies of the Turks.[64] The 1931 edition of the *Citizenship Education* book included a section called "Bad People," in which non-Muslim citizens of the republic were depicted as usurers, swindlers, and profiteers.

Despite all these drawbacks, schools maintained their importance for the maintenance and recovery of Armenianness. First of all, schools were allowed to teach the Armenian language and Armenian literature and music. According to state law, only ethnically Armenian children were allowed to attend Armenian schools and despite quotas for Turk teachers, most teachers, principals, and staff were Armenians. Although Armenian schools had to observe all Muslim and national holidays, they also celebrated Christian religious holidays as well, therefore closing on Armenian Christmas and Easter. Education in minority schools thus guaranteed a "syncopated temporality" because students would experience "a different rhythm of living and being"[65]—one of the main reasons why so many Armenian public figures emphasized its preservation. The first Armenian patriarch of the Republic of Turkey was among them.

Archbishop Mesrob Naroyan took office in the summer of 1927. Following tradition, the new patriarch's encyclical letter was read in all Armenian churches in Istanbul. The patriarch read the letter himself during his inaugural mass in the Kumkapı Armenian Church across from the patriarchate building. Even though his immediate audience was the congregation, he clearly had other targets in mind, mainly the Turkish authorities. The letter provides a perfect summary of how the Armenian representatives positioned their community in relation to their new rulers, and how they conceived the survival of Armenianness under and together with Turkishness.

In the opening paragraphs, Naroyan told his community that "we have to consider ourselves happy that we live under the paternal protection of our Turkish republican government, as witnesses of the important revolution that saved the Turkish homeland from true destruction and [...] put it on the level of a great, civilized nation."[66] Already, in this one sentence, the patriarch communicated his willingness to infantilize his community as harmless and inconsequential under the protection of an influential, giant-like father who was nonetheless civilized. He promised that the infant would follow the father in any direction he might choose to go. Naroyan added that Armenians were a "congregation," and that "thanks to the republican way of government," they were free in their "spiritual and moral development and progress." The rest of the letter explained what he meant by "spiritual and moral development and progress," basically the preservation of families, churches, schools, and charitable organizations, and the use of the mother tongue: "Dear people! Make sure that your children learn your mother tongue thoroughly, that beautiful and wondrous language that is the mirror of the genius and the creative capabilities of our race/nation [*tsegh*]." Naroyan was cautious not to be misread as dissenting or even disloyal. He must have been aware of how the Turkish political elite viewed Armenian schools negatively as bastions of Armenian nationalism and separatism. Recall MP Hamdullah Suphi's words during the drafting of Article 88 of the constitution during which he put the closing of schools as a condition for Armenians' inclusion in Turkness. Despite their loyalist stance, no Bolsahay ever suggested or agreed to the closing of Armenian primary schools. Patriarch Naroyan, who himself had worked in these schools before becoming the patriarch, felt the need to add immediately:

> It is never a hindrance for you to learn other languages as well both for your intellectual cultivation and your practical life. I exhort you and I command you to teach, with particular emphasis, the Turkish language, geography, history, and laws, embracing and putting into practice wholeheartedly the educational program of the republic. The Armenian school has always shown particular love and ability for the Turkish language, which is an essential condition for being good and conscientious citizens.[67]

In the last paragraph, Naroyan showed the same rhetorical strategy of promoting dual loyalties when he commanded his "Dear Armenian people": "You will contribute abundantly to Armenian charitable institutions, the Armenian National Hospital, and Armenian orphanages, and you will shine with your virtues of citizenship, you will remain a constructive and creative element in the great Republic of Turkey with fidelity and hard work."[68]

This letter shows that unlike Hamdullah Suphi, the patriarch was able to imagine a hybrid identity for Turkish Armenians. He, the most authoritative Armenian voice in Turkey, helped his community and Turkish officials believe that one could be a perfect Turkish citizen while still worshipping in the Armenian Church, going to an Armenian school, and continuing some distinctly Armenian traditions; that one could be equally conversant in Turkish and Armenian, and the two languages (and identities) were not mutually exclusive. Because a peaceful interweaving of the two identities was possible, Turkish Armenians' "hyphenated identity" should not be seen as seditious or threatening.

Even though the details of Naroyan's election are not clear, given the government's micromanaging tendencies in minority-related topics it is probable that the government had preapproved his election. He was known for his soft character and conformist nature, but his past was far from "clean" and fully pro-Turkish. During the postwar years, Naroyan had twice served as Patriarch Zaven's vicar when the patriarch was in Europe lobbying for Armenian territorial rights. As a bishop, Naroyan even penned a section called "Martyred Intellectual Clergymen" in the first collected volume dedicated to intellectuals murdered during the initial stages of the Armenian genocide.[69] In this volume, published in Istanbul in 1919, Naroyan had written, "In the hellish crime of dreadful butchery, the Armenian clergyman generally became immortal with the crown of martyrdom."[70] During that "butchery," he himself was the forty-year-old abbott-director of the Armash Seminary in Nicomedia/Izmit in western Anatolia. Along with other seminary staff, he was exiled to Konya, later arrested and brought to Istanbul, and then released. The conditions surrounding his release are not clear.[71] He served as a preacher and teacher in Istanbul until his rise to the patriarchate in 1927.

In early 1923, it was Bishop Naroyan who had written to Patriarch Zaven that the patriarch had best remain silent and retire (see Chapter 3). Keeping silent was what Naroyan himself did after he became the patriarch, as he witnessed the state's treatment and mistreatment of his congregation. Only occasionally and when he was certain that he was fully supported by tradition and by law did he raise his voice, usually to no avail. For instance, in 1932 the patriarchate sued the city government over the latter's desire to acquire the possession of the Pangaltı Armenian cemetery, a large and valuable property in the heart of the city. The case lasted about two years; in the end, the city confiscated the cemetery.[72] Currently a Hilton and the Turkish Radio and Television building are located in this space.

Overall, rather than dwelling on what his community no longer had, Naroyan paid attention to what it still possessed. He mastered the terms of secular dhimmitude, which equipped him with the golden rule of survival—that is, selectivity. He conformed to Turkification but did not let go of the ingredients that made one an Armenian. Naroyan was referred as "the author patriarch" because of the literary pieces he published both before and during his tenure as patriarch. He paid special attention to language and did not shy away from defending it, even at the height of the "Citizen, Speak Turkish!" campaigns. Notwithstanding comments here and there, even the "Citizen, Speak Turkish!" campaigns did not focus on what people spoke at home. This, in turn, helped to reify the household as the primary site for the enactment of difference. In 1930, Patriarch Naroyan wrote an article in which he made this point and singled out mothers as the primary agents responsible for preserving Armenian differences.

This piece was published in the 1930 issue of the Armenian National Surp Prgich Hospital's almanac and was titled "The Armenian Language and Its Study." The patriarch meant to alarm his congregation that parents were communicating with little children in "foreign [*odar*] tongues."[73] He did not clarify what *odar* referred to, probably leaving it purposefully vague so that it could mean Turkish as well as French, English, and other Western languages. He started by asserting that "the teaching and learning of the Armenian language is mandatory for every Armenian." The patriarch invited his congregation to learn their mother tongue well and to use it more often, especially at home and with children:

> The child has to imbibe the charm of his or her nation's/race's [*tsegh*] language through maternal love, as if he or she is drinking sacred mother's milk. It is the crucial responsibility of educated mothers to impress their beloved children with the marvelous language of Mashdots [the inventor of the Armenian alphabet]. Oh, those first impressions and those first maternal sensations [. . .] they are indelible and indestructible.[74]

The article was complemented by a small illustration that appeared on the cover page of that issue of the hospital's almanac (see Figure 17).

The visual focused on a mother and child in the privacy of a dark bedroom, in which the sleeping child is engulfed by her devoted mother's hands, arms, and body. Leaning close, the mother puts her mouth next to the child's ear. With a determined yet compassionate expression on her face, she communicates with the child through her body, and perhaps through words that she whispers. When viewed in conjunction with the patriarch's article, the message of the illustration was clear: the model mother transmitted maternal sensations and the charm of the Armenian language to her child. Her body was the prime transmitter, and that's why she wrapped it closely around her innocent, impressionable child: the mother knew she competed with "foreign" influences, but also that she had more control over the child, especially at this tender age. As the patriarch reminded his congregation, "Those first maternal sensations are indelible and indestructible."[75] To make the child resistant to forgetting or to any future obliteration, the patriarch assigned the mother the task of using her affective repertoire as well as words so that the child would don the Armenian difference and recover Armenia, albeit symbolically.

This image appeared only nine years after the *Sargavakin Daretsuytse* cover picture that opened Chapter 1 (Figure 3). Emblematic of the transformation that Armenians had gone through within the short space of a decade, the militant children of the earlier era, a boy dressed as a soldier and a girl dressed in a Red Cross uniform, both out in the field, switched to a picture of a bedroom in which a young mother hugs her sleepy child. Even though these images contrast with each other, the fact remains that in both periods the collective project (national/communal) could and was articulated through a gendered, age-conscious language that saw the relationship between Armenians along familial lines. The turn to the domestic sphere in post-1922 Turkey posed new challenges to feminism. The next chapter looks at the ways organized feminism, an ideology that by definition advocates change, survived for one more decade among Armenians in Turkey, a community whose most important goal was the preservation of who they were.

Figure 20. Keriman Halis (Ece), Miss Universe 1932, visiting with Hayganush Mark at *Hay Gin*'s office. Mark was a member of the jury that chose her as Miss Turkey. Yeghishe Charents Museum of Literature and Art (Hayganush Mark fond), Yerevan.

(CHAPTER 5)

CAN ARMENIAN FEMINISM SURVIVE THE NEW TURKEY?

Sometime in early December 1924, a "very well-known benefactor" scolded Kohar Mazlemian, a frequent contributor to *Hay Gin*, for a short story Hayganush Mark had penned in the journal's latest issue. Titled "A Woman's Confession," the piece profiled a newly married woman who confessed to her friend that despite her love for her husband she felt uneasy about her marriage. She did not like being referred to by her husband's last name because this made her feel objectified, "like a carpet, she was purchased from her father and given to her husband." She certainly was aware that her former last name was her father's. Her mother had comfortably lived with that last name all her life because, as "a woman of yesterday," she could not think of any alternative. "As a woman of today," however, Mark's heroine had difficulty putting up with this practice. She did not appreciate the double standards ingrained in other parts of her marriage, either. For instance, her husband was allowed to do what he wanted, but she was expected to inform him of everything she did.[1]

The benefactor asked Mazlemian to tell Mark that she should change course: "For a nation like us that is going through an era of misery, a woman's journal should publish pieces that encourage and *not* discourage marriage."[2] Mazlemian asked Mark to publicly respond to this criticism. Mark's answer was short and crisp: "Since benefactors [*parerar*] are clearly far from being able to understand how intellectuals think, they better focus on what they do best and build churches and schools." Moreover, she knew so many women who were unhappy in their marriages. And if its women did not feel happy, what ultimately would be the goal of "improving our nation's misery"? Last but not least, Mark questioned how Armenians who were so obsessed over mothers' sacred duties to the nation could so easily overlook the importance of fatherhood.[3]

Mark's encounter with the "benefactor" encapsulates the tensions that awaited Armenian feminists in the new, post-1923 Turkey, which increasingly pushed Armenians into communalism and traditionalism. Even though Hayganush Mark's overall goal of "putting an end to male domination" stayed basically the same in both periods, she adjusted her claim-making vocabulary to the new political context and *Hay Gin*'s content reflected these changes.[4]

Domesticity and Its Discontents

Hayganush Mark's ideas about domesticity can broadly be categorized into four strands of thought. First, she did not reject women's domesticity. Second, she contended that too much of it would be of no good to the nation. Third, she didn't see any reason why women's domestic responsibilities would hinder their public duties. Fourth, nature did not necessarily dictate that women be domestic and men be non-domestic.

From its first issue on *Hay Gin* felt the need to flag that this feminist journal approved of domestic responsibilities traditionally associated with women, such as cooking, housewifery, and mothering. Because *Hay Gin* hoped to appeal to the "new woman," it frequently featured sections on fashion and etiquette as well. If one reason for these choices was to expand the readership pool, the other was to negate the long-established fear among Armenian intellectuals that feminists meddled with the "natural" order of things and thus alienated women from the household where they rightfully belonged.[5] During the occupation years when *Hay Gin* concentrated on women's involvement in the causes related to the National Revival (such as lobbying, orphan care, relief work), Mark did not obsess over such accusations.[6] She seemed to have more important matters in mind than dealing with random antifeminist attacks at a time when Armenian Women's Association supporters, who included even the patriarch, significantly outnumbered her opponents, at least in theory.

But after the autumn of 1922, parallel with the general Armenian trend toward a retreat to the domestic and Mark's embrace of the church, *Hay Gin* dedicated many columns to setting the record straight, emphasizing again and again that feminists did not reject the home, the family, and motherhood. For instance, Mark devoted *Hay Gin*'s 1930 New Year's issue to the "Kitchen/Cuisine." It was explained that this topic was chosen to disprove the assumption that elite and intellectual women were not interested in kitchen talk and in cooking. After all, "for a New Year's Day, what could be more appealing than a yummy *anushabur* [Noah's pudding]?"[7] The issue featured the actress Digin Knar's *Diyarbakır keufte* (meatballs) and Kohar Mazlemian's *khavidz* (a kind of sweet porridge).[8] Sibil embellished her stuffed lamb (*letsvadz karnug*) recipe with an anecdote that featured a very important man in the history of Armenians and a very important woman in the history of Armenian feminists.[9]

Srpuhi Dussape, the first Armenian female novelist, in the 1880s wrote three feminist novels—dedicated to her mother and daughter—that advocated women's rights to education, employment, and choosing their own marriage partners.[10] Even more radically, Dussape's novels asked women and young girls to disregard traditions if they were prejudiced against the female sex. Inside the family unit, Dussape advocated a conjugal partnership in the wife and husband; rather than being locked in a slave-and-master relationship, the two complemented each other and were equal. Dussape excelled in exposing the paradoxes of patriarchal society. She questioned, for instance, why society would see women as inept and deny them education, employment, and public roles but would concomitantly trust them with the most important job for any society's continuation, raising the next generation and managing the household. She influenced all Armenian feminists coming after her, including Hayganush Mark, who would periodically publish Dussape's pieces in *Hay Gin*. Dussape had many opponents, most importantly Krikor Zohrab, one of the major Western Armenian writers of the late nineteenth century, who penned short stories and novels exploring the "female psyche." He was fundamentally against Dussape's ideas that women's nature did not dictate that they be domestic and nothing else. Zohrab was also a lawyer and a rising star of the Ottoman Armenian community.[11] He was a member of the Ottoman parliament from 1908 on and was one of four Armenian MPs who were massacred in the initial stages of the Armenian genocide. In *Hay Gin*'s New Year's special kitchen issue of 1930, Sibil, the most successful Armenian language teacher of the time, poet, and textbook writer, remembered Dussape and the polemics between her and Zohrab:

> When Srpuhi Dussape wrote *Mayda*, Krikor Zohrab got very angry with her. He claimed that educated women would not even know how to cook. Upon hearing this, a group of women baked a stuffed lamb meal, one that was hard to make and labor-intensive. On a sunny day in May, Zohrab was throwing an open-air feast. The women sent him the lamb to which they attached a note: "To our dear writer, from learned women [*kidun giner*]." In response, Zohrab admitted that it was the most delicious meal that he had ever eaten![12]

Sibil's above-quoted anecdote, real or manufactured, portrays traditional yet progressive Armenian women overcoming conservative men who could not think "out of the box." That Sibil in 1930 brought up this issue suggests that the conversation remained relevant for Armenians. Even though feminists around *Hay Gin* did not approve of Zohrab's politics on gender, they all embraced him as an Armenian giant lost to the Medz Yeghern, without, of course, being able to use this term in the early Turkish Republic. Perhaps another function of this anecdote was to quietly mourn Zohrab, who was Sibil's contemporary, and according to at least one neighbor of hers from Scutari, her one-time lover.[13]

In *Hay Gin* housewifery remained an important part of the discussion regarding the Armenian family. In her editorial titled "The Value of Home Economics" Mark first embraced housewifery as a beautiful and important thing and noted that feminists did not categorically negate it. But, she added, "it is a different thing to be a *woman* and an *individual* and a very different thing to be a *woman* and a *doll*. What we want is the former."[14] "Doll" was a metaphor Mark borrowed from Henrik Ibsen's play *A Doll's House* (1879).[15] In the play, instead of accepting her role as the passive, submissive, and inconsequential wife that society expected her to be—a doll—Nora, the heroine, deserts her husband along with her children. *A Doll's House*, "the *Uncle Tom's Cabin* of the women's rights movement," staged Nora as an *individual* who discovered she needed and had the right to "find the kind of person she [was] and to strive to become that person."[16] She was able, willing, and entitled to pursue freedom, and in the process to become an "individual."

According to Mark, the doll-type woman was a housewife and a mother but she viewed the home merely as a place to decorate and impress others. This was not the kind of sweet and patriotic home that Armenians needed to turn to in order to sustain their grouphood in the new Turkey and in the diaspora. Despite being the woman of the house, dolls lacked the education, commitment, and consciousness to make the house into a hearth that attracted all of its members "like a magnet."[17] That she was a housewife did not guarantee the doll's domesticity. Even worse, the doll was merely derivative of others' ideas, choices, and pleasures, what the heroine of Mark's story in the opening of this chapter did not want. She was a toy in the hands of men and a "parasite" dependent on the man for her finances. All she was interested in was his money, which she solicited in her own "tricky" ways. She always wanted to take, and never to give.[18] Therefore, she was subject to a man's decisions and was the object of his pleasures. Her husband was her master, but more than anything, she was a slave of fashion—one among many indications of her inability to make her own decisions. She lived a life whose terms were set by others, even though it was clear that "fashion was created by antifeminists who wanted to turn women into dolls."[19] The doll-woman busied herself all day trying to make herself beautiful for others.

According to Mark, dolls "blackened" the name of all women and gave antifeminists living proof that women were dependent, thus immature beings incapable of exercising social and political rights. This "sickly daydreamer" was "of absolutely no use to her nation."[20] Dolls were of no use to the nation because they did not care about other people's problems and were not motivated to go outside of their comfort zone and reach out to those who needed help. Returning to the story that opened this chapter, Mark defended the heroine of her story because she was a woman who found herself trapped in conventional circumstances but rejected being a doll; she wanted to be an individual. The Armenian nation, Mark believed, needed women who could think and act independently even and especially in this weakened, minoritized state trying to survive under a hostile regime. This was a difficult argument to make because of the many paradoxes that had to be resolved in its formulation.

In Mark's thinking, what defined an individual, the antithesis of the doll, was the ability to be independent. French feminists, especially Olympe de Gouges and Hubertine Auclert, had influenced Mark greatly. De Gouges's

1791 "Declaration of the Rights of Woman and the Female Citizen" aimed to expose and protest the French Revolution's paradox of simultaneously agreeing on the fundamental human sameness, thus equality, of everyone *and* the exclusion of women from this single, abstracted individual-citizen, thus denying her equality with humans.[21] In the liberal, secular humanism of the post–French Revolution era, the independent individual was being cast as the opposite of the dependent female, who lacked the nature, experience, and capacity to make political judgments of her own. Mark's feminist strategy, then, rested on proving that women could be independent and therefore individuals and citizens with rights equal to men's.

Hayganush Mark aimed to turn the dolls into individuals, but was extremely insistent that she did not want to do this at the expense of turning them into men or women indifferent to their Armenian heritage. Like many of her feminist counterparts worldwide, Mark had to grapple with the dilemma of arguing simultaneously for women's likeness to men (to qualify for rights and citizenship) and their difference from men ("to refute the prevailing equation of active citizenship with masculinity").[22] A strategy many *Hay Gin* writers employed in order to ease this tension was to provide proof after proof that responsibilities and attitudes associated with femininity could successfully coexist with public activism and therefore should not be seen as justification for women's inequality.

Mark saw herself as one such woman who proved that a public role could be reconciled with domesticity and femininity. A sentence that would be remembered as the summary of her feminism long after she died said it all: "For me, the needle, the ladle, and the pen have always stood side by side."[23] She never had children. If she had, she would likely have added to the list an object that reified motherhood. The pen symbolized both her writing career as a form of employment and her active and organized effort to effect change. By her own example, as well as through the examples of the many other publicly active mothers, wives, and accomplished young girls that *Hay Gin* featured, Mark sought to establish the irrelevance of sex to political participation.

Even if sex was irrelevant for engagement in the public sphere, however, this did not mean that sex had to disappear as a fundamental difference among humans and as an organizing principle of human society. On the contrary, Mark dreaded the idea that women must be masculinized in order become equal members of society, or that men had be feminized to acquire less aggressive, softer, more domestic roles. She continuously emphasized that she "had never wanted to put pants on women." Rather, she believed that both sexes had something different to contribute to society. These roles were complementary and should be considered equivalent in worth.[24] Women's domestic roles, or their "sacred motherhood," should not be used as a pretext for denying equality to "half of humanity." Therefore, "like the scientist, soldier, and the politician, the woman had a duty to fulfill for humanity and that duty was the very reproduction of humanity."[25] It was an injustice, she believed, that society appreciated men's more public—therefore easily visible—contributions while it left women's invisible labor inside the home in the dark. "There are many monuments to the unknown soldier but there is none dedicated to the unknown mother," she complained to her readers.[26]

In summary, according to Mark, a woman's devotion to, or even self-sacrifice, for family (or others) did not detract from her individuality and independence, so her dedication to her family could not be used as an pretext to exclude her from the sphere of the non-family. In an ideal society, a woman's domesticity should not result in her subjection to men. She wrote that if a household was of her choosing; if her husband was her lover and friend; and if instead of "enchaining her with their little arms," her children allowed her to pursue a meaningful life outside the home, then a woman would willingly devote herself to that household. "If the home were a shared possession for woman," Mark declared, "it would cease to be her prison."[27]

Despite the stark contrasts she posed between different categories of women (such as dolls vs. individuals), however, she did believe in an "essence" that all females shared regardless of time, space, and conditions. Women, *by nature*, were more tender, caring, and emotional than men. Yet Mark did not attribute explanatory power to nature: the contemporary inequality between the sexes was not caused by nature but was literally *man*-made. Both the past education in and performance of assigned (gendered) roles resulted in the hierarchical difference of intelligence that one observed among the sexes in the present. For instance, because girls and boys were educated differently at home and in school, their expectations, experiences, and capacities differed. In 1922, Mark wrote that "if a man and a woman were to be educated the same way, no significant difference would be observed in their brain development,"[28] and then in 1932, a more confident Mark noted, "The brain does not belong to this or that sex. The sex is in the brain, not vice versa." She could not help but add that "if we compare average women to average men, women would win."[29]

Women would win, Mark believed, because they had achieved so much *despite* the kind of education that society allowed them. She specifically blamed men for selfishly holding women back. For instance, not only did many sciences and occupations remain closed to women, but women who had shown interest in "men's spheres" were demeaned as arrogant or "blue stockings."[30] This was a double standard, one among many that *Hay Gin* worked to expose in order to reduce their power to convince. Another important double standard that Mark and her colleagues at *Hay Gin* continuously attacked related to the church and how it hindered woman from becoming individuals. Armenian canonical law required that during the wedding the wife vow to "obey" her husband and the husband vow to be her "master." Despite the support that Mark and *Hay Gin* usually offered to the Armenian Church, in this particular issue the journal severely criticized the church for allowing such a "backward" and discriminatory practice to continue.[31] Mark reasoned that because this law's roots went back to the Gospel of Paul and because Paul was a man, like all other men who made laws he had made them in a way that they worked to the benefit of men.[32]

Mark's social constructionist ideas allowed her to conclude and argue that women—and men—were changeable. This is why feminism was necessary and viable. Indeed, her feminism might not have made sense if she had not advocated the constructed nature (perhaps even artificiality) of gender roles. Her advocacy of understanding gender roles as created by society was important because the most prevalent antifeminist ideas invoked "nature" as the ultimate authority in women's exclusion from the public realm. She historicized the process by arguing that women had worked outside the home since "ancient times," but in the eighteenth and nineteenth centuries men had tried to "soften" women by enclosing them inside the home.[33] Hence, "her home became her prison, and the arms of her child her chains. Because no one else would do it, she took care of the child."[34]

Mark opposed the naturalization of the difference between mothers and fathers. She emphasized that men had to be domesticated. Her understanding of the "domestic" did not merely mean housekeeping nor refer only to the physical structure of the home; the "domestic" also included "family and social relationships, child-rearing practices, personal well-being, purchasing habits, recreation, schools and neighborhoods, gardening, civic involvement, food preferences, health, and personal appearance."[35] Some of these duties could be perfectly undertaken by men. She criticized society for thinking that fatherhood simply meant disciplining the children. The "new man" of the modern, bourgeois household that *Hay Gin* promoted was not only a less-demanding husband but a father involved in the upbringing of his children and a participant in their daily lives.[36] For instance, he came home early and played with his children. He helped with gardening and repairing broken items at home. *Hay Gin* advised husbands to appreciate their wife's efforts with frequent kisses and presents. A most important domestic duty for men, however, was to remain faithful to their wives, an increasingly difficult task, it seemed, in an Istanbul that was home to countless young and rebellious women ready for pleasurable adventures.

La Garçonne's Threat to Armenians and Their Feminism

At the same time that feminists were coming to terms with the cessation of the causes associated with the National Revival and the commencement of a new, minority identity for Turkish Armenians, they were hit by a different kind of challenge, this time from faraway France. *Manch-aghchig* (boy-girl), a creation of Victor Margueritte's 1922 novel *La Garçonne*, gave a name to the postwar flapper type that had been the concern of several Armenian writers during the occupation years.[37] These writers had expressed their concerns especially in the context of "the dance craze," by which they meant girls and boys doing sexually suggestive "foreign dances" such as the foxtrot, the Charleston, and the shimmy. By 1924, the novel's Armenian (*Manch-Aghchige*) and Turkish (*Erkek Kız*) translations already filled the bookshelves, further inspiring youth, many a *Hay Gin* contributor feared, to disrespect well-established social norms, especially sexual propriety.[38]

The character type manch-aghchig, as discussed and depicted in the press of the time, fundamentally rejected all forms of modesty attached to her sex.[39] She frequented bars, drank alcohol, danced until the wee hours, smoked, drove cars, and had multiple lovers, both men and women. It was easy to recognize her for she embodied the opposite of the traditional female body. She cut her hair short, lost her curves to become cigarette-thin, put on exaggerated makeup, and wore short skirts and revealing clothing; but she could also be found in men's dress, for she did not shy away from cross-dressing. She read promiscuous novels, liked the movies, and loved shopping. Her most threatening characteristic, however, was her indifference; she did not care what others thought of her, and instead lived a life driven by her own desires. If she had parents, they did not seem alarmed by her immorality, thus being complicit in her "moral fall." Regardless of her social class—she could be from a modest background or be high class—she sometimes exchanged sexual favors with men for money. Yet she was no prostitute: her goal was not daily sustenance but the power to consume luxury goods such as makeup and cars. Most critically, the manch-aghchig was not interested in marriage or motherhood, and therefore utterly useless for Armenians.[40]

Monique, the heroine of *La Garçonne*, posed a threat to Mark's ideology for a number of reasons. First, people confused the individualist Monique with the "new woman" and the "feminist" that *Hay Gin* promoted. Second, she had no value for the metamorphosed post-1923 Armenian cause in Turkey. Third, she represented the wrong kind of Armenian womanhood to the outside world. *Hay Gin*'s "new Armenian woman" did not negate the "old Armenian woman" but simply found her inadequate and inappropriate for the changing times. Indeed, both types of women were featured on the journal's cover illustrations. Mark and her feminist comrades were not ready to fully get rid of the traditionalism represented by the "old woman." The problem with the doll, the ultimate Other of the new woman, was her complicity in "male domination" as well as her neglect of age-old Armenian traditions at the expense of her interest in beauty and fashion. Usually depicted as a married woman, the doll could have been the manch-aghchig's mother, for she was so invested in her *own* body that she failed to recognize the immoral course her daughter had taken. She might even have felt a sense of pride in her Europeanized daughter. The manch-aghchig, almost always depicted as a young, unmarried girl like Monique, represented a full negation of the Armenian tradition, and therefore was radically dangerous.

In an editorial titled "Let's Kill the Manch-Aghchig," Mark declared that as a woman's journal that worked for the equality of men and women, *Hay Gin* condemned the manch-aghchig, a disgrace to the name of womanhood.[41] Even a cursory look at the Armenian press indicates why Mark used such sharp language to note feminists' difference from what the manchaghchig represented. The caricatures of the time show that many journalists and cartoonists blurred the line between the "feminist" and the "modern girl."[42] It seemed as though many antifeminists felt vindicated: the manchaghchig confirmed their fears that revolutionizing womanhood would lead to societal collapse. Many caricatures attributed the same body type and clothing for both subversive modern girls (Figure 21 and 22) and revolutionary feminists (Figure 23), accusing both of the demise of morals and the dangerous intermixing of men's and women's spheres.

Figure 21.

— Waiter, why is this champagne diluted with water?

— Just so that you don't lose your mind completely because once you get the check you'll stay here for a long time.

Anushabur–Badger, July 14, 1927.

Figure 22. "Duration of Love."
— Is the romantic novel you're reading based on a true story?
— No way! I've been reading it for three days and it has yet to end.
Anushabur–Badger, June 23, 1927.

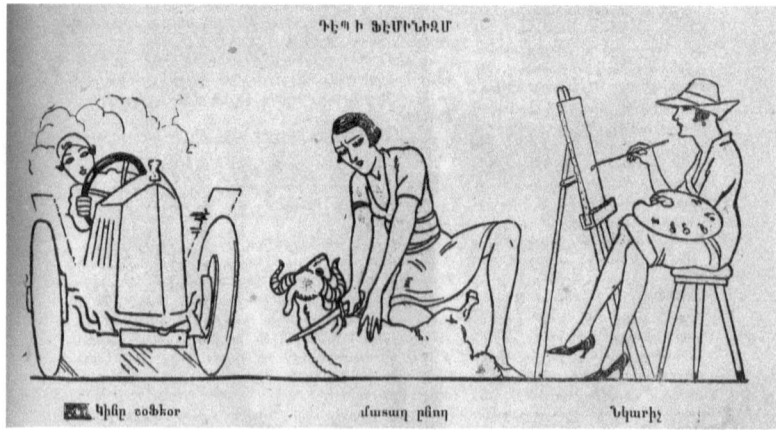

Figure 23. "Toward Feminism." The press frequently employed the same type of female figure to depict both decadent and dangerous modern girls and feminists. The three women depicted here (*from left to right*: as a motorist, as a ritual butcher, and as an artist) represent anxieties associated with the mixing up of traditional gender roles. *Anushabur–Badger*, September 1, 1927.

Ironically, one of the most significant challenges the modern girl posed to Mark's feminism was her love of books. Since the early nineteenth century, Armenian intellectuals with growing national consciousness had equated the nation's progress with the enlightenment of its girls, the future mothers of the nation. Books had been the ultimate symbols of an Armenian nation awakening to its rights and marching toward "civilization." Many family photographs in urban centers of both Bolis and the interior provinces included books placed on a little girl's lap, indicating the importance of her schooling for the family's self-image. The growing consciousness of an ethno-national Armenianness (separate from religious identification) had prioritized girls' education and had therefore presented endless possibilities for girls who were lucky enough to receive the new kind of education. The new and modern girls' schools produced thousands of Armenian young women literate not just in Armenian but also in at least one more European language.

By the time *Hay Gin* started publication, books still carried the same symbolic importance, as indicated by *Hay Gin*'s cover illustration in which the new woman holds a book, though not as an accessory but in order to read it (see Figure 14). In Mark's discursive constructions the ideal woman reads to get informed about life so that she can improve it. By the mid-1920s, however, the symbolic meaning of the book began to change, because there were too many of them and not all of them contained appropriate messages for young girls.

Every Armenian newspaper serialized novels (*terton*), which were especially well received by women and girls. At times women readers protested and threatened to boycott if a given newspaper skipped a day's *terton* because of big advertisements. Newspapers seem to have yielded to their requests.[43] Even though many contributors to *Hay Gin*, including the patriarchal *locum tenens* Kevork Aslanian, had urged girls to be "selective" in their reading and not read "trashy literature" (meaning promiscuous novels, of which *La Garçonne* was the prime example), it was clear that many women and girls did read whatever they found, especially promiscuous literature.[44] One *Hay Gin* contributor complained that "if there were four different editions of *La Garçonne* they would devour them all."[45]

Modern girls were frequently depicted with books, but given their clothing, background, and words, it was clear that these girls were not reading for deep knowledge but for pleasure. One caricature (Figure 22) summarized all the anxieties associated with the sexuality of the modern girl and her reading habits. Two modern girls are side by side. One of them asks, "Is the romantic novel you're reading based on a true story?" The reply: "No way! I've been reading it for three days and it has yet to end."

With its emphasis on writing, Mark's feminism differentiated itself from the male-dominated Armenian public sphere and also from the manch-aghchig. If reading a book was a passive activity through which one received, then writing was an active engagement through which one gave back, acquiring in the process a voice (thus becoming an individual) and the ability to push for change. In Mark's motto, "the needle, the ladle, and the pen," the pen was not only a literal reference to her own activism as an editor, but also the symbol of women's *active* entry into the public sphere of ideas and

Figure 24. Hayganush Mark working in her office, 1924. *Angudineru Zvarjali Darekirke* 6 (1924): 23.

practices traditionally reserved for men. Remember that Takuhi Kalantar, the teacher posed with her students on *Hay Gin*'s cover page in 1921, too had a ready-to-be-used pen on her table (Figure 15).

It seemed as if Mark's self-identification with the pen was revered by at least some sectors of society. A caricature published in a satirical almanac in 1924 depicted Mark in her office (Figure 24). In the drawing, she is thinking, reading, and writing. The clock behind her is ticking, suggesting that she might be trying to finish an editorial before the issue goes to print. The curtains are fully shut, indicating that she is cut off from the outside world. The highlight of the piece, other than Mark herself, is the oversized quill pen she holds.

It is striking that a photo of Mark, taken about a year after this caricature, posed her in similar setting (Figure 25). It is important to note, however, that in the caricature, the exemplar woman that Mark embodied does seem to

Figure 25. Hayganush Mark working in her office, 1925. *Hayganush Mark, Gyankn U Kordze* (Istanbul: n.p., 1954), 22.

share some characteristics with the modern girl. Even though Mark is curvy (thus female by tradition), her V-neck is rather deep and her arms are showing, unlike in the real photo. But more significantly, like the manch-aghchig, her hair is cut short; this reflects the reality, for in the photo she wears it bobbed. Mark did criticize manch-aghchig for smoking, but it was known that she and many of her feminist friends smoked.

That the new woman was married (like herself) but the modern girl was single accounted for the different criteria by which Mark judged them. Armenian girls, Mark asserted, had to become individuals without losing their traditional attributes associated with innocence, inexperience, and modesty—such as the "capability to blush," something that the manch-aghchig so clearly lacked.[46] This was especially important for Armenians, she argued, who had to rely on their women for self-preservation. The fact that the Catholic Church banned *La Garçonne* and that its author, Margueritte, the honorary president of the Société des Gens de Lettres, was expelled from the Légion d'Honneur further convinced Mark that Armenians could not tolerate the manch-aghchig.[47] She was almost relieved that even a civilized, European country that she admired did not approve of this much promiscuity. In a 1924 editorial she expressed her contempt for the increase in dance halls and the type of girls that danced there until early in the morning:

> Nowadays it is not important anymore that a girl knows how to boil an egg or take the temperature of the sick. All that matters is that she knows how to dance. Of course we are not promoting backwardness! Even the author of *La Garçonne*, in his response to the Légion d'Honneur, told them that rather than accusing him they should look at the dance halls which are full of *la garçonnes*. Anatole France agreed with him. Mind you, these are big countries that have all the means to perpetuate themselves, such as a state, a military, a large population, and financial power. If even they are bothered with this issue we have to be alarmed because we cannot afford voluntary losses [*gamavor gorusd*]. Who is going to tell our youth that dance halls are not places for our mourning souls?[48]

In light of my discussion so far, it should be easy to contextualize the message of this passage: because Armenians lacked a state, a military, a relatively large population, and money, and because they had experienced a major catastrophe, girls' sexual misconduct jeopardized the perpetuation of the Armenian grouphood.

Another problem with manch-aghchig revolved around the harmful and derogatory image of the Armenian woman it reflected to the outer world. The 1920s were a time in Istanbul when cultural critiques hotly contested Turkish women's dress, mobility, and habits, all in the context of the uncertain turn the nascent republic had taken toward "modernity." The jazz clubs, dance halls, bars, theaters, and cocaine dens—especially in Pera, the historically cosmopolitan district in the European part of the city—were marked by decadence as well as the unwanted interethnic mixing and the polyglot atmosphere these establishments provided.[49] Mark and her colleagues knew that as Christians, Armenian women in urban Istanbul had long been branded in the popular mind as Westernized or Europeanized, and therefore potentially immoral and impure. After 1923, when the community had to control its public image to prevent unsolicited attention, the bodies of women and girls acquired an added meaning. As a symptom of the overall Armenian turn toward keeping a low profile, females were to avoid attention, cover their difference, and keep their voices low.

The issue was clearly expressed in the context of mixed-sex beaches, a novelty for Istanbul in the mid-1920s. In 1925, Mark reported how a Turkish periodical was annoyed that Christian women were frequenting mixed-sex beaches in Florya, wearing swimsuits and behaving improperly. Instead of criticizing the Turkish writer for singling out Christian women, Mark wrote that "unfortunately what these Armenian and Greek women do blackens the name of all Christian women."[50] Not only did she call on Armenian teachers and parents to be more alert about this issue, she also wished that the Turkish government would ban mixed-sex beaches; she saw this as the ultimate solution to the problem. This issue had clearly occupied the Jewish community as well, for around the same time a certain Ms. Cuence was dismissed from her position as a teacher at the Jewish Orphanage at Ortaköy because of rumors that she had been seen in a bathing suit on the beach at Moda.[51]

In a 1925 *Hay Gin* article Kohar Mazlemian emphasized the burden placed on every Armenian, but especially the young girls, to represent themselves in a certain way. She looked at Armenian girls through the eyes of non-Armenians, and warned girls that they should represent their nation with decorum. In a piece titled "Womanly Sermons for Some of Our Girls," Mazlemian expressed her dissatisfaction with girls who had artificial, Europeanized manners, and who spoke loudly in public, mixing foreign words while speaking Armenian in saloons, ferries, or trains.⁵² She warned girls that their bad manners would cause foreigners to ridicule the Armenian nation. Linking the problem to the dispersion of Armenians, Mazlemian added that Armenians should adjust to the conditions of the country where they live, and because they were in Turkey, they had to abide by its norms, which emphasized female modesty.⁵³ Mazlemian could not help but add that if these girls really wanted to become Europeanized, they had better work for the education of their less fortunate counterparts.

About a month later, Mazlemian found the perfect medium to restate her point. She compared *La Garçonne* to Turkish novelist Reşat Nuri Güntekin's 1922 novel *Çalıkuşu* (The Wren), which Mazlemian read in Armenian translation in the *Marmara* daily as a serialized novel with the title *Tsakhsarig*.⁵⁴ She contrasted the narratives and characters of the two novels. They both revolved around young women cheated by their fiancés. Even though Monique's response to betrayal was sexual misconduct, Feride, the protagonist of Güntekin's novel, left Istanbul to devote herself to orphaned children and began teaching at girls' schools in remote corners of Anatolia.⁵⁵ Mazlemian applauded Güntekin for representing such a good role model for young girls and reprimanded all those girls, Armenian or not, who tried to follow the footsteps of Monique. In addition to expressing admiration for the kind of girls Güntekin promoted, Mazlemian's essay had the function of aligning herself (thus her community) with the Turks and disassociating Armenians from a Europeanness that did not fit Armenians' and Turks' shared notions of modesty and propriety.

The Women of the Other

In June 1931, Dr. Tiulian of the Armenian National Assembly advocated women's participation in the Board of Directors of the Armenian National Hospital and National Trusteeship. Once again, Mark took it upon herself to write an article in response to those who opposed this idea. In the article, first published in *Nor Lur* daily edited by Vahan Toshigian and later reprinted in *Hay Gin*, Mark employed arguments she had used previously in defending women's political rights. First, she stated that the Armenian National Constitution was almost obsolete and therefore in need of revision; second, the constitution did not categorically reject women's political participation.[56] What differentiated this piece from its predecessors was that Mark felt the need to boost her argument with a forceful reference to the Republic of Turkey and its women. A year earlier, in 1930, Turkish women acquired the right to elect and be elected in municipal elections. Mark wrote:

> What fear, Gentlemen! Let's assume that it is necessary to change the laws [of the National Armenian Constitution]. Is it really such a fearful thing to approach an ancient institution of seventy years with the force of the laws of evolution? [...] Our country [Turkey] has witnessed such reversal in the course of ten to twenty years. The despotic order has been overthrown and the ample breath of the republic has enlivened our beautiful Turkey. With a great gesture, our enlightened and modern government has taken down the veil of the Turkish woman and given her a wide range of rights; it has taken her out of the shadows of the cages and exposed her to the free world.
>
> This is the case even though the Turkish woman was not ready; she was not accustomed, like us, to pursuing national philanthropic tasks even in times of despotism.
>
> On the other hand, we, Armenian women, have long demonstrated that we have hearts and minds and that we have the [necessary] experience.
>
> [...] Our [Turkish] state authorities have recently bestowed upon women the right to participate in municipal elections. Is the [Armenian] National Assembly a fortress more unreachable, more impregnable than the former?[57]

This piece is telling from a variety of angles. First, it shows that despite her emphasis on the fact that the National Constitution gave political rights to "all" Armenian taxpaying men and women, Mark continued to theorize political rights as compensation for numerous sacrifices and accomplishments for the nation (as indicated in her reference to how experienced Armenian women were in philanthropy). Her reference to Turkish women as inexperienced and unready effectively silences Turkish women's past and contemporary organized feminist, philanthropic, benevolent, and educational activities. Here Mark indirectly argues that even though Turkish women did not deserve their rights as much as Armenian women, they were still enfranchised by an "enlightened and modern government," which she discursively constructed as the binary opposite of the "despotic" Ottoman state. Mark's argument suggests that she sought to shame Armenian men by positioning them as inferior to the Turkish government. She equated the absence of women on community boards with despotism. This reasoning is noteworthy because Armenian intellectuals, both male and female, had been trying to "modernize" their nation along Western lines for more than a century. Indeed, Mark's rhetorical assaults were not only deliberate, they were meant to hurt. Her affirmative reference to the Turkish government aimed to put Turkish and Armenian men of power into a civilizational competition with regard to their willingness and ability to share power with women.

Strikingly, therefore, Mark found a feminist ally in the Turkish state. But this alliance wasn't enough for Mark to identify with the state nor with "Turkish women." The above quote demonstrates that Mark did not consider herself "Turkish." Legally speaking, when "Turkish women" gained their political rights Armenian women too were given suffrage as Turkish citizens. Mark, however, did not consider this gain as one for Armenians in Turkey. In the two editorials that she wrote after Turkish women received the right to vote and stand for election in municipal elections in 1930, she congratulated the republican government and its leader, Mustafa Kemal Atatürk, and expressed her happiness for Turkish women. She did not mention that this development would also positively affect Turkish Armenians.[58] That Mark conceived Armenian women, including herself, in a category different from "Turkish women" is telling in terms of the changing and unchanging aspects of Armenian belonging in Turkey from the occupation years to the early Turkish Republic. Indeed, when Mark referred to "our governmental body," during the preceding decade (in 1919 and 1921) she meant the independent Republic of Armenia.[59] In 1931, when she wrote "our country" and "our government," she was referring to Turkey. She identified with the Turkish state as her own only to advocate women's political equality with their men *in* the Armenian community—the only place she felt she owned, the only place in which she felt the desire and ability to intervene.

Mark omitted, perhaps purposefully, the fact that from the 1880s on Turkish women intellectuals had been actively trying to awaken their counterparts to their rights and responsibilities.[60] Moreover, by the early 1920s Turkish women had a well-organized and effective movement for the recognition of their rights. Most noticeably, together with her friends in the Turkish Women's Association, Nezihe Muhiddin had intensely worked for Turkish women's suffrage. Mark mentioned the movement of her Turkish counterparts only rarely with praise. On the contrary, in both of the editorials written right after Turkish women gained rights in municipal elections, she explicitly mentioned that Turkish women had not worked toward this end: "[Turkish women] must be so happy that, unlike their counterparts in other countries, they are given rights without any effort on their part."[61]

Given the lack of scholarly attention to this issue, it is hard to account for Mark's indifference and silence.[62] Since *Hay Gin* occasionally reported news related to the Turkish women's movement, specifically referring to the Turkish Women's Association and its leader, Nezihe Muhiddin, it appears to have been intentional.[63] But even though most such reporting was in a neutral tone, one of Mark's 1927 editorials referred to the Turkish Women's Association rather sarcastically.[64] The unpleasant experience generated by this editorial, discussed below, might have caused her unwillingness to later acknowledge Turkish women's efforts.

In 1927, Mark wrote that the mayor of Istanbul gave a speech at the Turkish Women's Association arguing against women's suffrage because women do not join the military and die for the nation.[65] In an editorial, Mark challenged the mayor's perspective; she suggested that women's motherhood equaled men's military service: "men die only in occasional wars. Women, however, die frequently during childbirth, which is their military duty. In addition, women always go to wars as nurses and they too die."[66] Both the mayor's argument that killing and dying for the nation are the ultimate rationales for full citizenship and Mark's counterargument that motherhood is an alternative, and a better justification, for membership in the nation were shared by many intellectuals worldwide as well as Turkish feminists in the 1920s.[67] The end of the editorial is relevant for this discussion. Mark hinted that surely the Turkish Women's Association would deal with the issue. She was disappointed that the association had provided the space for the mayor to give an anti-suffrage speech.

According to Mark's autobiography, her editorial immediately caught the attention of the Turkish press; it was translated and reprinted in Turkish the next day.[68] Subsequently, Mark was invited to join the Turkish Women's Association. However, she was upset that she was not invited directly by her fellow (Turkish) nationals but through the mediation of a certain Ann Stis, a feminist from Geneva and the secretary of the International Feminist Women's Association, who happened to be in town.[69] Despite her feelings, Mark accepted the invitation. In her autobiography, Mark notes that many Turkish newspapers did not mention Ann Stis's invitation but reported the news as if Mark herself initiated her membership. Utterly disappointed once again, she immediately withdrew her membership; "this incident had dishonored not only herself but all Armenian women."[70] Given the lack of sources on the subject, it is not clear why the Turkish Women's Association never repeated the invitation or why Mark did not criticize the Turkish press for misrepresenting the sequence of events or for their divisive politics. With this episode, however, a possible channel for cooperation and solidarity between Armenian and Turkish feminists was closed off.

In 1932 a public show of sympathy was expressed between Turkish women and Armenian women. Markedly, this rapprochement was not about feminist solidarity but a sisterly solidarity around modernity and Westernization. As such, it provides a telling example of how secular modernism, a project that is always somewhat related to the female body (its dress, its conduct, its mobility), helped women of the two groups bridge a gap. In 1932 Mark was invited to be a jury member in Turkey's beauty pageant. The winner, Keriman Halis (Ece), later won the world's beauty pageant in Belgium. When she returned home, Keriman Halis and her father visited *Hay Gin*'s office, which was in Mark's house (Figure 20). In Mark's crowded salon, Halis's father communicated his good will to all Armenians who celebrated his daughter's success from all over the world.[71] Mark appreciated Halis's modesty and showcased her as an example of the "inner beauty" that she recommended for all women. Halis represented the right kind of young girl: she was Europeanized and modern but was not degenerate like the manch-aghchig. She was modest, domestic enough to seek her father's company when she moved about in town, and perhaps most importantly for Hayganush Mark, open to interactions with non-Turkish women who shared similar values.

In the End

The Turkish government ordered *Hay Gin* closed in early 1933. The new press law passed in 1931 stated that those who had served the "enemies of the Turks" during the War of Independence or those who had been working against the Turkish state would no longer be allowed to publish newspapers or journals.[72] Even though nothing published in *Hay Gin* after 1923 could be suspect, its pre-1923 support of occupation forces and Armenian territorial claims could easily be interpreted as "work against the Turkish state."[73] According to an unpublished 1948 letter that Mark wrote to Zaruhi Kalemkearian, the Turkish authorities were able to track down *Hay Gin* because Suren Shamlian reported on her to the Turkish authorities.[74] Mark did not explain why Shamlian, whom she described as an informer for the Turkish state, would do such a thing. Even though more extensive research is needed on the topic, it is likely that the cause was the intense competition between Shamlian and Mark's husband, Vahan Toshigian.

Shamlian was the founder and editor of the newspaper *Marmara* and Toshigian published *Nor Lur*. The two men published the two most popular Turkish Armenian newspapers in Turkey and represented opposite political views: while Toshigian's *Nor Lur* was a left-leaning periodical in support of Soviet Armenia (however cryptic the support may have been), *Marmara* represented the anti-Soviet section of the community, a division that is outside of the scope of this study.[75] Ara Kochunian, the editor of the third most important newspaper of the time, *Zhamanag*, similarly referred to Shamlian in his recollections as an informer who would use unethical measures to eliminate his rivals.[76] Because *Nor Lur* had started publication after the establishment of the republic and did not publish anything explicit that could be easily described as "against the Turkish state," it was not possible to close down this newspaper while it was rather easy to find evidence against Mark since her journal was vocal and active during the occupation years.[77]

Hay Gin's abrupt closing traumatized Mark. She had devoted all her energy to this journal over the preceding thirteen years. As someone who never had children, Mark had considered *Hay Gin* her daughter who was killed at the tender age of thirteen.[78] She refused to hold a pen for the next three years, responding to friends' letters in pencil. Given the symbolic importance of the pen to her feminist philosophy and politics, it is significant that she protested *Hay Gin*'s closing by refusing to participate in the public life of ideas. In her memoirs she did not mention why and how *Hay Gin* had come to an end; she had to censor herself, which she did by noting simply that everyone already knew the reasons. Her comrades and friends who left Bolis in 1922 (Anayis, Zaruhi Kalemkearian, Vahram Papazian) wrote about *Hay Gin*'s closing in their memoirs.[79] While they noted that it was the state that order the journal closed, they did not flag the Shamlian connection. Effectively, *Hay Gin* became the victim of an Armenian man who collaborated with the Turkish authorities to bring an end to Armenian women's activism.

Mark returned to the literary scene in 1936 by contributing to the women's pages in *Nor Lur*. After a few years, she decided that her writing in *Nor Lur* was not attracting the attention she expected, and so was not worth continuing. The Armenian community had already lost its interest in the women's movement. This does not mean, however, that *Hay Gin*'s legacy was short lived. In May 2013 I conducted an interview with Armine Bagdiken, who was born in Istanbul in 1918.[80] When I asked her if she had heard about Hayganush Mark, she first expressed surprise that I thought she might not have heard of Mark before. She told me that her father, who was an intellectual and occasional writer in the Armenian press, had all issues of *Hay Gin* bound like an encyclopedia. Her older sisters had loved reading the journal and when she came of age, she too devoured everything in the journal. Without me asking her about what she remembered from Hayganush Mark's writings the most, she mentioned the quote about the ladle and needle. Armine Bagdiken thought it was a great message for girls like herself that Mark did not want them to get an artificial education ("some piano lessons, some French lessons") but know how to handle the home as well. Mrs. Bagdiken referred to Mark as a feminist and did not seem to think that feminism and domesticity might ever conflict with each other.

In 1954 a group of Armenian women formed a commission to organize Mark's jubilee marking the fiftieth anniversary of her involvement in active public life. Sponsored by Archbishop Karekin Khachadurian, the Armenian patriarch of the time, the event took place at the luxurious Park Hotel with the presence of well-known intellectual figures. It was for this occasion that the same commission, made up of seven women including the famed composer and pianist Koharig Ghazarosian, who was a good friend of Mark's, published a volume dedicated to the life and work of Hayganush Mark. They also convinced Mark to pen an autobiography to be included in the volume, *Gynank U Kordze*.[81]

In 1954 Mark's partner of forty-seven years died at the age of seventy-four. According to his grandnephew Ara Toshigian, who now lives in Montreal, Vahan Toshigian had always wanted to visit Soviet Armenia. At the age of seventy-four he finally found an appropriate reason and procured the necessary documents to visit Yerevan on the occasion of the death of Kevork VI, Catholicos of All Armenians (Supreme Patriarch of the Armenian Apostolic Church) and report the funeral to Armenian newspapers. Ignoring his doctors' advice against such a long trip (given his poor health), he embarked on the train in Istanbul but died in Kars before making it to the other side of the border, to Armenia.[82] Upon his death, an Armenian photographer, Ara Güler, visited Hayganush Mark and took two photos. In the coming years Güler would became Turkey's most famous photograph artist and an internationally acclaimed photojournalist. With these pictures he not only paid tribute to the passing of Toshigian but also to the long years that the couple devoted to the Armenian press. Güler put two issues of *Nor Lur* on Vahan Toshigian's now empty desk, commemorating the paper at the same time that he mourned its editor. Then he posed Mark in front of the *Hay Gin* sign that had graced the walls of Mark's apartment for twenty-one years following the journal's folding (Figure 26). The picture is reminiscent of the youthful "new woman" that sat at the center of *Hay Gin*'s cover image (Figure 14) and held a paper and read it. In Güler's picture Mark similarly holds a paper (it is *Hay Gin*) even though her seasoned eyes face not the journal but the objective. The pen is noticeable only by its absence.

Mark's identification with *Hay Gin* continues even after her death. Her epitaph in the Intellectuals' Section at the Şişli Armenian Cemetery (Figure 27) mentions *Dzaghig*, the first journal she edited, and *Hay Gin*, and includes a quote from one of her *Hay Gin* editorials, entitled "Do Not Lie, Woman":

Do not lie woman, do not renounce yourself
Do not lie in moral, material and social matters.
Be who you are.

Figure 26. Hayganush Mark in 1954. Photo by Ara Güler, taken days after the passing of Vahan Toshigian. Mark is posed in front of the *Hay Gin* sign, holding an issue of the journal, twenty-one years after the Turkish state closed it down. Yeghishe Charents Museum of Literature and Art (Hayganush Mark Fond), Yerevan.

While this quote is probably not the best representation of her career as an Armenian feminist, it is still evocative of her feminist ideology. Below is the section in her 1932 *Hay Gin* editorial from which the epitaph was taken:

> Woman, when you do not love for sure, do not lie. Do not lie, when you love. Do not lie when you do not have the appetite for one thing or another. Do not lie when people are annoying you. Do not lie and renounce yourself.

> Do not lie by borrowing other people's ideas. Do not lie in moral, material, and social matters. The only way to make your voice heard is by using your own voice. Be who you are. Do not lie.[83]

Effectively in life as in death, then, Mark encouraged women to find their authentic, emancipated voices, irrespective of others' assumptions and ideas. The kind of Armenian woman that she hoped to mold through her writings shined with her individuality but was not individualistic. Unlike the manch-aghchig who was led by her passions and the doll who conformed to societal expectations but did not have any other meaningful purpose in life, the new women that *Hay Gin* promoted formed their voices through education and exploration and used that voice for the benefit of Armenians *and* women. Throughout her long career as a social critic Mark insisted that feminist women (like herself) were more important assets for the Armenian national cause than non-feminist women because feminists knew how to simultaneously preserve tradition and actively participate in the public life of the nation and shape its future.

When Armenian feminists looked at the image of the mother and her sleepy baby in the bedroom that accompanied Patriarch Naroyan's article in 1930 (Figure 17), like the patriarch they saw an Armenian mother consciously and dutifully passing on her group identity to her child. Yet, feminists saw other things in that mother that likely evaded the patriarch. They saw an educated, selfless yet feminist Armenian mother who might or might not have worked outside the home all day. Even if she wasn't employed, she must have spent some part of her day in a community-related activity, volunteering at an orphanage, hospital, or school. She expected that her husband, the father of the baby, would share her responsibilities of childcare and housework to the extent that a male could. This young mother was as capable as her husband, her father, or her butler or boss of having a say in the ways her community was governed.

In 1929 the noted writer Gosdan Zarian wrote to a friend that "the Ottoman Empire bequeathed two things to the new Turkey: the muddy streets of Pera and *Hay Gin*."[84] That continuity became exactly what led the government to close *Hay Gin*. Even though *Hay Gin*'s legacy has continued in other countries, most remarkably in Lebanon with Siran Seza's *Yeridasart*

Hayuhi (Young Armenian Woman), no Armenian women's journal has been published in Turkey ever since.[85] The conditions surrounding the journal's closing, that its call for accountability for the Armenian massacres in 1918–1922 led to *Hay Gin*'s silencing in 1933, are thus emblematic of how history became destiny not just for Hayganush Mark and Vahan Toshigian but for all Armenians who remained in the perpetrating society.

Figure 27. The tombstone of Hayganush Mark and Vahan Toshigian, in the Intellectuals' Section of the Şişli Armenian Cemetery. The inscription at the top of the stone reads *Hay Gin*. Photo by Umut Vedat. February 2015.

WHEN HISTORY BECAME DESTINY
A Conclusion

How can a people survive a genocide? What does it take for a group to reinvent itself after an onslaught on its very existence? What is the role of that group's pre-genocide past in making post-genocide reconstruction possible?

The first part of this book has tried to answer these questions by focusing on Armenian spokespeople in Istanbul in the first few years immediately following World War I. Irrespective of their ideological backgrounds, everyone who took it upon themselves to write and talk on behalf of "Armenians" agreed that the *veraganknum* (restoration) of Armenianness had to have an indispensable gendered dimension. They saw Armenians as one big family that, like all families, might have had long-running feuds but in the end was made up of mothers, fathers, sisters, and brothers who sprang from the same roots and therefore shared the same destiny. They perceived the Ottoman Turkish attack against Armenians during the Great War as an attempt to uproot the Armenian nation and foreclose the possibility of an Armenian future. In the aftermath of the war, the Armenian leadership felt the need to prove "the Turk" wrong simply by surviving as a nation, hopeful and stronger than ever. The survivor nation had to reestablish the family, both the big Armenian national family and its smaller units composed of individual Armenian families. The women of the family, specifically the mother, had the most important role in the restitution of the family, thus of the nation. She was seen as the liaison between the roots and the present. As a biological figure, the female body reproduced the new generation, those who would make the Armenian future possible. As a socially constructed figure, the mother raised the children and transmitted all things Armenian to them, the future citizens of an independent, united, Greater Armenia for which they all worked.

Mother Armenia was never established. The Turks emerged as the ultimate victors of the postwar clash over territory in what is generally referred as "Anatolia" today. During the postwar fighting, remnants of the Armenian nation once again experienced ethnic cleansing in the form of massacre and forced deportations. Some of them, especially those in Bolis, fled voluntarily in anticipation of violence. Others chose to stay and face the new challenges. Many others did not have the means to escape. Once the dust of the chaos settled, the remaining Armenians had to find ways of cohabiting with onetime exterminators of their nation who now accused them of treachery and continued not to want them. How did Armenians survive the new Turkey?

As the second part of the book shows, as they began a new phase in their relationship, the state and its Armenians had a script to rely on. They reenacted the pre-genocide past in how they interacted in the present. Even though the present was structurally different from the past, it bore enough resemblance that made Armenians' Ottoman dhimmi repertoires transferable to the Turkish nation-state republic. Armenians chose to perform submissive loyalty and unconditional gratitude in the hope of ensuring security in everyday life. This notion of "security" also included the capability of protecting their religion, native tongue, and other traditions that marked them as different from the majority. Even though multilateral treaties theoretically guaranteed the preservation of these differences, in practice they became a constant site of negotiation between the state and the Bolsahay elite. Like those dispersed throughout the globe, the community that remained in Istanbul had to find a balance between integrating with the host society without disappearing as Armenians. This concern forced Bolsahay political, religious, and intellectual leaders to pay extra attention to the household and the home, a space in which the Turkish state did not intervene aggressively. The traditional patriarchal family and gendered relationships thus continued their critical importance for the maintenance of Armenian grouphood in Turkey. Mothers remained the trunks that connected the Armenian roots with the new branches.

When the nation was but a gendered project that divided identity labor between its male and female members based on their assumed traditional duties, how can those who were committed to the nation but opposed to its hierarchically organized gendered structures argue for change? How could an Armenian be a feminist in Turkey? Could a feminist be an Armenian in a Turkey that had squeezed Armenianness into an enclave and forced conservatism on it as the only avenue for existence thus resistance?

A third dimension of this book pertains to post-genocide feminists who simultaneously pursued the Armenian cause and the woman's cause. Even though their objective remained the same—equality between the sexes—the formulation of their demands metamorphosed according to the changing political circumstances. One particular feminist, who, in addition to an unshakable devotion to women's emancipation benefitted from the support of a loving husband-colleague, bore the flag of the cause for long years. In the beginning, Hayganush Mark had several equally devoted comrades with whom she worked for orphan relief and the sheltering of kidnapped girls and women. These feminists lobbied among high commissioners for Greater Armenia and among Armenian males for the political representation of women in the Armenian National Assembly. Their feminist journal *Hay Gin* featured pieces from the most renowned male and female writers of the time and was widely popular, with many advertisements and a steady body of subscribers.

The situation took a drastically different turn in late 1922 when most of Hayganush Mark's companions left the city. Mark did not stop being a feminist and *Hay Gin* continued publication. Yet, reflecting the broader changes in the Armenian community itself, the journal's tone and content waned into domestication, if not invisibility. In 1933 the Turkish government silenced the voice of *Hay Gin*.

If we were to envision this book as a matryoshka doll, Hayganush Mark would stand as the tiny core around which all other dolls circle and unfold. Each layer/doll has a history of its own that future scholars will excavate in more detail and nuance. The existence of each layer/doll corresponds to layers and layers of deliberate erasure and unintentional omitting in the various historical narratives that have been constructed around the place called Turkey and the people called Armenians.

After her death in 1966, not many people remembered Hayganush Mark and her journal. She did not make it into Armenian literature or history textbooks perhaps because her literary pieces largely remained in the pages of the press.[1] Another reason was that she was a woman, and as such remained outside of the canon.[2] She, like other women and feminists, also did not make it into Armenian historiography. This was not only because of her sex but also because she was among those who remained in post-genocide Turkey.[3] Until very recently, the mainstream, "national" history of Armenians, even those versions that included a discussion of the Armenian diaspora, did not have much to say about Armenians who remained among "the enemy."[4] Hayganush Mark, like all other Armenian feminists, was missing also from the historiography of the Ottoman and Turkish women's movement that has burgeoned since the early 1980s. Equating "Ottoman" with "Turkish" and remaining blind to non-Muslim, non-Turkish feminist activism inside the borders of the Ottoman Empire and then the Turkish Republic, this women's historiography thus has shared the assumptions and mistakes of the larger gender-blind historiography against which it had originally emerged.[5] Until about a decade ago "Ottoman history" and "Turkish history" meant the history of ethnic Turks and Muslims. This has been the case not just for official Turkish historiography but for the kind of histories that are produced outside of Turkey, such as in North America, which has, until very recently, peripheralzied, if not omitted, the violence that Armenians endured in the Ottoman Empire from 1890s on.[6]

Hayganush Mark reappeared in the Armenian public sphere in March 2000 when a group of young women, including this author, studied her and Zabel Asadur (Sibil) to give a presentation in the Esayan Armenian School's alumni association building in celebration of the March 8 International Women's Day.[7] Both Mark and Sibil had worked at the Esayan School as teachers. During a repetition of the event at the alumni association of the Pangaltı Armenian School, much to our surprise Archbishop Mesrob Mutafian, recently elected Armenian patriarch of Istanbul (then forty-four years old), honored the evening with his presence. Known for his intellectualism, the patriarch made a point of publicly congratulating the young women for unearthing the experiences of their feminist ancestors. Our amazement with the patriarch did not last long. Only a few months after our presentation, at a sermon in Kınalıada's Surp Krikor Lusavoriç Armenian Church, the patriarch warned his congregation that out-marriage was on the rise among youth. He singled out girls. Because girls were continuing their education into universities and thus postponing marriage, this was taking a toll on the community as a whole since it was leading young men to marry non-Armenians. Girls had to be tamed into marrying early. Our young and passionate hearts were infuriated by this expression of misogyny and the double standards in the patriarch's ideology.

It took me a decade of research on the formative years of the Turkish Armenian community to be able to understand Patriarch Mutafian's dilemma, which was in fact quite similar to that of Hayganush Mark's in the 1920s and '30s. This dilemma sits at the core of the limits within which one could become and stay Armenian in post-genocide, post-minoriticization Turkey. Because the terms of the Turkish domination over the Armenian minority have remained more or less the same throughout the republic's history, and because that domination has a gendered history and implications, it would be impossible for the patriarch to remain a persistent feminist. Perhaps this was not a huge problem for this member of the clergy. But for Hayganush Mark and all other Armenian feminists that came after her, the broader political framework did not leave them much choice but "only paradoxes to offer."[8] Liberal progressivism that roots for gender equality is a threat to the hierarchically ordered "tradition" that Armenians insist on conserving in order to continue their presence in a Turkey that insists on structurally discriminating against them. As long as the power imbalance between the Turkish state and its Armenians remains intact, paradoxes will remain the best friends of feminists.

NOTES

Introduction

1. Her certificate of graduation from the Esayan Armenian School notes Mark's date of birth as 1882 but her birth year is marked as 1885 on her tombstone (see Figure 27).

2. *Bolis*, the shortened form of *Gosdantinobolis*, is the Armenian for Constantinople or Istanbul. Throughout this book, depending on the context, I will use all three names. In general, and in order to emphasize the cosmopolitan outlook of the city, I will refer to it as Constantinople during the 1918–1922 era, when the city was occupied by the Allies. In 1923, as a result of the Turkish War of Independence, the Allies evacuated and the city was "reconquered" by the Turks. After this date, I refer to it as Istanbul, to emphasize its consciously Turkish character. Officially the city's name was changed to Istanbul with the 1930 Turkish Postal Service Law, a step in the overall campaign to "Turkify" all social, political, and economic life in Turkey. While official Ottoman Turkish correspondence referred to the city as "Konstantiniye," "Istanbul" had been in use in Ottoman Turkish even before the Ottoman conquest of the city in 1453. Armenians had always referred to the city as Bolis regardless of the changing political conditions and official names, and I use it both to emphasize their subjective perspective as well as the continuity of their presence in the city, a core theme of this book.

3. See Figure 27 for Hayganush Mark and Vahan Toshigian's tombstone. The tombstone mistakenly identifies the last year of *Hay Gin* as 1932 even though the journal continued until January 1933. Every bibliography or any other kind of source that mentions *Hay Gin* provides the wrong date.

4. Throughout this book instead of using "Constantinopolitan Armenian" I will use the Armenian translation of the term, *Bolsahay*, which is the word the main historical actors of this work used to refer to themselves.

5. I borrow Andre Patrick's definition of elites as "people who have the ability to make themselves heard in the public sphere because they have acquired status, either through gaining wealth and standing from one's family or through the securing of societal positions deemed important, often gained through the attainment of an education." It also encompasses people who have the power to make decisions on behalf of their community. Andrew Patrick, "'These People Know about Us': A Reconsideration of Attitudes Towards the United States in World War I–Era Greater Syria," *Middle Eastern Studies* 50, no. 3 (2014): 397–411. As for the term "identity," I am aware of Rogers Brubaker and Frederic Cooper's criticism, but am using it here to mean something more active than what they assume the term can mean. Rogers Brubaker and Frederick Cooper, "Beyond 'Identity,'" *Theory and Society* 29, no. 1 (2000): 1–47.

6. It should be noted that what is conventionally referred to as the "1915 Armenian genocide" did not neatly end at 1915 or 1916. Many scholars rightfully include in the "genocidal era" the massacres that Armenians experienced during the Kemalist national resistance in the 1919–1922 period. I use the term "post-genocide" because this book also includes the decade after the establishment of modern Turkey. Moreover, the "post-" in front of "genocide" does not mean that the genocide belongs to a bygone era. Given the fact that the Turkish state has continued to reject the use of this term with regard to the "1915 Armenian deportations," apologize, or pay any kind of reparations, one can legitimately argue that the genocidal effects of the Turkish policies continue up to the present. Many genocide scholars see denialism as the "last stage of genocide." See, for an example, Israel W. Charny, "The Psychology of Denial of Known Genocides," in Israel Charny, ed., *Genocide: A Critical Bibliographical Review / 2* (New York: Facts on File, 1991), 22–23. Nonetheless, there is a marked difference in the political climate of the post-1918 era that warrants its own study without being included under the umbrella term of "genocide." It is in this spirit that I use the "post-," that is, as the aftermath.

7. The issue of how "constructed" the idea of a historical homeland was/is remains unresolved in Armenian historiography. For a recent sample of scholarship that discusses where "the fatherland" was for some Armenians in the early nineteenth century, see Dzovinar Derderian, "Mapping the Fatherland: Artzvi Vaspurakan's Reforms through the Memory of Past," in Vahé Tachjian, ed., *Ottoman Armenians: Life, Culture, Society*, vol. 1 (Berlin: Houshamadyan e.V., 2014), 144–69. Razmik Panossian provides a textbook-like definition: "The historic territory on which the Armenian people lived stretched between the Kur river to the east, the Pontic mountain range to the north, the Euphrates river to the west and the Taurus Mountains to the south." Razmik Panossian, *The Armenians: From Kings and Priests to Merchants and Commissars* (New York: Columbia University Press, 2006), 34.

8. This is obviously a much more complicated story than depicted here. The historiography on the Armenian genocide is very large. For the most recent work on the topic that provides a good summary, see Ronald Grigor Suny, *They Can Live in the Desert But*

Nowhere Else: A History of the Armenian Genocide (Princeton, NJ: Princeton University Press, 2015). Raymond Kévorkian's *The Armenian Genocide: A Complete History* (New York, I. B. Tauris, 2011) is a good reference book in view of its geographical breadth. For a thorough study of the genocide that uses the currently available Ottoman Turkish state archives, see Taner Akçam, *Young Turks Crime Against Humanity: The Armenian Genocide and Ethnic Cleansing in the Ottoman Empire* (Princeton, NJ: Princeton University Press, 2012). For a study that focuses on one region during a longer period of religious and ethnic homogenization, see Uğur Ümit Üngör, *The Making of Modern Turkey: Nation and State in Eastern Anatolia, 1913–1950* (Oxford: Oxford University Press, 2011). For a study that focuses on the role of external powers, see Donald Bloxham, *The Great Game of Genocide: Imperialism, Nationalism, and the Destruction of the Ottoman Armenians* (New York: Oxford University Press, 2005).

9. According to a table prepared by the patriarchate in Istanbul in April 1921, the number of orphaned children who were "slaves in the service of Mesopotamian races that live in the deserts" was 5,800, "orphaned children enslaved among Anatolia's Turks" numbered 58,000, and women kept in "harems of the Anatolia" numbered more than 50,000. *Amenun Daretsuytse* 15 (1922): 261–65. This table, which is reproduced in *Hikmet Özdemir, Ermeniler: Sürgün ve Göç* (Ankara: Türk Tarih Kurumu, 2004), was circulated among American diplomatic circles in the Ottoman Empire (p. 123). Titled "The Number of Armenians in the Boundaries of the Turkish Empire" (pp. 124–26), the table does not include the women in harems. Instead, a separate section notes that the total number provided in the table "does not represent the entire number. Many Armenians had adopted Islam to get rid of the unspeakable crime and of the persecution organized by the Ittihad [the governing Ottoman party]" (p. 126).

10. Thousands of unmarried Armenian men who were born outside of Istanbul but for some reason resided in the city in 1915 and 1916 were also deported. The German archives mention that their numbers reach ten thousand. See Akçam, *Young Turks Crime Against Humanity*, 401–5.

11. For more on the etymology and historical usage of the term *Medz Yeghern*, see Vartan Matiossian's eleven articles in *Armenian Weekly* (accessible online at http://armenianweekly.com) that began on October 25, 2012, with his "The Birth of 'Great Calamity': How 'Medz Yeghern' Was Introduced onto the World Stage" and ended on December 16, 2013, with "What I Choose It to Mean: On 'Yeghern' as the Armenian Translation of 'Genocide.'"

12. Four Armenian members of the Ottoman parliament (Krikor Zohrab, Hovhannes Serengiulian [Vartkes], Onnik Tertsagian [Vramian], and Stepan Chirajian) and three former Armenian MPs (Nazaret Daghavarian, Hampartsum Boyajian [Murad], Dr. Garabed Pashaian) were among the murdered. For the most recent study, see Nesim Ovadya Izrail, *24 Nisan 1915 İstanbul, Çankırı, Ayaş, Ankara* (Istanbul: İletişim Yayınları, 2014).

13. Teotig, *Azke Che Meradz yev Anhnar e Vor Merni: Pandi yev Aksori Dariners* (Antelias, Lebanon: Gatoghigosutiun Hayots Giligio, 1985), 19–21.

14. In 1919, the population of Istanbul was between one and 1.2 million: 120,000 were Armenian, 380,000 Greek, 45,000 Jewish, and 550,000 Turkish. The number of Armenians was provided by the Armenian patriarch in 1919. Clarence Johnson, *Constantinople To-day or, The Pathfinder Survey of Constantinople. A Study in Oriental Social Life* (New York: Macmillan, 1922), 18.

15. Zabel Yesayan is a giant of Armenian history and literature and has been studied relatively well. She survived the genocide and settled in Soviet Armenia but fell to Stalin's purges in the late 1930s. Mari Beylerian, on the other hand, is in near-complete darkness. For a preliminary analysis of her work, see Lerna Ekmekcioglu, "*Ardēmis*: An Armenian Women's Journal Published in Egypt, 1902–1904," *Journal of Armenian Studies* 8, no. 1 (2004): 11–28.

16. There are numerous but thus far untapped accounts in Armenian memoirs about the war years in Constantinople. For a sample, see Hagop Siruni, *Inknagensakragan Noter* (Yerevan: Sarkis Khachents, 2006); and Berdjouhi (Barseghian), *Jours de Cendres à Istanbul* (Paris: Paranthèses, 2004).

17. Anahid Tavitian provides a vivid narrative of how the Armenians in Kınalıada, one of the Prince's Islands near Istanbul heavily populated by Armenians, celebrated the news of the establishment of the Republic of Armenia in the Caucasus. Anahid Tavitian, *Yergu Dziranner (Arvesde yev Engerayin Dzarayutiune)* (Beirut: Sipan, 2006), 35–45. Kınalıada, which was also known as Hay Ghghzi (Armenian Island), was distant enough from the center that Armenians could celebrate the news openly. It is likely that Armenians in the city heard the news at mass on Sunday. In her memoir, Anayis (Yevpime Avedisian) narrated how during the first divine liturgy after the establishment of an independent Armenia the priest uttered the name "the Republic of Armenia" (*zHanrabedutiunn Hayots*), which caused shock waves and barely suppressed cries among the attendants. Anayis [Yevpime Avedisian], *Hushers* (Paris: n.p., 1949), 242. Soon after the declaration of independence, the new country's National Council dispatched a mission to Constantinople to negotiate a treaty. The group, composed of Avedis Aharonian (chairperson), Alexander Khadisian, and Mikael Papajanian, arrived in the Ottoman capital in June 1918, and stayed at the luxurious Tokatliyan Hotel, all expenses covered by the Ottoman minister of the interior Talat Pasha, the mastermind of the Armenian genocide. Until their departure in early November, many local Armenians secretly or openly communicated with the members of the commission, especially with Avedis Aharonian, long known to Ottoman Armenians as a masterful novelist and poet. The most detailed description of these interactions is in Dr. Vahram Torkomian's chronicles serialized in *Vem, Hantes Mshaguyti yev Badmutyan*, published in Paris. His pieces start in 1936, in *Vem*'s fifteenth issue, and end in 1938 with the twentieth issue.

18. Initially the city was occupied informally but in March 1920 the occupation was

made formal. Greek's also welcomed the Allied warships and soldiers as depicted in Yorgos Theotokas's memoir-novel *Leonis: Bir Dünyanın Merkezindeki Şehir, 1914–1922* (Istanbul: İstos Yayınları, 2013), 118–35. The Armenian and Greek welcoming of the Allied warships is much exploited in the field as a moment proving Ottoman Christians' "treachery." In contrast, the literature assumes that Constantinopolitan Jews' reception of the Allied forces had been negative. For an new study that shatters this myth, see Devi Mays, "Recounting the Past, Shaping the Future: Ladino Haggadot of the War in Occupied Constantinople," blog entry at the National Endowment for the Humanities Summer Seminar, *World War I in the Middle East*, convened in 2014, https://blogs.commons.georgetown.edu/world-war-i-in-the-middle-east/seminar-participants/web-projects-2014/devi-mays/.

19. The note reads: "In the face of these fresh crimes committed by Turkey against humanity and civilization, the Allied Governments announce publicly to the Sublime Porte that they will hold all the members of the Ottoman Government, as well as such of their agents as are implicated, personally responsible for such massacres." As Peter Holquist's research shows, this note represents the first use of the term "crimes against humanity" in a penal sense even though the term had existed as an expression of opprobrium previously. The note was drafted and initiated by Imperial Russia. Holquist, "'Crimes against Humanity': Genealogy of a Concept (1815–1945)," paper presented at the conference "From the Armenian Genocide to the Holocaust: The Foundations of Modern Human Rights," University of Michigan, Ann Arbor, April 2–4, 2015.

20. Alexis Alexandris, *The Greek Minority of Istanbul and Greek-Turkish Relations, 1918–1974* (Athens: Center for Asia Minor Studies, 1983), 102.

21. See Bedross Der Matossian, *Shattered Dreams of Revolution: From Liberty to Violence in the Late Ottoman Empire* (Stanford, CA: Stanford University Press, 2014); Gerard J. Libaridian, "What Was Revolutionary about the Armenian Revolutionary Parties in the Ottoman Empire?," in Ronald Grigor Suny, Fatma Müge Göçek, and Norman M. Naimark, eds., *A Question of Genocide: Armenians and Turks at the End of the Ottoman Empire* (New York: Oxford University Press, 2011), 82–112.

22. CNN Turk, February 3, 2014, Enver Aysever's "Aykırı Sorular."

23. This is one of the oldest rules of sharia that pertain to dhimmis and is also inscribed in the Quran (Q 2:221). See Milka Levy-Rubin, *Non-Muslims in the Early Islamic Empire: From Surrender to Coexistence* (Cambridge: Cambridge University Press, 2011), 123.

24. Anne McClintock, "Family Feuds: Gender, Nationalism and the Family," *Feminist Review*, no. 44 (Summer 1993): 61–80. One of the most important early works in this sub-field of nationalism studies that maintains its relevance is Nira Yuval-Davis, *Gender and Nation* (London: Sage, 1997).

25. Partha Chatterjee, "The Nationalist Resolution of the Women's Question," in Kumkum Sanari and Sudesh Vaid, eds., *Recasting Women: Essays in Indian Colonial*

History (New Brunswick, NJ: Rutgers University Press, 1990), 233–53; Mrinalini Sinha, "Reading Mother India: Empire, Nation, and the Female Voice," *Journal of Women's History* 6, no. 2 (1994): 6–44.

26. See chapter 1 of Melissa Bilal's dissertation, "Thou Need'st Not Weep, For I Have Wept Full Sore: An Affective Genealogy of the Armenian Lullaby in Turkey," (PhD dissertation, University of Chicago, 2013).

27. Victoria Rowe, *A History of Armenian Women's Writing, 1880–1922* (London: Cambridge Scholars, 2003); Anahid Harutyunyan, *Yereveli Dignants Tare: Hay Ganants Hasaragagan Kordzuneutiune XIX Tarum yev XX Tarasgzpin* (Yerevan: Hokevor Hayasdan, 2005).

28. Lerna Ekmekçioğlu and Melissa Bilal, eds., *Bir Adalet Feryadı: Osmanlı'dan Türkiye'ye Beş Ermeni Feminist Yazar, 1862–1933* (Istanbul: Aras Yayıncılık, 2006); Hasmik Khalapyan, "Woman's Question and Women's Movement among Ottoman Armenians 1875–1914" (PhD dissertation, Central European University, 2008).

29. This does not mean that the state did not try to reshape various intra-family relationships such as those pertaining to gender. It certainly did, for instance by stipulating in the law who the breadwinner (husband) was. The point here is that the state did not regulate the family as the *Armenian* family but like any other family in the Republic of Turkey.

30. "İsmet Paşa Hazretlerinin Nutukları," *Muallimler Birliği* 1, no. 1 (October 1925): 147–55.

31. This is a phrase from the poem "Awake! My People" by Yehuda Leib Gordon (1831–1892). It is generally used to summarize how secular states expect citizens to confine the exercise of their religion to the private sphere of home and church. Michael W. McConnell, "Believers as Equal Citizens," in Nancy Rosenblum, ed., *Obligations of Citizenship and Demands of Faith: Religious Accommodation in Pluralist Democracies* (Princeton, NJ: Princeton University Press, 2000), 90–110.

32. Balakian brought the boxes to Marseilles in 1927 when he moved there. In 1938 they were transferred to the Armenian patriarchate in Jerusalem. The patriarchate's archives are closed to outside researchers. The Armenian General Benevolent Union's Nubar Library in Paris has the microfilms of at least part of these archives. Zaven Der Yeghiayan (Armenian Patriarch of Constantinople, 1913–1922), *My Patriarchal Memoirs* (Barrington, RI: Mayreni, 2002), 189. In preparing his memoirs, which include original documents, the former patriarch visited the Jerusalem patriarchate's archives in the summer of 1938. The Armenian original of the memoir was published a few months after his death in 1947. Zaven Der Yeghiayan, *Badriarkagan Hushers: Vaverakirner yev Vgayutiunner* (Cairo: Nor Asdgh Dbaran, 1947).

33. This number includes periodicals that had been closed down on the orders of the Ottoman government but were later published under a new name. For example, *Zhamanag/Zhoghovurti Tsayne, Ariamard/Jagadamard,* and *Nor Lur/Verchin Lur/Marmara*.

M. Babloyan, *Hay Barperagan Mamule: Madenakidagan Hamahavak Tsutsag, 1794–1980* (Yerevan: Haygagan SSH GA Hradaragchutiun, 1986).

34. The practice still continues in the Armenian press and on websites, although with decreasing frequency.

35. The scholarly literature still lacks a detailed study of the everyday lives of Armenians in the first decades of the Turkish Republic. In her work on Armenians' musical practices, Melissa Bilal discusses how Armenians born in the 1920s and '30s remember their childhood and youth in Turkey. See chapters 1 and 4 of her dissertation, "Thou Need'st Not Weep."

36. Interview with Knar Makkasian (1926–2014), December 29, 2010, in Cliffside Park, New Jersey.

Chapter 1

1. The almanac was published in Istanbul for one issue (1920–1921) by Harutyun Manavian, whose penname was Sargavak, that is, Deacon. Despite its name, the almanac did not target a religious leadership and was not spiritual in content. It tried to reach a broader readership and constantly argued for the much-needed unity of Armenian political parties, lay people and Armenian Apostolic, Catholic, and Protestant religious authorities in order to realize a bright Armenian future, which the editor believed would be under a mandate run by the United States. Manavian resumed the publication of the almanac in Egypt, in the 1940s.

2. Orphans are central to discussion in almost all post-genocide, postwar, post-catastrophe societies. For a comparative sample, see Tara Zahra, *The Lost Children: Reconstructing Europe's Families after World War II* (Cambridge, MA: Harvard University Press, 2011).

3. The Ottoman government began permitting the return of Armenians earlier, though in a more limited fashion. A general decree promulgated on October 18, 1918, declared that the Council of Ministers had decided that anyone who had been "removed from a place by a military decision as a result of war" could return to the places from which they had been expelled. Taner Akçam, *Young Turks Crime Against Humanity: The Armenian Genocide and Ethnic Cleansing in the Ottoman Empire* (Princeton, NJ: Princeton University Press, 2012), 333n175.

4. Vahram L. Shemmassian, "The Repatriation of Armenian Refugees from the Arab Middle East, 1918–1920," in Richard Hovannisian and Simon Payaslian, eds., *Armenian Cilicia* (Costa Mesa, CA: Mazda Publishers, 2008), 419–55.

5. "Exiled people," that is *aksoraganner*, was also used, though more rarely. After 1923 Turkish Armenians would usually remember them with the politically more neutral term *kaghtaganner*, that is, "emigrants."

6. This number is provided both by the patriarch, Zaven Der Yeghiayan, *My Patriarchal Memoirs* (Barrington, RI: Mayreni, 2002), 180; and by Clarence Johnson, *Constan-*

tinople To-day or, The Pathfinder Survey of Constantinople. A Study in Oriental Social Life (New York: Macmillan, 1922), 18 (the latter gives the number of 32,000).

7. Raymond Kévorkian, *The Armenian Genocide: A Complete History* (New York: I. B. Tauris, 2011), 540.

8. *Azkayin Khnamadarutiun: Enthanur Deghegakir Arachin Vetsamsya, 1 Mayis 1919–31 Hogdemper 1919* (Constantinople: M. Hovagimian, 1920).

9. For a recent study of the history of international humanitarianism that pays due attention to Armenian relief, see Keith David Watenpaugh, *Bread from Stones: The Middle East and the Making of Modern Humanitarianism* (Berkeley: University of California Press, 2015).

10. The Armenian Church follows Christian Orthodoxy, but is independent from the Greek and Russian Orthodox Churches, and because of the tradition that the apostles St. Thaddeus and St. Bartholomew evangelized and were martyred in Armenia, it calls itself "Apostolic." It is also often referred to, although incorrectly, as the "Gregorian" Church after St. Gregory the Illuminator, who was its first official head in the fourth century A.D.

11. For an informative comparison between the versions that Armenians drafted and the Ottoman state approved, see Masayuki Ueno, "The First Draft of the Armenian Millet Constitution," *Japan Association for Middle East Studies* 23, no. 1 (2007): 213–51. For a fine discussion of the earliest stage of constitutionalism in the Ottoman Empire, see Aylin Koçunyan, "Negotiating the Ottoman Constitution, 1856–1876" (PhD dissertation, European University Institute, Florence, 2013), esp. 117–40.

12. Of the 120 lay members of the National Assembly, 40 were set aside to be elected from the Anatolian provinces and others were to be elected from Constantinople. Vartan Artinian, *The Armenian Constitutional System in the Ottoman Empire, 1839–1863: A Study of Its Historical Development* (Istanbul: Isis Press, 1988).

13. Only a few of the patriarchate's commissions, such as those dealing with religious, educational, and philanthropic affairs of the community, remained open. Der Yeghiayan, *My Patriarchal Memoirs*, 123.

14. We should note that the first Ottoman parliament convened after the Mudros Armistice included Armenian members who put forward motions to bring the perpetrators of the massacres to justice. These attempts did not produce any results. In any case, in less than a couple of months, on December 21, 1918, Sultan Mehmed VI dissolved the Ottoman parliament. Ayhan Aktar, "Debating the Armenian Massacres in the Last Ottoman Parliament, November–December 1918," *History Workshop Journal* 64, no. 1 (2007): 241–70. The dissolving of the Ottoman parliament meant that Armenians did not have an Ottoman umbrella under which to express their grievances and seek justice. The next Ottoman elections took place in January 1920 but non-Muslims were not given the right to stand for election or hold office. During the Allied occupation of Constantinople four informal elections were held inside the Armenian community

producing national administrations that dealt with a wide spectrum of affairs. For more, see Levon Marashlian, "Finishing the Genocide: Cleansing Turkey of Armenian Survivors, 1920–1923," in Richard Hovannisian, ed., *Remembrance and Denial: The Case of the Armenian Genocide* (Detroit: Wayne State University Press, 1999), 116.

15. For a detailed description of this organization's activities, see the published report: *Deghegakir Daregan Kordsarnutyants Azk. Yelevm. Getr. Hantsnazhoghovo 1 Sept. 1919–31 Okosdos 1920* (Constantinople: M. Hovagimian, 1921).

16. Madteos Eblighatian, *Gyank Me Azkis Gyankin Mech: Aganadesi yev Masnagtsoghi Vgayutiunner 1903–1923* (Antelias, Lebanon: Gatoghigosutiun Medzi Dann Giligio, 1987), 174.

17. The tax law is printed in *Deghegakir Daregan Kordsarnutyants Azk. Yelevm. Getr. Hantsnazhoghovo*, 5–6. Those who did not pay the tax would lose all their privileges in the Armenian Church. For example, they would be denied wedding, baptism, and funeral services. Moreover, their names would be announced on posters in the churches.

18. This number is from *Azkayin Khnamadarutiun: Enthanur Deghegakir Arachin Vetsamsya*. Johnson, *Constantinople To-day*, 255–57; *Amenun Daretsuytse* 16 (1922), 380–81. For detailed discussions, see Hramyag Kranian, "Hay Vorputiune," in Kersam Aharonian, ed., *Hushamadean Medz Yegherni, 1915–1965*, 3rd ed. (Beirut: Zartonk Oratert, 1987), 926–52; and Libarid Azadian, *Hay Vorpere Medz Yeghnerni* (Glendale, CA: L. Azadian, 1995), esp. 25–40.

19. "Mer Vorpere," *Amenun Daretsuytse* 15 (1921): 161. Teotig himself was a survivor who returned to Constantinople after the war and devoted himself wholeheartedly to the Greater Armenia cause, with particular attention to orphan relief. He gave a speech on the nearby island of Kınalıada on December 30, 1920, and donated all the income from the day to orphan relief. The text of the speech was published and its income also went to orphan relief. *Zulume yev Hay Vorpere* (Constantinople: D. Keshishian Vorti, 1921).

20. Lyrics from the Howard Karageuzian Home Orphanage's anthem ("Homi Yerke," written by Paylag-Sanasar), "Aytselutiun Me Howard Karageuzian Homi," *Hay Gin* 3, no. 20 (August 16, 1922).

21. For a similar discussion in the context of Jewish displaced persons in occupied Berlin, see Atina Grossmann, *Jews, Germans, and Allies: Close Encounters in Occupied Germany* (Princeton, NJ: Princeton University Press, 2007), 184–235.

22. Zaruhi Bahri, *Gyankis Vebe* (Beirut: n.p., 1995), 146.

23. Payladzu A. Captanian, *Tsavag* (New York: Armenia Dbaran, 1922), 37 (italics in the original). Captanian (pp. 31–37) provides a vivid account of how, in the earliest stages of the deportation of Armenians from Samsun, the Greek bishop of the town secretly sent word to Armenians that they could bring their children to the diocese to be distributed among willing Greek families. The Zachariadis family who received Payladzu's two sons, the five-year-old Hrant and three-year-old Aram, took good care of the boys. In the summer of 1918 the boys were united with their mother in Constantinople. By that time,

Payladzu had another baby, whom she named Tsavag, meaning "little pain," a made-up name that is also the title of her memoir. On the last page of the memoir Payladzu emphasizes that the father of the baby was her husband, who had been deported and killed right before Armenians' deportation from Samsun. In his memoirs, Patriarch Zaven made a point of emphasizing that during the war and deportations, "[Greek] Metropolitans did not spare [any effort to help] our people" and that "we have a particular debt of gratitude to the Metropolitans of Samsun and Trabizon." Der Yeghiayan, *My Patriarchal Memoirs*, 195. In postwar Constantinople, when Armenians found Greek children inside a Muslim household they returned them to the Greek patriarchate. Konstantina Adrianopoulou, "Social Policy and 'National Mission': 'Little Ethnomartyrs' in the Christian Orthodox Community of Istanbul during the First World War," paper presented at the Princeton University Hellenic Studies seminar, 2007. Captanian's memoirs were written in Armenian but were first published in French. Payladzu Aragel Captanian, *Mémoires d'une Déportée* (Paris: M. Filinikavski, 1919).

24. Atina Grossmann, "Victims, Villains, and Survivors: Gendered Perceptions and Self-perceptions of Jewish Displaced Persons in Occupied Postwar Germany," *Journal of the History of Sexuality* 11, nos. 1 and 2 (April 1, 2002): 291–318.

25. For example, a contributor to *Hay Gin* proposed that the Armenian patriarchate should collect extra taxes from singles and decrease taxes on families with multiple children. Armenag Salmaslian, "Pnagchutiun yev Amurineru Vra Durk," *Hay Gin* 1, no. 21 (September 1, 1920).

26. Hayganush Mark, "Dzpankner Gyankes," in *Hayganush Mark, Gyankn U Kordze* (Istanbul: n.p., 1954), 56.

27. On Turkish better baby contests, see Kathryn Libal, "National Futures: The Child Question in Early Republican Turkey" (PhD dissertation, University of Washington, 2001), 101.

28. Dokt. Derorti, "Ur Gertas Hay Gin," *Hay Puzhag* 3, no. 9 (July 1922): 150 (emphasis in the original).

29. Eric Weitz, "From the Vienna to the Paris System: International Politics and the Entangled Histories of Human Rights, Forced Deportations, and Civilizing Missions," *American Historical Review* 113, no. 5 (2008): 1313–43.

30. Der Yeghiayan, *My Patriarchal Memoirs*, 205.

31. Ibid., 207.

32. For more on Armenian delegations in the Paris Peace Conference, see Houri Berberian, "The Delegation of Integral Armenia: From Greater Armenia to Lesser Armenia," *Armenian Review* 19 (Autumn 1991): 39–64.

33. For a memoir of an Armenian boy who was forcibly Islamicized in a Turkish orphanage in wartime Lebanon, see Karnig Panian, *Goodbye Antoura: A Memoir of the Armenian Genocide* (Stanford, CA: Stanford University Press, 2015).

34. For more on this policy and the historical repertoire that made it possible, see

Lerna Ekmekcioglu, "A Climate for Abduction, a Climate for Redemption: The Politics of Inclusion during and after the Armenian Genocide," *Comparative Studies in Society and History* 55, no. 3 (2013): 522–53.

35. In Muslim households, abducted boys usually served as laborers working the land. It was more common for boys than girls to be taken into institutions such as orphanages and military schools. Girls and women were usually absorbed into households, where they worked as domestic helpers, concubines, or wives.

36. After the British conquest of these territories, together with the Armenian General Benevolent Union (AGBU), Allied authorities began to collect Armenian women and children who were forcefully kept by Bedouin tribes. For a detailed discussion of this subjects and the ways the AGBU and British intelligence officers collaborated to help liberate captive Armenians, see Vahé Tachjian and Raymond Kévorkian, "Reconstructing the Nation with Women and Children Kidnapped during the Genocide," *Ararat* 45, no. 185 (2006): 4–16. For a rare memoir of a *vorpahavak*, an orphan collector agent, in Mesopotamia, see Levon Yotnakhparian, *Crows of the Desert: The Memoirs of Levon Yotnakhparian* (Tujunga, CA: Parian Photographic Design, 2012).

37. Zaruhi Bahri, "Inch er Chezok Dune?," *Aysor* 1, no. 705 (May 3, 1953). I thank Vahé Tachjian for bringing this article to my attention and providing me a copy. Anahid Tavitian, *Yergu Dziranner (Arvesde yev Engerayin Dzarayutiune)* (Beirut: Sipan, 2006), 161–179; Bahri, *Gyankis Vebe*, 242–46.

38. Der Yeghiayan, *My Patriarchal Memoirs*, 185.

39. Aram Haygaz, *Bantog* (Beirut: Mshag, 1967), 138. Responsible authorities' memoirs either refute the accusations or remain silent on the topic. Madteos Eblighatian italicized the following in his memoirs: "*I affirm that we had no wish to Armenianize any Turk's child*" (*Gyank Me Azkis Gyankin Mech*, 185).

40. For example, see Varteres Garougian, *Destiny of the Dzidzernag: Autobiography of Varteres Mikael Garougian* (Princeton, NJ: Gomidas Institute, 2005), 96.

41. Isabel Kaprielian-Churchill, "Armenian Refugee Women: The Picture Brides, 1920–1930," *Journal of American Ethnic History* 12, 3 (1993): 3–29, here 22n54, 29.

42. The patriarch would not easily give away orphaned girls even to their Armenian relatives, even when they provided extensive proof of their relationship. Haygaz, *Bantog*, 133.

43. Hayganush Mark, "Khmpakragan: Angyal Gineru Hamar," *Hay Gin* 3, no. 4 (December 16, 1921).

44. Varteni Mosdichian (b. 1953) recounts that her grandmother's aunt, Adrine Aghababian (formerly, Indjian), who had lost her husband and two daughters during the genocide, was abducted by a Turk. She was raped and gave birth to a son. After the Armistice, the mother took her son and felt compelled to leave Constantinople because the Armenian community "was not prepared to accept such situations." They went to Marseilles. Personal correspondence with Varteni Mosdichian in June 2012, in

Watertown, Massachusetts. Zaruhi Bahri, the Armenian manager of the neutral house in Şişli, noted in her memoirs how a young man approached her for a bridal candidate. Even though he was willing to marry a previously kidnapped girl, he asked that Bahri keep the girl's background a secret from his own family. Bahri, *Gyankis Vebe*, 186.

45. *Yergamia Deghegakir H. G. Khachi Getr. Varchutian, 1918 Noy. 18–1920 Teg. 31* (Constantinople: M. Hovagimian, 1921), 24. Mabel Evelyn Elliott, an American physician who was the representative of the American Women's Hospitals in the Near East and a one-time medical director of the Near East Relief, treated many of the rescued women in this shelter. She detailed their experiences in her memoir: Mabel Evelyn Elliott, *Beginning Again at Ararat* (New York: Fleming H. Revell, 1924), 20–35.

46. John Minassian, *Many Hills Yet to Climb: Memoirs of an Armenian Deportee* (Santa Barbara, CA: J. Cook, 1986), 236.

47. It should be noted that it was not unprecedented for Armenian men to marry a woman formerly kidnapped by Kurds or Turks. The best-remembered precedent was Kegham Der Garabedian's marriage to Gulizar, a young girl who had fled from the household of the Kurdish Musa Bey, into which she had been kidnapped in 1893. Der Garabedian, a writer and a member of the Armenian Revolutionary Federation (ARF, *Tashnagtsutiun*), was elected as a deputy to the Ottoman parliament in the 1909 elections. For a sample of how Armenians remembered the case in postwar Istanbul, see "Musa Bey yev Gulizar," *Amenun Daretsuytse* 10–14 (1916–1920): 151–52. For the memoirs of Giulizar, see Arménouhie Kévonian, *Giulizar* (Paris: Imp. Der Agopian, 1946). The book has also been translated into French: Arménouhie Kévonian, *Les Noces noires de Gulizar*, trans. by Jacques Mouradian (Rocquevaire: Parenthèses, 2005).

48. One such girl, then nineteen, remembered how she would go to Muslim households with two male guards and, even when the lady of the house claimed that there were no "infidels" (non-Muslims) in the house, she would forcibly enter the household and find children hidden in basements. Eliz Sanasarian, "Gender Distinction in the Genocidal Process: A Preliminary Study of the Armenian Case," *Holocaust and Genocide Studies* 4, no. 4 (1989): 449–61, here 455.

49. "Ganants Asharhen," *Hay Gin* 1, no. 3 (December 1, 1919).

50. "Hay Ganants Engeragtsutyun," *Hay Gin* 1, no. 3 (December 1, 1919); "Hay Ganants Engeragtsutyan Kodsuneutyune, Yergrort Yeramsya Deghegakir Varchagan Zhoghovi," *Hay Gin* 1, no. 8 (February 16, 1920); Huliane Sarkisian, "Patsadrutyun Me," *Hay Gin* 1, no. 11 (April 1, 1920).

51. "Ganants Asharhen: Hay Ganants Engeragtsutyun," *Hay Gin* 1, no. 19 (August 1, 1920).

52. Kalemkearian narrated this incident as an essay titled "Badmutiun me Tornigis Hamar, Yerp vor Medznas," which she wrote in New York in 1927. The piece is included in her memoir, *Gyankis Jampen* (Antelias, Lebanon: Dbaran Gatoghigosutian Giligio, 1952), 293–98.

53. Kohar Mazlemian recounted Nazeni's story in two articles in *Hay Gin*: "Prni Mayrutyan Bardatrvadz Teradi Mayreru Hokegan Vijage yev Anonts Yerakhanerun Zrganknere," *Hay Gin* 1, no. 11 (April 1, 1920), and "Iragan Badmutiun Me," *Hay Gin* 3, no. 11 (April 1, 1922).

54. Dr. Yaghubian, "Hay Gnoch Aroghchabahagan Tere Hayasdani Mech," *Hay Gin* 1, no. 19 (August 1, 1920).

55. Some kidnapped women did not want to return to their natal community. Others were willing to return but did not want to leave their new children behind. Even though Armenian relatives were usually willing to accept kidnapped women back into their communities, these women's "Muslim children" were not accepted as easily. This issue points to yet another layer of dissonance between the elite administration, which did not care about children's paternity, and survivors who did. For example, a certain Azaduni was kidnapped by an Arab during the deportations who later married her. She had a son by her new husband. When the return of Armenians to their former places of origin was allowed, her Muslim husband let her leave with her son. However, even though Azaduni's former Armenian husband was willing to take her back, he did not want to have the son with them. Azaduni decided to stay with her new family. See Tachjian and Kévorkian, "Reconstructing the Nation."

56. Zaruhi Kalemkearian tells how a refugee woman insisted that her three-year-old son should be taken away from her to be sheltered in an orphanage to prevent her from committing infanticide since he was conceived as a consequence of rape during the deportations. The mother had not killed her son before because she was not sure whether the father was her Armenian husband (who was killed) or the rapist. Since the boy grew up looking like the rapist, she was then assured about the real father. "Zavage," in Kalemkearian, *Gyankis Jampen*, 272. For a comparative case of mothering and communal responses to "wrong children," see Veena Das, "National Honor and Practical Kinship: Of Unwanted Women and Children," in *Critical Events: An Anthropological Perspective on Contemporary India* (Delhi: Oxford University Press, 1995).

57. Only very rarely did the feminists disagree with the highest administrative authorities regarding the fate of a given refugee woman or orphan. Zaruhi Bahri tells of a case in which the patriarch did not authorize the return of a recently rescued 18-year-old Armenian woman to her beloved Iranian husband whom she married during the deportations in Mosul, despite the young man's promises to convert to Christianity and immigrate to Europe to live as a Christian family. Bahri pointed out that this was a remarkable case since around the same time this Iranian young man's brother got married to an Armenian girl in Istanbul without any trouble; that Armenian woman, however, was not a refugee but a local. Bahri, *Gyankis Vebe*, 186–91.

58. It is noteworthy that women's memoirs, especially if they are not in the "eyewitness accounts of the genocide" genre, were either self-published or published posthumously by their families. Unlike the male memoirists whose works were published by

regular presses and are comparatively readily available, these women's memoirs are hard to find. As a consequence they have remained outside the canon of primary sources, and have not been utilized by historians, except for a few studies that focus on the Armenian women's movement.

59. For a rare instance where survivors talk about how they neglected or abandoned their rape babies, see Donald E. Miller and Lorna Touryan Miller, *Survivors: An Oral History of the Armenian Genocide* (Berkeley: University of California Press, 1999), 101–2.

60. Mazlemian, "Iragan Badmutiun Me."

61. "Hay Ganants Engeragtsutyun," *Hay Gin* 1, no. 12 (April 16, 1920).

62. *Hay Gin* 4, no. 20 (October 1, 1923).

63. Kaprielian-Churchill, "Armenian Refugee Women," 3. For a glimpse of such women's experiences as they transitioned from orphanages to North American households to perform wifely and motherly duties, see David Kherdian, *The Road from Home: The Story of an Armenian Girl* (New York: Greenwillow Books, 1979); David Kherdian, *Finding Home* (New York: Greenwillow Books, 1981).

64. Anayis [Yevpime Avedisian], *Hushers* (Paris: n.p, 1949), 264.

65. Harutiun Khachadurian, "Hayun Vrezhe," *Amenun Daretsuytse* 15 (1921): 134.

66. Ibid., 135.

67. For example, Varteres Garougian, an Armenian American volunteer in the French Legion d'Orient, wrote in his memoirs that when their French ship approached Mersin, a port city occupied by the French, all the soldiers were "so eager to be among the first to set foot on Armenian soil in Cilicia that they pushed and shoved each other to get to the head of the line." He continued: "After all that had happened to us during the past several years, we were finally in our homeland, lined up in the modern custom house. However our men were excited, acting like enraged tigers roaring to pounce on any Turks in sight as if to eat them alive. Our officers were warning us to remain calm, to avoid bloodshed since the Armistice was now in effect. They reminded us that the Turkish Government had surrendered unconditionally, that we must wait for the decisions of the peacemakers. But, to whom do you direct these logical arguments? All of the soldiers had members of their family whom this Ottoman Government had commanded to be murdered—father, mother, brother, sister, wife, children, relations, an entire nation. The Armenian Legionnaire's pent up rage and frustration could no longer be contained. 'Revenge, Revenge!' was the outcry." Garougian, *Destiny of the Dzidzernag*, 31.

68. Lyrics by Mgrdich Der-Bedrosian, musical composition by Tavit Khachigian. "Hayun Yerke," *Aravodi Darekirk* 1, no. 1 (1921): 16–17.

69. It should be noted that under the leadership of the Armenian Revolutionary Federation (*Tashnagtsutiun*) Armenians organized a covert mission to assassinate the masterminds of the Armenian genocide. For the most recent research on Operation Nemesis, see Eric Bogosian, *Operation Nemesis: The Assassination Plot That Avenged the Armenian Genocide* (New York: Little, Brown, 2015); and Marian M. MacCurdy, *Sacred*

Justice: The Voices and Legacy of the Armenian Operation Nemesis (New Brunswick, NJ: Transaction Publishers, 2015).

70. Greek-Armenian Joint Declaration reproduced in Der Yeghiayan, *My Patriarchal Memoirs*, 195–97.

71. "Havadkin Uzhe," *Arakadz* 1, no. 2 (February 1, 1919).

72. There certainly was variation in terms of how Armenians of different political persuasions in and outside of the Ottoman territories related to the Republic of Armenia in Transcaucasia but no political party rejected it as a legitimate nucleus.

73. For a study of the role of Armenian nurses in Western-run medical institutions in the Ottoman Empire and the Middle East before and after World War I, see Isabel Kaprielian-Churchill, *Sisters of Mercy and Survival: Armenian Nurses, 1900–1930* (Antelias, Lebanon: Armenian Catholicosate of Cilicia, 2012).

74. "The Little Army against Disease," *New Near East* (September 1922): 12. I thank Vicken Babkenian for sharing this source with me.

75. *Hay Gin* 3, no. 18 (July 16, 1922).

76. Nargiz Kipritjian, "Goch Me Hay Mayrerun," *Hay Gin* 1, no. 10 (March 16, 1920).

77. *Sargavakin Daretsuytse* (n.p., 1921), 30–31.

78. Teotig, ed., *Hushartsan Abril Dasnemegi* (Constantinople: O. Arzuman, 1919). The book was sponsored by the Committee for the April 24 Mourning Ceremony (*Abril Dasnmegi Skahantesi Hantsnakhump*) and edited and published by Teotig. The book's revenue reportedly went to the newly established Armenian Intellectuals' Foundation (*Hay Mdavoraganneru Fond*) to provide financial support for the widows and orphans of Armenian intellectuals killed during the genocide. The Committee for the April 24 Mourning Ceremony was composed of seven men and five women. Anayis, Zaruhi Kelemkearian, and the Armenian Red Cross vice president Mari˙ Stambulian, who was also a frequent *Hay Gin* contributor, were among them.

79. Lerna Ekmekcioglu, "The Armenian National Delegation at the Paris Peace Conference and 'The Role of the Armenian Woman during the War,'" blog entry at the National Endowment for the Humanities Summer Seminar, *World War I in the Middle East*, convened in 2012, https://blogs.commons.georgetown.edu/world-war-i-in-the-middle-east.

80. Henry Morgenthau, *Ambassador Morgenthau's Story* (Garden City, NY: Doubleday Page, 1918).

81. Henry Morgenthau, *Tesban Morgentaui Badmadznere: Ksanvets Amis Turkio Mech Kdnvadz Henri Morgentaoui Badmadznere Diezeragan Baderazmen Arach yev Baderazmi Michotsin Miatsyal Nahankneru*, trans. by Mikael Shamdanjian (Constantinople: Asadurian yev Vortik, 1919); Henry Morgenthau, *Amerigan Tesban Mr. Morgentaui Hishadagnere yev Haygagan Yeghernin Kaghdniknere*, trans. by Yenovk Armen (Constantinople: Arzuman, 1919).

82. *Hay Gin* 1, no. 2 (November 16, 1919). In the next issues the book was also ad-

vertised as a decoration and a "book for the salon" (*zhshmarid zart yev saloni kirk*), and therefore "the best Christmas gift that one could buy for Armenian mademoiselles." *Hay Gin* 1, no. 5 (January 1, 1920).

83. *Hay Gin* 2, no. 2 (November 16, 1920). The book in question was Sevag Aguni, ed., *Milion Me Hayeru Charti Badmutiune* (Constantinople: Asadurian, 1920).

84. For a comprehensive study of these tribunals, see Vahakn N. Dadrian and Taner Akçam, *Judgment at Istanbul: The Armenian Genocide Trials* (New York: Berghahn Books, 2011).

Chapter 2

1. *Hay Gin* 2, no. 18 (July 16, 1921).
2. *Hay Gin* 2, no. 19 (August 1, 1921).
3. *Hay Gin* 2, no. 18 (July 16, 1921).
4. *Hay Gin* 2, no. 20 (August 16, 1921).
5. *Hay Gin* 2, no. 21 (September 1, 1921).
6. Yenovk Armen, "Hay Gini Nor Hartsume," *Hay Gin* 2, no. 23 (October 1, 1921).
7. For instance, *Aghkadakhnam Dignants Engerutiun* (Society of Charitable Ladies), established in 1864, and *Azkanver Hayuhyats Engerutiun* (Patriotic Armenian Women's Society) and *Throtsaser Hayuhyats Engerutiun* (Armenian Women's Pro-Educational Society), both established in 1879.
8. Zaruhi Bahri, *Gyankis Vebe* (Beirut: n.p., 1995), 183.
9. Hervé Georgelin, "'La Renaissance' and the Aftermath of World War I, December 9, 1919–February 10, 1920," in Richard Hovannisian, ed., *Armenian Constantinople* (Costa Mesa, CA: Mazda Publishers, 2010), 401–30.
10. Kohar Mazlemian, "Inch Erav Trkuhin Baderazmi Ampoghch Entatskin," *Hay Gin* 1, no. 14 (May 16, 1920).
11. Grigoris Balakian, *Armenian Golgotha* (New York: Alfred A. Knopf, 2009), 419.
12. Mevhibe Celalettin, *Geçmiş Zaman Olur Ki . . . : Prenses Mevhibe Celalettin'in Anıları* (Istanbul: Çağdaş Yayınları, 1987), 261–69.
13. Bahri, *Gyankis Vebe*, 183.
14. "Dzrakir Nakhakidz Hay Ganants Engeragtsutyan," *Hay Gin* 1, no. 1 (November 1, 1919) (italics in the original). *Mayr Hayrenik* might be thought of as the archetypal combination of the mother and father figures. In this particular case, *mayr* might also designate *klkhavor*, that is, "main." Therefore, the phrase *Mayr Hayrenik* could also be translated as "the main homeland."
15. Bahri, *Gyankis Vebe*, 184.
16. "Bolso Hay Ganants Engeragtsutyun," *Hay Gin* 1, no. 10 (March 16, 1920).
17. "Ganants Ashkharhen," *Hay Gin* 2, no. 16 (November 16, 1920). This news item also mentioned that for the same purposes the Kadıköy Davros women's society had written an open letter to the American Senate.

18. Société des Dames Arméniennes, *Témoignages inédits sur les atrocités turques commises en Arménie suivis d'un récit de l'épopée arménienne de Chabin-Karahissar* (Paris: Imprimerie Dubreuil, 1920).

19. "Ganants Ashkharhen," *Hay Gin* 1, no. 4 (December 16, 1919).

20. For a detailed account of this visit and the "independence loan" campaign, see Richard Hovannisian, *The Republic of Armenia: Volume 3, From London to Sèvres, February–August 1920* (Berkeley: University of California Press, 1996), 284–89.

21. "Mer Desagtsutiune Hayasdani Nakhort Varchabedin Hed," *Zhoghovurti Tsayne* (June 29, 1920).

22. Bahri, *Gyankis Vebe*, 180.

23. "Ganants Ashkharhen: Baron Khadisian," *Hay Gin* 1, no. 17 (July 1, 1920).

24. Hayganush Mark, "Khmpakragan: 'Angakhutyan Pokharutiun' yev Vosgi Or," *Hay Gin* 1, no. 18 (July 16, 1920); Hayganush Mark, "Khmpakragan: Hayasdani Pokharutiune," *Hay Gin* 1, no. 21 (September 1, 1920).

25. "Ganants Asharhen: Jshmarid Hayuhin," *Hay Gin* 1, no. 24 (October 16, 1920).

26. *Hay Gin* 2, no. 2 (November 16, 1920). Another such example appeared in the following issue of *Hay Gin*. As well as printing her photo, the journal promoted Mrs. Takuhi Khosrovian as a role model. *Hay Gin* 2, no. 3 (December 1, 1920).

27. Kohar Mazlemian, "Vosgi Ori Artiv," *Hay Gin* 1, no. 21 (September 1, 1920).

28. Nargiz Kipritjian, "Hayuhiner Oknetsek Hay Zinvorin," *Hay Gin* 1, no. 14 (May 16, 1920). Similar themes are employed also in other pieces such as: Nargiz Kipritjian, "Hay Oriortnerun Bardke Hay Zinvorin," *Hay Gin* 1, no. 9 (March 1, 1920); Mark, "Khmpakragan: Hay Gnoch Bardaganutiune Hanteb Hay Panagin," *Hay Gin* 2, no. 1 (November 1, 1920).

29. "Hay Ganants Engeragtsutyun yev Panage," *Hay Gin* 1, no. 10 (March 16, 1920); "Ganants Ashkharhen: Hay Ganants Engeragtsutyun yev Hay Zinvor," *Hay Gin* 2, no. 3 (December 1, 1920); "Ganants Ashkharhen: Kahirei Hayuhyats Miutiune," *Hay Gin* 1, no. 7 (February 1, 1920).

30. For a detailed account, see Richard Hovannisian, *Republic of Armenia: Volume 4, Between Crescent and Sickle: Partition and Sovietization* (Berkeley: University of California Press, 1996).

31. Teotig, "Tumanian Mer Mech," *Amenun Daretsuytse* 16 (1922): 401.

32. "Ganants Ashkharhen: Tumanian," *Hay Gin* 2, no. 2 (November 16, 1921).

33. Anayis vividly details the visit in her memoir: Anayis [Yevpime Avedisian], *Hushers* (Paris: n.p., 1949), 266–72.

34. *Hay Gin* 1, no. 1 (November 1, 1919), 1.

35. Ibid.

36. Anayis, *Hushers*, 262.

37. Hayganush Mark, "Dzpankner Gyankes," in *Hayganush Mark, Gyankn U Kordze* (Istanbul, n.p., 1954), 58.

38. "Digin Hayganush Mark," *Dzablvar Darekirk* (Istanbul: n.p., 1921), 39–41.

39. Mark, "Dzpankner Gyankes," 25.

40. Victoria Rowe, *A History of Armenian Women's Writing, 1880–1922* (London: Cambridge Scholars, 2003); Lerna Ekmekçioğlu and Melissa Bilal, eds., *Bir Adalet Feryadı: Osmanlı'dan Türkiye'ye Beş Ermeni Feminist Yazar, 1862–1933* (Istanbul: Aras Yayıncılık, 2006).

41. Mark, "Dzpankner Gyankes," 41.

42. For more on Marguerite Durand (1897–1914), one of the leading feminists of her time in France, see Mary Louise Roberts, *Disruptive Acts: the New Woman in Fin-de-Siècle France* (Chicago: University of Chicago Press, 2002).

43. She finally gave in and let male writers use their own names. It was only in her 1954 autobiography that Mark disclosed the real names of the male contributors to *Dzaghig*. Mark, "Dzpankner Gyankes," 42.

44. Interestingly, she changed the orthography from her father's last name which starts with "Marg" to "Maṟk". It is also important to note that legally she did not have the right to do so and must have changed her name to Hayganush Toshigian. But until the very end she signed her pieces as Hayganush Mark. Her tombstone bears the name "Hayganush Mark Toshigian" (Figure 27). I thank Nilgün Gökgür for alerting me to this nuance.

45. Hayganush Mark, "Gnoch Tade," *Hay Gin* 3, no. 3 (December 1, 1921). She repeated the same definition in "Dzpankner Gyankes," 57. The quotation is from Laguerre's booklet, *Qu'est-ce que le féminisme?* (Lyon: Société d'éducation et d'action féministes, 1905), 1–3, quoted in Karen M. Offen, *European Feminisms, 1700–1950* (Stanford, CA: Stanford University Press, 2000), 117. Mark might have accessed Laguerre's original pamphlet or read it in Ottoman Turkish translation in Bahâ Tevfik Bahâ, *Feminizm: Âlem-i Nisvân* (Istanbul: Müşterekü'l-Menfaa Osmanlı Şirketi Matbaası). The publication date of the volume, however, is not noted in the book. Irvin C. Schick maintains that since the earliest dated book printed at Müşterekü'l-Menfaa Osmanlı Şirketi Matbaası bears the date 1909, *Feminizm: Âlem-i Nisvân* was most probably published after the restoration of the second Ottoman Constitution in 1908. In addition to an Ottoman Turkish translation of Laguerre's above-mentioned pamphlet, the book includes an appendix entitled "İslâmiyet ve Feminizm" (Islam and feminism) written by Bahâ Tevfik. Irvin Cemil Schick, "Print Capitalism and the Emergence of New Norms of Sexuality in the Ottoman Empire during the Second Constitutional Period, 1909–1922," *Comparative Studies of South Asia, Africa and the Middle East* 31, no. 1 (2011): 196–216.

46. Mark, "Gnoch Tade."

47. A near-complete list of *Hay Gin* contributors is in Yeprem Boghosian, *Hay Gin Khmpakruhiner* (Vienna: Mkhitarian Dbaran, 1953).

48. The "new woman" as a phenomenon has been studied in various contexts. For

example, see Mary Louise Roberts, *Civilization without Sexes: Reconstructing Gender in Postwar France, 1917–1927* (Chicago: University of Chicago Press, 1994); and Elizabeth A. Wood, *The Baba and the Comrade: Gender and Politics in Revolutionary Russia* (Bloomington: Indiana University Press, 1997), especially the fourth chapter.

49. Around the same time Khachadurian had opened an exhibition at the Russian Club and dedicated all the income to the AWA.

50. Mark, "Dzpankner Gyankes," 56.

51. In this regard, Armenian feminism is comparable to other postwar European feminist movements where women claimed political rights because of their role as social and biological mothers, and because they had filled men's jobs in their absence during the war. See, for example, Kathleen Canning and Sonya O. Rose, eds., *Gender, Citizenships and Subjectivities* (Oxford: Blackwell, 2002).

52. Hayganush Mark, "Khmpakragan: Mer Jampan," *Hay Gin* 1, no. 1 (November 1, 1919) (italics mine).

53. Hayganush Mark, "Khmpakragan: Ginere Azkayin Zhoghovi Mech," *Hay Gin* 1, no. 4 (December 16, 1919).

54. Ibid. The three women MPs—Berjouhi Parseghian, Katarine Manugian, and Varvara Sahagian—were elected to the first Armenian parliament in 1918. See Victoria Rowe, "Women as Political Actors in the First Republic of Armenia and in the Creation of International Networks of Refugee Relief, 1918–1925," paper presented at the conference "Legacy of the First Republic of Armenia, 1918–1920," Boston, 2008.

55. Parseghian (1883–1949) was among the intellectuals who had been deported from Istanbul in April 1915. He survived through the efforts of the US ambassador Henry Morgenthau.

56. This was the Armenian National Delegation that was headed by Boghos Pasha Nubar and represented the Armenians in the diaspora. Others sent from Istanbul to Paris in support of the delegation included the former patriarch Archbishop Yeghishe Turian and Professor Abraham Der Hagopian of Robert College.

57. Mark, "Khmpakragan: Ginere Azkayin Zhoghovi Mech."

58. For more on Halide Edip's election, see Hülya Adak, "Suffragettes of the Empire, Daughters of the Republic: Women Auto/biographers Narrate National History (1918–1935)," *New Perspectives on Turkey* 36 (Spring 2007): 27–51, here 41n50.

59. Hayganush Mark "Khmpakragan: Amusnaludzumnere," *Hay Gin* 2, no. 11 (April 1, 1921).

60. Mark, "Dzpankner Gyankes," 61–62.

61. Ibid.

62. Hayganush Mark, "Khmpakragan: Tebi Panaganutiun," *Hay Gin* 2, no. 12 (April 16, 1921).

63. Article 10 of Olympe de Gouges, "Declaration of the Rights of Woman and the Female Citizen," in *The French Revolution and Human Rights: A Brief Documentary His-*

tory, translated, edited, and with an introduction by Lynn Hunt (Boston: St. Martin's, 1996), 124–29.

64. Turkish women students were officially admitted to universities beginning in 1915. We do not know exactly when Christian and Jewish women started attending institutions of higher learning in the Ottoman Empire/Turkey. Before 1915 and after that, Armenian girls who wanted (and were able) to pursue university education went abroad. *Hay Gin*, in its usual "From the Women's World" (*Ganants Ashkharhen*) section, provided news about Armenian female university students who graduated from universities in Europe and America.

65. Hayganush Mark, "Khmpakragan: Mer Desagede," *Hay Gin* 2, no. 16 (June 16, 1921).

66. Mark was mistaken about the age requirement. The Armenian Constitution states that voters should be at least twenty-five years old.

67. It is important to note that in this piece Mark formulates an argument that she would not repeat anywhere else. She mentioned that women's political equality should be accepted in principle and women who were not mothers or did not have any domestic responsibilities could perform political roles. "Gineru Medz Haghtanage," *Hay Gin* 1, no. 24 (October 16, 1920). Mark might have meant to reject the *Gochnag* reporter's insistence on reducing women to motherhood or domestic responsibilities. As a woman who never become a mother, she was especially alert about the non-mother woman. For the original *Gochnag Hayasdani* article to which *Hay Gin* referred, see the newspaper's September 11, 1920, issue (no. 37), 1171–72.

68. Yenovk Armen, "Hay Gnoch Gochume," *Hay Gin* 3, no. 23 (October 1, 1922). Another dissident male *Hay Gin* contributor, Ardashes Kalpakjian, once admitted that if he were a woman, he would prefer to be an antifeminist, not wanting to enjoy equal rights with men. Ardashes Kalpakjian, "Yete Yes Gin Ellayi," *Hay Gin* 1, no. 4 (December 16, 1920). Many of his antifeminist articles, published in *Hay Gin* and other periodicals, were harshly criticized by other *Hay Gin* contributors and Mark herself. For a few examples, see Ardashes Kalpakjian, "Gine Iprev Gurk," *Hay Gin* 2, no. 12 (April 16, 1921); Hayganush Mark, "Khmpakragan: Gardzikner Arti Endanegan Gyanki Masin," *Hay Gin* 9, no. 6 (March 16, 1928); Hovhannes Asbed, "Namagner," *Hay Gin* 9, no. 9 (May 1, 1928).

69. Kegham Krikorian, "Feminizmi Nbadage yev Gnoch Gochume," *Hay Gin* 4, no. 1 (December 16, 1922) (italics in the original).

70. Hayganush Mark, "Khmpakragan: Vomants Irarantsume," *Hay Gin* 2, no. 14 (May 16, 1921). Here Mark is probably referring to Anayis. When Mark was promoting women's participation in the Judicial Commission, Anayis serialized a study entitled "The Situation of Women in Human Societies" (*Gnoch Vijage Martgayin Engerutyan Mech*), dating from February 15, 1921 to May 1, 1921.

71. Anayis, *Hushers*, 261. Shirvanzade (Alexander Movsesian), the well-known Rus-

sian Armenian playwright and novelist, visited Constantinople in November 1919 and stayed there for three months. He was in communication with the Armenian Women's Association. In his recollections he mentioned how Yervant Odian ridiculed the association's president (most probably Anayis at the time) and how Odian was sick and tired of "public women" who were so active in the city and kept organizing fundraisers. Shirvanzade, *Gyanki Povits Husher* (Yerevan: Hayasdan Hradaragchutiun, 1982), 493–510.

72. Zabel Berberian, "Nshanavor Giner: Harriet Beecher Stowe," *Hay Gin* 2, no. 12 (April 16, 1921).

73. "Voghpatsyal Digin Takuhi Tavit Kalantar yev Ir Grtagan Huntske," *Hay Gin* 2, no. 15 (June 1, 1921).

74. Zaruhi Bahri, "Digin Takuhi Kalantar," *Hay Gin* 2, no. 15 (June 1, 1921).

75. Takuhi Kalantar, "Garevor Kordze," *Hay Gin* 1, no. 23 (October 1, 1920).

76. *Hay Gin* 1, no. 8 (February 16, 1920); Teotig, *Azke Che Meradz yev Anhnar e Vor Merni: Pandi yev Aksori Dariners* (Antelias, Lebanon: Gatoghigosutiun Hayots Giligio, 1985), 23.

77. Her memoirs provide a detailed account of the interaction of women of different ethnic and class backgrounds in the Turkish prison. "Getronagan Pandi Gineru Pazhine" appeared in *Hay Gin*, intermittently from March 1, 1920, until April 16, 1920. After her mother's death, Vartuhi Kalantar left for America (in 1921, at the age of twenty-one). In 1923, she married Zaven Nalbandian, an ARF delegate. In 1926, under the pseudonym "Zarevand," the couple published a famous treatise about pan-Turanism in Armenian (later translated into Russian). The treatise was translated into English and reprinted in 1971. Zarevand, *United and Independent Turania: Aims and Designs of the Turks* (Leiden: Brill, 1971).

78. Vartuhi Kalantar, "Tserke," *Hay Gin* 2, no. 16 (July 16, 1921).

79. Mark, "Khmpakragan: Mer Desagede."

80. For a few examples, see Araksi Terzian, "Yerp Gine Dirana Ir Iravunknerun," *Hay Gin* 1, no. 11 (April 1, 1920); Zabel Berberian, "Amerigatsi Gnoch Engeragan Gyanke," *Hay Gin* 2, no. 18 (July 16, 1921); Hayganush Mark, "Khmpakragan: Tasdiaragutiun Hin Hayots Kov," *Hay Gin* 5, no. 15 (August 1, 1924).

81. According to Vahan Toshigian's grandnephew, who frequented the couple's house, Mark had a significant hearing difficulty and was almost deaf but could read lips. This disability prevented her from pursuing a career in teaching. Interview with Ara Toshigian, May 26, 2013, Montreal, Canada.

82. Hayganush Mark, "Khmpakragan: Zhest Me," *Hay Gin* 6, no. 21 (November 1, 1925). In the same issue Kohar Mazlemian's piece asserts that Mark's calls had been effective in ensuring the formation of the women's auxiliary body in the hospital. Kohar Mazlemian, "Gnoch Tsayne," *Hay Gin* 6, no. 21 (November 1, 1925).

83. It was in Sibil's salon in the 1890s and early 1900s that Mark, a girl from a humble background, had found the opportunity to meet with the leading intelligentsia

of the time. Vahram Papazian likened Mark in this "Olympian literary assembly" to a hopping sparrow, who by "passing an ashtray to a guest, handing matches to another," aspired to make her presence felt. Soon, she would make a name for herself. Vahram Papazian, "Sibili Mod . . . Mi Khntrankov," in *Srdis Bardke* (Yerevan: Hay Bed. Hrad, 1959), 62–63.

84. Hayganush Mark, "Khmpakragan: Azkayin Hivantanotsi Hamar," *Hay Gin* 6, no. 18 (September 16, 1925).

85. Hayganush Mark, "Khmpakragan: Garke Mern E," *Hay Gin* 6, no. 20 (October 16, 1925). In the same issue, Nevrig Sebuhian wrote a piece to support Mark and criticize the Education Commission for not having any women members. Nevrig Sebuhian, "Ganatsi Tserkere Hanrayin Kordzeru Mech," *Hay Gin* 6, no. 20 (October 16, 1925).

86. "Hay Ginere yev Azkayin Hivantanotse," *Hay Gin* 7, no. 21 (November 1, 1926); Hayganush Mark, "Khmpakragan: Azkayin Hivantanotsi Ozhantag Masnajiughere," *Hay Gin* 7, no. 22 (November 16, 1926).

87. Mark, "Dzpankner Gyankes," 63 (italics in the original).

88. *Hay Gin* had many male contributors, some of whom were outspoken feminists, such as Dikran Aslanian, Stepan Shahbaz, Kegham Grigorian, and Hovannes Asbed (Onnik Chifte-Saraf). Mark repeatedly pointed out that despite a few individual men who supported feminism, men as a group were against it. Hayganush Mark, "Khmpakragan: Baronneru Ngadman," *Hay Gin* 3, no. 14 (May 16, 1922); Mark, "Khmpakragan: Mer Ayrere yev Menk," *Hay Gin* 3, no. 19 (August 1, 1922).

89. Even a basic narrative of how these developments unfolded is missing from the literature.

Chapter 3

1. Gosdan Zarian, *The Traveller and His Road* (New York: Ashod Press, 1981), 28–29.

2. According to a Greek diplomat, about 70 percent of the Turkish population in Istanbul supported the nationalist cause. Alexis Alexandris, *The Greek Minority of Istanbul and Greek-Turkish Relations, 1918–1974* (Athens: Center for Asia Minor Studies, 1983), 78.

3. *Vakit*, September 9, 1922.

4. *Jagadamard*, "Editorial," September 12, 1922. Three full paragraphs were censored in this editorial, like many other columns in Armenian newspapers of the time. They appear blank.

5. *Vakit*, September 11, 1922.

6. *Jagadamard*, September 12, 1922, first page.

7. Anayis [Yevpime Avedisian], *Hushers* (Paris: n.p., 1949), 282.

8. Ibid., 283–84. Similar feelings of terror and helplessness are depicted in other memoirs as well. Kerop Bedoukian, *Some of Us Survived: The Story of an Armenian Boy* (New York: Farrar Straus Giroux, 1979), 209; Arshavir Shirakian, *The Legacy: Memoirs of an Armenian Patriot* (Boston: Hairenik Press, 1976), 211–12.

9. For an example, see the last page of the October 5, 1922, issue of *Jagadamard*. The page has five ads of ferry companies and ticket sellers and no other ads. The ferries were the *King Alexander*, the *Akropolis*, and the *Madonna*.

10. Vahan Tekeyan, *Namagani* (Watertown, MA: Tekeyan Mshagutayin Miutiun, 1983), 214 (letter dated October 12, 1922).

11. Alexandris, *The Greek Minority of Istanbul*, 82.

12. Ibid., 80.

13. Ibid., 102.

14. An Anglo-Turkish war was avoided. This is the famous Chanak Affair of late September and early October 1922, which resulted in the resignation of British prime minister Lloyd George and put an end to his career. For further details on the evacuation of the city, see Bilge Criss, *İşgal Altında İstanbul, 1918–1923* (Istanbul: İletişim Yayınları, 1993), 209–31.

15. For an important discussion of why and how the British ceased to support the Armenian cause, see Michelle Tusan, "'Crimes against Humanity': Human Rights, the British Empire, and the Origins of the Response to the Armenian Genocide," *American Historical Review* 119, no. 1 (2014): 47–77.

16. Charles Harington, *Tim Harington Looks Back* (London: J. Murray, 1940), 137.

17. Sources are silent on whether women were present at the ceremonies and, if they were, what kind of headgear they wore.

18. Anayis's archives, which also include her correspondence with Hayganush Mark, are in the Yeghishe Charents Museum of Literature and Art in Yerevan, Armenia.

19. Zaruhi Kalemkearian's archives are also in the Yeghishe Charents Museum of Literature and Art in Yerevan, Armenia.

20. "Ganants Ashkharhen," *Hay Gin* 9, no. 15 (August 1, 1928).

21. Zaven Der Yeghiayan, *My Patriarchal Memoirs* (Barrington, RI: Mayreni, 2002), 241.

22. All this information is from Bahri's memoir, *Gyankis Vebe*, which was posthumously published (any only in very limited numbers) by her daughter Anahid and her daughter's husband, Nubar Tavitian.

23. Zaruhi Bahri had four grandchildren, Roland Tavitian, Tavit Tavitian, Jacques Bahri, and Aline Elmayan. I thank them for talking with me about their family history in Paris in July 2011. Their insight was very useful and will form the basis of another study.

24. Der Yeghiayan, *My Patriarchal Memoirs*, 253.

25. Alexandris, *The Greek Minority of Istanbul*, 144–54.

26. Hayganush Mark, "Khmpakragan: Gin yev Yegeghetsi," *Hay Gin* 3, no. 1 (December 16, 1922).

27. Ibid.

28. *Hay Gin* 4, no. 2 (January 1, 1923).

29. Zaven Arzumanian, "Naroyan Badriark," in *Azkabadum, Volume Four, Book One (1919–1930)* (New York: St. Vartan Press, 1995), 329.

30. "Nazenian Mayranotse," *Hay Gin* 6, nos. 23–24, (December 1–16, 1925).

31. Hayganush Mark, "Khmpakragan: 'Hay Gin'i 4rt Darelitse," *Hay Gin* 5, no. 1 (January 1, 1924) (emphasis in the original).

32. The treaty was signed between "Turkey" (the Ottoman Empire) and "the Allied Powers," meaning the British Empire, France, Italy, Japan, Greece, Rumania, and the Serb-Croat-Slovene State. The United Stated participated in the conference as an observing party but was not a signatory. The full text is in *The Treaties of Peace 1919–1923*, vol. 2 (New York: Carnegie Endowment for International Peace, 1924), 959–1052.

33. The most detailed treatment of the Armenian delegation in the years 1920–1923 is Levon Marashlian, "The Armenian Question from Sèvres to Lausanne: Economics and Morality in American and British Policies, 1920–1923" (PhD dissertation, UCLA, 1992). On the Lausanne Conference, see pp. 647–815.

34. The hearing took place on December 26, 1923. The Armenians who presented their case were Gabriel Noradungian (from the Armenian National Delegation), Alexander Khadisian, and Avedis Aharonian (from the Delegation of the Republic of Armenia).

35. Alexander Khadisian, "The Lausanne Conference and the Two Armenian Delegations," *Armenian Review* 14, nos. 4–56 (Winter, January 1962): 58–65.

36. The patriarch discusses these developments in Der Yeghiayan, *My Patriarchal Memoirs*, 238–55.

37. For further details, see Lerna Ekmekcioglu, "Mecbur," in Fikret Adanır and Oktay Özel, eds., *1915: Öncesi ve Sonrasıyla Ermeni Siyaseti, Tehcir ve Soykırım* (Istanbul: TESEV, 2015).

38. According to the Armenian delegation at Lausanne, as of December 1922 the population of Soviet Armenia was 1,400,000, of which 1,200,000 were Armenians and 60,000 Muslims. Marashlian, "The Armenian Question from Sèvres to Lausanne," 719.

39. Bilal Şimşir, *Lozan Telgrafları I (1922–1923)* (Ankara: Türk Tarih Kurumu Basımevi, 1990), s. xiv.

40. Fahri Çoker, *Türk Parlamento Tarihi: Millî Mücadele ve T.B.M.M. I. Dönem, 1919–1923*, Cilt 2 (Ankara: Türkiye Büyük Millet Meclisi Vakfı, 1995), 348.

41. Seha Meray, *Lozan Barış Konferansı Tutanaklar, Belgeler*, Takım 1, Cilt 1, Kitap 1 (Ankara: Ankara Üniversitesi Basımevi, 1969), s. 199.

42. Telegram dated December 7. 1922. Şimşir, *Lozan Telgrafları I*, 172.

43. For a recent study of the birth and trajectory of the idea of self-determination, see Eric D. Weitz, "Self-Determination: How a German Enlightenment Idea Became the Slogan of National Liberation and a Human Right," *American Historical Review* 120, no. 2 (2015): 462–96.

44. Liliana Riga and James Kennedy, "Tolerant Majorities, Loyal Minorities and

'Ethnic Reversals': Constructing Minority Rights at Versailles 1919," *Nations and Nationalism* 15, no. 3 (2009): 461–82.

45. İsmet Pasha emphasized this point at the Lausanne Conference but was not taken seriously, not only because of the orientalist biases of his audience but also because of the wartime massacres of Ottoman Christians and the fact that not imposing minority protections would elevate Turkey to a level equal to that of the victorious Allies. For İsmet Pasha's tirade during the December 12, 1922, session of the Lausanne Conference, see Meray, *Lozan Barış Konferansı*, 187–200.

46. For a discussion of how the Ottoman ghost would continue to haunt the new Turkey and inform anti-diversity measures, see Yeşim Bayar, *Formation of the Turkish Nation-State (1920–1938)* (New York: Palgrave Macmillan, 2014).

47. Meray, *Lozan Barış Konferansı*, 200.

48. The former chief rabbi Haim Nahum went to Lausanne to support the Turkish delegation's stance. On December 10, 1922, Turkish Jews established in Switzerland organized a reception in Geneva in honor of İsmet Pasha. For more on Nahum, see Haïm Nahoum and Esther Benbassa, *Haim Nahum: A Sephardic Chief Rabbi in Politics, 1892–1923* (Tuscaloosa: University of Alabama Press, 1995).

49. Since the 1880s, Asian and Middle Eastern intellectuals have criticized similar kinds of double standards. See Cemil Aydın, *The Politics of Anti-Westernism in Asia: Visions of World Order in Pan-Islamic and Pan-Asian Thought* (New York: Columbia University Press, 2007), esp. chap. 3.

50. Mark Mazower, "Minorities and the League of Nations in Interwar Europe," *Daedalus* 126 (1997): 53.

51. Treaty of Lausanne VIII: Declaration of Amnesty, www.mfa.gov.tr/viii_-declaration-of-amnesty.en.mfa (accessed January 5, 2014).

52. Taner Akçam, *A Shameful Act: The Armenian Genocide and the Question of Turkish Responsibility* (New York: Metropolitan Books, 2006), 362–64. For an important discussion of how Mustafa Kemal supported the perpetrators of the Armenian genocide, see Fatma Ülgen, "Reading Mustafa Kemal Atatürk on the Armenian Genocide of 1915," *Patterns of Prejudice* 44, no. 4 (2010): 369–91.

53. Erik Jan Zürcher, "Renewal and Silence: Postwar Unionist and Kemalist Rhetoric on the Armenian Genocide," in Ronald Grigor Suny, Fatma Müge Göçek, and Norman M. Naimark, eds., *A Question of Genocide: Armenians and Turks at the End of the Ottoman Empire* (New York: Oxford University Press, 2011), 306–16. For recent studies of Turkish denialism, see Fatma Müge Göçek, *Denial of Violence: Ottoman Past, Turkish Present and Collective Violence against the Armenians, 1789–2009* (New York: Oxford University Press, 2015); G. Gürkan Öztan and Ömer Turan, "Türkiye'de Devlet Aklı ve 1915," *Toplum ve Bilim* 132 (April 2015): 78–131; and Jennifer M. Dixon, "Turkey's Narrative of the Armenian Genocide: Change within Continuity," in Annette Becker et al., eds., *Le Génocide des Arméniens: Cent ans de recherche 1915–2015* (Paris: Armand Colin, 2015), 249–56.

54. Soner Çağaptay, *Islam, Secularism, and Nationalism in Modern Turkey: Who Is a Turk?* (London: Routledge, 2006), 37.

55. Meray, *Lozan Barış Konferansı*, 155, 161.

56. For more on how the Armenian properties were appropriated by the Turkish state, see Nevzat Onaran, *Emval-i Metruke Olayı: Osmanlı'da ve Cumhuriyette Ermeni ve Rum Mallarının Türkleştirilmesi* (Istanbul: Belge Yayınları, 2000); Uğur Ümit Üngör and Mehmet Polatel, *Confiscation and Destruction: The Young Turk Seizure of Armenian Property* (London: Continuum, 2011); and Taner Akçam and Ümit Kurt, eds., *Kanunların Ruhu: Emval-i Metruke Kanunlarında Soykırımın İzini Sürmek* (Istanbul: İletişim, 2012).

57. Letter of Mr. Aharonian to the Powers, August 13, 1923, Archives of Delegation of the Armenian Republic. Quoted in Mary Mangigian Tarzian, *The Armenia Minority Problem, 1914–1934: A Nation's Struggle for Security* (Atlanta, GA: Scholars Press, 1992), 28–29.

58. 2 March 1229 (1923), *TBMM Gizli Celse Zabıtları*, Devre: 1, İçtima Senesi: III, Cilt 4, p. 13.

59. Ibid., 7.

60. Ibid., 8.

61. According to the first census of Turkey, which was conducted in 1927, of the country's total population of about 13.5 million people, around 110,000 were Greek, 77,000 were Armenian, and 82,000 were Jewish. Non-Muslims made up 2 percent of the population. Their numbers declined to 1.6 percent according to the second census, in 1935. Ahmet İçduygu, Şule Toktaş, and B. Ali Soner, "The Politics of Population in a Nation-Building Process: Emigration of Non-Muslims from Turkey," *Ethnic and Racial Studies* 31, no. 2 (2008): 368–69. Note that the census figures are not completely reliable given how the questions were phrased, categories offered, etc. For more on this issue, see Fuat Dündar, *Türkiye Nüfus Sayımlarında Azınlıklar* (Istanbul: Doz Yayınları, 1999).

Chapter 4

1. Hayganush Mark, "Khmpakragan: Mer Yegeghetsin yev Menk," *Hay Gin* 5, no. 3 (February 1, 1924).

2. According to Anne-Marie Fortier, the "diasporic moment" includes "not only a type of diasporic consciousness—expressed in forms of longing and memory that are common to displaced people—but also actual practices that take place within transnational networks of dispersed 'communities.' These practices may circulate within a system of exchange [. . .] or they may be disconnected and isolated from one another, yet occur simultaneously in different places." Anne-Marie Fortier, *Migrant Belongings: Memory, Space, Identity* (Oxford: Berg, 2000), 142.

3. The other difference was that the 1924 constitution replaced the 1876 constitution's "sect" with "race."

4. A. Ş. Gözübüyük and Z. Sezgin, *1924 Anayasası Hakkındaki Meclis Görüşmeleri* (Ankara: AÜSBF İdari Bilimler Enstitüsü, 1957), 436–40.

5. Ibid., 436.

6. Ibid., 437.

7. Ibid. (emphasis added).

8. Ibid., 438–39. The transliteration of the text does not capitalize the terms *musevi*, *ermenilik*, and *rum*, which mean "Jewish," "Armenianness," and "Greek," respectively. Terms such as "Türk," "Fransa," and "İngiliz" are capitalized.

9. Will Kymlicka, *Multicultural Citizenship: A Liberal Theory of Minority Rights* (Oxford: Clarendon Press, 1995); Iris Marion Young, *Justice and the Politics of Difference* (Princeton, NJ: Princeton University Press, 1990).

10. Jay R. Berkovitz, *Rites and Passages: The Beginnings of Modern Jewish Culture in France, 1650–1860* (Philadelphia: University of Pennsylvania Press, 2004), 89.

11. Joan W. Scott, *The Politics of the Veil* (Princeton, NJ: Princeton University Press, 2007), 11.

12. Gözübüyük and Sezgin, *1924 Anayasası*, 441.

13. Ibid. (emphasis added).

14. Mesut Yeğen, "Citizenship and Ethnicity in Turkey," *Middle Eastern Studies* 40, issue 6 (2004): 51–66.

15. Gözübüyük and Sezgin, *1924 Anayasası*, 439.

16. For a more in-depth discussion of the processes covered in this part of the chapter, see Lerna Ekmekcioglu, "Republic of Paradox: The League of Nations Minority Protection Regime and the New Turkey's Step-Citizens," *International Journal of Middle East Studies* 46, no. 4 (2014): 657–79.

17. For a discussion of how these changes were experienced on the ground, see Hale Yılmaz, *Becoming Turkish: Nationalist Reforms and Cultural Negotiations in Early Republican Turkey, 1923–1945* (Syracuse, NY: Syracuse University Press, 2013).

18. Nükhet A. Sandal, "Public Theologies of Human Rights and Citizenship: The Case of Turkey's Christians," *Human Rights Quarterly* 35, no. 3 (2013): 631–50.

19. For more, see Anver Emon, *Religious Pluralism and Islamic Law: "Dhimmīs" and Others in the Empire of Law* (Oxford: Oxford University Press, 2012). In Emon's words, dhimmis can be thought of as "permanent resident aliens" of states ruled by sharia. They have rights but because Islamic law finds religious belief relevant for legal differentiation, their rights are different from those of Muslims and are not equal to theirs. Ibid., 34.

20. Before 1934, citizens in Turkey did not have to register a last name (though most of them did so willingly) and many were known by their nicknames, which often denoted their ethnic background or native town. The Surname Law aimed at various targets: it would flatten onomastic differences, erase any residual hierarchical denominations from Ottoman times, cut any potentially competing loyalties, and in general render the administration of the population more efficient. The law (Law No. 2525, "Soy

Adı Kanunu," June 21, 1934) stipulated that everyone in Turkey must acquire a last name, that last names be adopted from the Turkish language, and that "names denoting rank, tenure, official position and those belonging to foreign races and nations" not be adopted. The ensuing Surname Regulation (*Nizamname*) forbade the adoption of patronyms not only associated with certain Muslim groups (that is, *-veled, -bin, -madumu, -zade*) but also those of non-Muslims (e.g. *-yan* for Armenians and *-dis* for Greeks).

21. Yet the whole process of getting a last name was characterized by irregularity and chaos. Since we lack in-depth studies of the law, some unanswered questions remain. However, it seems that because the law lacked clarity, if it applied to people who had already registered last names with such endings or only to those who were going to register a last name for the first time, the law did not apply to everyone uniformly and this led to a variety of outcomes. Moreover, from anecdotal evidence it appears that Armenians in Istanbul had kept their original last names while those in Anatolia changed them. But even in Istanbul while some non-Muslim families kept their ethnic last names, some chose to Turkify them, some were forced to Turkify them, while others simply dropped the linguistic patronymic ending. The only extensive study thus far on the surname law does not solve this puzzle. See Meltem Türköz, "The Social Life of the State's Fantasy: Memories and Documents on Turkey's 1934 Surname Law" (PhD dissertation, University of Pennsylvania, 2004).

22. ʾA. Afetinan, *Atatürk Hakkında Hatıralar ve Belgeler: Anı*, 6th ed. (Istanbul: Türkiye İş Bankası Kültür Yayınları, 2007), 213.

23. Dhimmi rules date back to the precedent of the Prophet Mohammed and his dealings with the Jewish tribes of Arabia in the seventh century. Muslim jurists codified the rules in the ninth century in response to the second caliph Omar's negotiations with Christians residing in contemporary Syria who asked for protection (*aman*) during the conquest. The emerging document, the Pact of Omar, which is essentially a surrender document, is, despite its dubious authenticity and multiple versions, important because it remained the blueprint for future Islamic states', including those of the Ottomans', legislation on their Christian and Jewish subjects. For a detailed discussion, see Milka Levy-Rubin, *Non-Muslims in the Early Islamic Empire: From Surrender to Coexistence* (New York: Cambridge University Press, 2011).

24. For the only in-depth study of this society, see Silvart Malhasyan, "İstanbul'da 1922 Yılında Kurulan Türk-Ermeni Teali Cemiyeti ve Faaliyetleri" (M.A. thesis, İstanbul Üniversitesi Atatürk İlkeleri ve İnkılap Tarihi Enstitüsü, 2005).

25. Ibid., 20–21.

26. Mıgirdiç Agop, *Türkiye Ermenileri* (Istanbul: Ali Şükrü Matbaası, 1922). The brochure is transliterated to modern Turkish and published in full in Fikret Adanır and Oktay Özel, eds., *1915: Öncesi ve Sonrasıyla Ermeni Siyaseti, Tehcir ve Soykırım* (Istanbul: TESEV, 2015). "SETA Member Mıgirdiç Agop" was probably a nickname. Because SETA was established on December 24, 1922, the pamphlet was either written and published in

one week or published in 1923 but stamped with the previous year's date. Both are possible. Given its propaganda value for the Lausanne Conference's Turkish delegation, it is not unimaginable that it was produced in the space of seven days. In addition, the text itself mentions that "this pamphlet had to come out in a short period of time" (ibid., 12).

27. *Sezâ-yı tîğ olur haddin tecâvüz eyleyen mûlar*. The next line is: *Anın'çün tîğdan âzâdedir müjganla ebrûlar*: "That is why the eyelashes and eyebrows remain free of the knife."

28. The general elections were held on June 29, 1923. SETA's tea party at the Tokatliyan was on July 20, 1923.

29. He was elected president of the Armenian National Assembly's Civil Council on February 17, 1922. Arshag Alboyajian, *Badmutiun Hay Gesario. Deghakragan, Badmagan yev Azkakragan Usumnasirutiun*, vol. 2 (Cairo: Hradaragutiun Gesario yev Shrchagayits Hayrenagtsgan Miutyan Kahirei Varchutyan), 2121–25.

30. *Verchin Lur*, July 21, 1923. Mosdichian was elected vice president of SETA at the association's July 4, 1924, meeting.

31. *Hay Gin* 3, no. 6 (January 16, 1922).

32. *Hay Gin* 8, no. 13 (July 1, 1927).

33. In 1936, the paper claimed that new scientific research had found that Armenians were in fact Turks. The title of the article was "Turk Oghlu Turk Yenk," that is, "We Are Turk-born Turks." A. C., "Turk Oghlu Turk Yenk," *Nor Huys* 1, no. 46 (February 22, 1936).

34. M. Vankaya, "Inchbes Grnank Harazad Turk Hayrenagitsner Ellal?," *Nor Huys* 1, no. 2 (April 20, 1935).

35. M. Vankaya, "Nasıl Hakiki Türk Vatandaşı Olabiliriz?," *Nor Huys* 1, no. 3 (April 27, 1935).

36. Ibid.

37. "Türkiye Cumhuriyeti Ölmez," *Nor Huys* 1, no. 29 (October 26, 1935).

38. "Ardasahmani Hay Mamule yev Turkia," in Toros Azadian and Mardiros Kochunian, eds., *Armağan, Türkiye Cumhuriyeti 15 İnci Yıldönümü, Armaghan Turkio Hanrabedutyan 15 Amyagin Artiv 1923–1938* (Istanbul: Gutemberg, G.N. Makasjian, 1938), 78–79.

39. "Turk Krakedner Ge Bandzatsnen Hay Midke," *Sharzhum* 1, no. 1 (January 27, 1930).

40. Kevork Terzibashian (1859–1929) was an Armenian Catholic ecclesiastic who published a two-volume study of Fuzûlî in Armenian in Istanbul: *Nmuysh Arevelian Misdig Panasdeghdzutyan gam Fuzuli Megnapanvadz* (Istanbul: Asadurian, 1928 and 1929).

41. Badrig, "Hay yev Turk Mdavoragan Haraperutiunnere: 'Hayere Mius Darreren Aveli Zpaghadz En Turk Kraganutiamp'; Mdavoragan Gamurch Me Hasdadel Anhrazheshd E' Gese Celal Nuri Beye," *Sharzhum* 1, no. 2 (February 3, 1930). Mehmet Fuad Köprülü (1890–1966) was a well-known Turkish politician, historian of the Ottoman

Empire, and scholar of Turkish and Azerbaijani literature. He served as Turkish foreign minister from 1950 to 1956. "Menk yev Turkere—'Hay yev Turk Kraganutiants Michev Zoravor Gaber Gan . . .' 'Yergu Azkeru Michev Mdavoragan Mertsetsume Mishd Okdagar Ge Ngadem' Gse Köprülü Zade Fuad Bey," *Sharzhum* 1, no. 3 (February 10, 1930).

42. Marion Kaplan analyzes Jewish daily life in Nazi Germany and argues that as long as Jews were able to continue a more or less "normal" daily life, they did not clearly see the dangers that they were experiencing every day. Marion A. Kaplan, *Between Dignity and Despair: Jewish Life in Nazi Germany* (New York: Oxford University Press, 1998).

43. Senem Aslan rightfully maintains that the whole Turkification/homogenization process cannot be explained solely through a state-centered approach. The social engineering projects were created, reproduced, enriched, and carried out through the state's missionaries such as students, professionals, intellectuals, and the like. Senem Aslan, "'Citizen, Speak Turkish!': A Nation in the Making," *Nationalism and Ethnic Politics* 13, no. 2 (April 2007): 245–72.

44. Cemil Koçak, "Ayın Karanlık Yüzü: Tek-parti Döneminde Gayri Müslim Azınlıklar Aleyhinde Açılan Türklüğü Tahkir Davaları," *Tarih ve Toplum Yeni Yaklaşımlar* 1 (March 2005): 147–208.

45. Agop J. Hacikyan, *My Ethnic Quest* (London: Gomidas Institute, 2012), 94.

46. Ibid., 98. In my interview with Agop Hacikyan (born in Istanbul in 1931), without my asking he brought up the subject of language, telling me that his mother did not know Turkish and when they were outside of the home his mother spoke a caricaturized form of Turkish which was both funny and embarrassing. Hacikyan wished his mother would keep silent and leave the talking to her young son Agop. Interview with Agop Hacikyan, May 27, 2013, Montreal, Canada.

47. Franz Werfel, *The Forty Days of Musa Dagh* (New York: Modern Library, 1933).

48. Soner Çağaptay, *Islam, Secularism, and Nationalism in Modern Turkey: Who Is a Turk?* (London: Routledge, 2006), 136.

49. For a detailed discussion, see Rıfat N. Bali, *Musa'nın Evlatları, Cumhuriyet'in Yurttaşları*, 2nd ed. (Cağaloğlu, Istanbul: İletişim Yayınları, 2001), 116–34.

50. Without my raising the subject, Agop Hacikyan told me that his family owned a copy of Werfel's book in Armenian translation but that they hid it like it was a "federal state secret." He never knew where his parents' hid the book because, in his words, "They were afraid that they could come and find it." Interview with Hacikyan, May 27, 2013, Montreal, Canada. For a recent discussion of Armenians' book hiding and burning practices in Turkey, see Talin Suciyan, "Dört Nesil: Kurtarılamayan Son," *Toplum ve Bilim* 132 (2015): 132–49, esp. 147. The first Armenian translation of Werfel's book was published in Sofia in 1935. Frants Verfel, *Haygagan Herosabadum. Musa Leran Karasun Orere*, trans. by Yervant Antreasian (Sofia: Masis Dbaran, 1935), 2 vols.

51. Interview with Shakhe and Ardashes Shelemian, March 19, 2013, Watertown, Massachusetts. Ardashes Shelemian and many of the elderly people whom I talked

with mentioned that they despised the prime minister İsmet İnönü, otherwise known as Milli Şef, but liked Mustafa Kemal. Only future work can elucidate the reasons. Agop Hacikyan mentioned that among Armenians the expression "Ismet Pashayin namag krel" (writing a petition to Ismet Pasha) meant going to the bathroom and using the toilet paper. Interview with Agop Hacikyan, May 27, 2013, Montreal, Canada.

52. For a detailed discussion, see Erik Jan Zürcher, "Renewal and Silence: Postwar Unionist and Kemalist Rhetoric on the Armenian Genocide," in Ronald Grigor Suny, Fatma Müge Göçek, and Norman M. Naimark, eds., *A Question of Genocide: Armenians and Turks at the End of the Ottoman Empire* (New York: Oxford University Press, 2011).

53. Zeynep Kezer, "Of Forgotten People and Forgotten Places: Nation-Building and the Dismantling of Ankara's Non-Muslim Landscapes," in D. Fairchild Ruggles, ed., *On Location: Heritage Cities and Sites* (New York: Springer, 2011), 169–91, here 169.

54. Ibid, p. 181.

55. Martayan was well-versed in many other languages, including his mother tongue, Armenian. He wrote for *Hay Gin* as well. Hagop Martayan, "Gnoch Yes'e," *Hay Gin* 3, no. 20 (August 16, 1922).

56. The 1926 "Law on Civil Servants" specified that "being a Turk" was a primary criterion for eligibility to work as a civil servant. During parliamentary deliberations, "the Turk" was defined as a non-Armenian and non-Greek citizen of Turkey. For more, see Yeşim Bayar, *Formation of the Turkish Nation-State (1920–1938)* (New York: Palgrave Macmillan, 2014), 131–32.

57. Hayganush Mark, "Khmpakragan: Klkhargi Mdahokutiun," *Hay Gin* 2, no. 1 (November 1, 1921); Hayganush Mark, "Khmpakragan: Mskhumner," *Hay Gin* 7, no. 17 (September 1, 1926).

58. Vartan Parunagian, "Mortsvads Nor Darin," *Hay Gin* 5, no. 4 (February 16, 1924).

59. Hayganush Mark, "Khmpakragan: Vorperun Vaghe," *Hay Gin* 5, no. 10 (May 16, 1924).

60. Matilda Jelal, "Mderim Namag," *Hay Gin* 5, no. 3 (February 1, 1924) (italics in the original).

61. "Khmpakragan: Ushakrav Yerevuytner," *Hay Khosnag* 1, no. 3 (October 1924).

62. Hidayet M. Vahapoğlu, *Osmanlı'dan Günümüze Azınlık ve Yabancı Okullar: Yönetimleri Açısından* (Istanbul: Millî Eğitim Bakanlığı Yayınları, 2005), 151–52.

63. Mehmet Deri, *Türkiye'de Azınlıklar ve Azınlık Okulları: Rum-Yahudi ve Ermeni Cemaatleri* (Istanbul: IQ Kültür Sanat Yayıncılık, 2009), 169–71.

64. Many of these laws are still in effect. For an unprecedented memoir (in novel form) of a "Turk" teacher working in minority schools in the 1990s and early 2000s, see Emin Keşmer, *Bir Poşet İstanbul Toprağı* (Istanbul: Siyah Beyaz Kitap, 2012).

65. Paul Gilroy, *The Black Atlantic: Modernity and Double Consciousness* (Cambridge, MA: Harvard University Press, 1993), 281.

66. Mesrob Naroyan, "Mesrob Arch. Naroyan Badriark G. Bolso 1927—Antranig

Gontag," in *Nshkharner Mesrob Arkebis. Naroyani (Harmag) Kragan Kordsere* (Istanbul: Becid Basımevi, 1948), 247. Naroyan was elected by the National Assembly on June 26, 1927. His encyclical letter is dated August 15, 1927.

67. Ibid., 253.

68. Ibid., 254–55.

69. Mesrob Bsh. Naroyan, "Nahadag Mdavoragan Yegeghetsagannere," in Teotig, ed., *Hushartsan Abril Dasnmegi* (Istanbul: O. Arzuman, 1919).

70. Ibid., 122. Translation from Rita Soulahian Kuyumjian, *Teotig: Biography & Monument to April 11 by Teotig* (London: Taderon Press, 2010), 219.

71. According to the memoirs of Patriarch Zaven Der Yeghiayan, he was saved thanks to the efforts of Reshad Bey, the chief of the Istanbul Police Department's Police Section. Patriarch Zaven mentions that Reshad Bey was "capable of occasional acts of kindness" toward Armenians since he had many friends among them (and spoke Armenian well) and that "many Armenians owe their salvation to him." Zaven Der Yeghiayan, *My Patriarchal Memoirs* (Barrington, RI: Mayreni, 2002), 118. According to Kevork V Surenian, Catholicos of All Armenians, Naroyan was able to return to Istanbul thanks to the former patriarch Yeghishe Tourian's successful mediation. Kevork V, "Naroyan Badriark," in Zaven Arzumanian, *Azkabadum, Volume Four, Book One (1919–1930)* (New York: St. Vartan Press, 1995), 331. Mesrob Naroyan never published his memories pertaining to the 1914–1923 era.

72. Armaveni Miroğlu, "Pangaltı Ermeni Mezarlığı (Surp Hagop Mezarlığı)," *Toplumsal Tarih* 187 (2009): 34–39.

73. Archbishop Naroyan, "Hayeren Lezun yev Ir Usume," *Entartsag Daretsuyts Surp Prgich Azkayin Hivantanotsi* 6 (1930): 231–33.

74. Ibid., 233.

75. Ibid.

Chapter 5

1. Hayganush Mark, "Gnoch Me Tavananke," *Hay Gin* 5, no. 22 (November 16, 1924).

2. Kohar Mazlemian and Hayganush Mark, "'Gnoch Me Tavanank' in Artiv," *Hay Gin* 5, nos. 23–24 (December 1–16, 1924).

3. Ibid.

4. Hayganush Mark, "Gnoch Tade II—Gnoch Tasdiaragutiune," *Hay Gin* 3, no. 4 (December 16, 1921).

5. Ardashes Kalpakjian, "Yete Yes Gin Ellayi," *Hay Gin* 1, no. 4 (December 16, 1920).

6. Mark's first editorial in which she notes that feminism does not negate domesticity is "Khmpakragan: Ardnin Dndesutiun," *Hay Gin* 2, no. 10 (March 16, 1921).

7. Hayganush Mark, "Khmpakragan: Khohanotse," *Hay Gin* 11, no. 1 (January 1, 1930).

8. Digin Knar, "Diyarbakir Keufte," *Hay Gin* 11, no. 1 (January 1, 1930); Kohar Mazle-

mian, "Khohanotsi Garevorutiune yev Ir Khnamke," *Hay Gin* 11, no. 1 (January 1, 1930). Digin Knar appears to have been especially close to the kitchen. Mevhibe Celalettin, who toured with Digin Knar's theater group in different parts of Anatolia in the 1920s and '30s, noted in her memoir that Digin Knar would have the most luggage because she carried her pans with her wherever she went. Mevhibe Celalettin, *Geçmiş Zaman Olur Ki . . . : Prenses Mevhibe Celalettin'in Anıları* (Istanbul: Çağdaş Yayınları, 1987), 288.

9. Sibil, "Namag Me," *Hay Gin* 11, no. 1 (January 1, 1930).

10. Srpuhi Dussape, *Mayda* (Constantinople, 1883); Srpuhi Dussape, *Siranush* (Constantinople, 1884); Srpuhi Dussape, *Araksia gam Varzhuhin* (Constantinople, 1887). As early as 1901, Arshag Alboyajian published a volume that analyzed Dussape's works. Arshag Alboyajian, *Usumnasirutiun Srpuhi Dussapei* (Venice, 1901).

11. On Zohrab's antifeminism, see Rita Vorperian, "A Feminist Reading of Krikor Zohrab" (PhD dissertation, UCLA, 1999).

12. Sibil, "Namag Me."

13. Zohrab was born in 1861 and died in 1915. Sibil was born in 1863 and died in 1934. Armine Bagdiken, born in Istanbul in 1918, told me that Sibil and Krikor Zohrab had a love affair, something that I could not corroborate in secondary sources. In any case it is clear that Zohrab appreciated "educated women" simply because he invested very much in his daughters' education. Interview with Armine Bagdiken on May 13, 2013, Jamaica Plains, Massachusetts.

14. "Khmpakragan: Ardnin Dndesutian Arzheke," *Hay Gin* 4, no. 11 (May 16, 1923) (italics in the original).

15. The first translation of *A Doll's House* into Armenian was in 1892. Tiruhi Kostaniantz translated the play under the title *Nora* and serialized it in Tbilisi's Armenian weekly *Ardzagang* (Echo) from May 1 to June 24, 1892. A fragment of *Nora* was published in Constantinople's *Luys* (Light) paper in May 2, 1898. The first performance of *Nora* in Armenian was on December 18, 1903, in Tiflis. The first performance of *Nora* in Constantinople was on October 17, 1922, at the Theatre de Petit-Champs, by the Theatrical Union of Constantinople. This was the swan song of the group, which emigrated to Soviet Armenia three days later on the initiative of its director, Vahram Papazian. Papken Harutiunian, *XIX–XX Tareri Hay Tadroni Darekrutiun* (Erevan: Haykakan SSH GA Hradarakchutiun, 1980–1981), 350–55.

16. Joan Templeton, *Ibsen's Women* (Cambridge: Cambridge University Press, 1997), 112.

17. Hayganush Mark, "Khmpakragan: Tebi Endaneganutiun," *Hay Gin* 4, no. 7 (March 16, 1923).

18. Hayganush Mark, "Khmpakragan: Magapuydser Artyok," *Hay Gin* 7, no. 5 (March 1, 1926).

19. Hayganush Mark, "Khmpakragan: Noratsevutyan Harvadse Gnoch Tadin," *Hay Gin* 4, no. 13 (June 1, 1923).

20. Hayganush Mark, "Khmpakragan: Kich Me Amen Pan," *Hay Gin* 7, no. 3 (February 1, 1926).

21. For the best treatment of the subject, see Joan Wallach Scott, *Only Paradoxes to Offer: French Feminists and the Rights of Man* (Cambridge, MA: Harvard University Press, 1996).

22. Ibid., 33.

23. Hayganush Mark, "'Lav Dndesuhi' yev 'Feminizm,'" *Hay Gin* 6, no. 6 (March 16, 1925). Stepan Shahbaz, a long-time friend of Mark and a frequent contributor to *Hay Gin* from various Middle Eastern cities, emphasized the same point and repeated the same phrase in the introductory essay he wrote for the book that came out in honor of Mark's fiftieth anniversary of her intellectual activities in 1954 and contained her short autobiography as well. Stepan Shahbaz, "Hayganush Mark yev ir Kordze," in *Hayganush Mark, Gyankn U Kordze* (Istanbul, n.p., 1954), 11.

24. Hayganush Mark, "Khmpakragan: Gin Yeghir Gin," *Hay Gin* 13, no. 14 (July 16, 1932).

25. Hayganush Mark, "Engeraparoyagan Hartser/Partsr Gine," *Hay Gin* 5, no. 4 (February 16, 1924).

26. Ibid.

27. Hayganush Mark, "Gnoch Tade I—Inch e Gnoch Tade" *Hay Gin* 3, no. 3 (December 1, 1921).

28. Hayganush Mark, "Gnoch Tade VI—Gnoch Kaghakagan Iravunknere," *Hay Gin* 3, no. 9 (March 1, 1922).

29. Mark, "Khmpakragan: Gin Yeghir Gin."

30. Mark, "Gnoch Tade II—Gnoch Tasdiaragutiune."

31. The discussion started with a *Hay Gin* essay ("Hnazantil," by Huguette, *Hay Gin* 1, no. 15, June 1, 1920) that was a translation from the magazine *Eve* where the author asked if it was fine for brides to vow to "obey" during a church wedding. Aside from Hayganush Mark, others joined the discussion as well. See, for example, Simon Khoren, "Gin yev Hnazantutiun," *Hay Gin* 1, no. 16 (June 16, 1920); Kohar Mazlemian, "Bashdonagan Geghdsike," *Hay Gin* 5, no. 15 (August 1, 1924); A. Dirazan, "Hnazantatyun te Hamerashutyun," *Hay Gin* 5, no. 18 (September 16, 1924).

32. Hayganush Mark, "Gnoch Tade V. Gine Yegeghetsiin Archev," *Hay Gin* 3, no. 8 (February 16, 1922).

33. Hayganush Mark, "Khmpakragan: Ashkhade Gin," *Hay Gin* 13, no. 8 (April 16, 1932).

34. Hayganush Mark, "Khmpakragan: Yedit Naye Gin," *Hay Gin* 13, no. 2 (January 16, 1932).

35. Nancy A. Walker, *Shaping Our Mothers' World: American Women's Magazines* (Jackson: University Press of Mississippi, 2000), viii.

36. For a representative sample of Mark's ideas about the importance of father-

hood, see her "Khmpakragan: Gardsikner Arti Endanegan Gyanki Masin," *Hay Gin* 9, no. 6 (March 16, 1928).

37. Victor Margueritte, *La Garçonne, Roman* (Paris: E. Flammarion, 1922).

38. The Armenian translation is: Viktor Margrit, *Manch-Aghchige La Garçonne* (Istanbul: Gutemberg, G.N. Makasjian, 1924). The Turkish translation is: Margueritte and Kemaleddin, *Erkek Kız: La Garçonne* (Istanbul: Cihan Biraderler Matbaası, 1923). *Hay Gin* had already published a book review in 1923 since many of the journal's writers and readers were well versed in Turkish or French.

39. The novel and its reception in France are discussed extensively in chapter 2 of Mary Louise Roberts, *Civilization without Sexes: Reconstructing Gender in Postwar France, 1917–1927* (Chicago: University of Chicago Press, 1994).

40. For a discussion of how the Turkish-reading public sphere responded to the "new woman," see D. Fatma Türe, *Facts and Fantasies: Images of Istanbul Women in the 1920s* (Newcastle: Cambridge Scholars Publishing, 2015).

41. Hayganush Mark, "Khmpakragan: Sbannenk Manch-Aghchige," *Hay Gin* 7, no. 21 (November 1, 1926).

42. The "modern girl" was a truly transnational phenomenon in the 1920s. Alys Eve Weinbaum, ed., *The Modern Girl Around the World: Consumption, Modernity, and Globalization* (Durham, NC: Duke University Press, 2008).

43. Hrant Samvel, "Inchbes Mda Zhamanagi Mech?," in Toros Azadian, ed., *'Zhamanag'i Karasnamya Hishadagaran, 1908–1948* (Istanbul, 1948), 156.

44. Bishop Kevork Aslanian, "Entertsanutyan (Inknazarkatsman) Bagase," *Hay Gin* 8, no. 22 (November 16, 1927).

45. Hrant Shahnur, "Sevamorti Me Namaganin II," *Hay Gin* 6, no. 15 (August 1, 1925).

46. Hayganush Mark, "Khmpakragan: Garmrelu Entunagutyune," *Hay Gin* 6, no. 14 (July 16, 1925).

47. Roberts, *Civilization without Sexes*, 48.

48. Hayganush Mark, "Khmpakragan: Dansingnere yev Mer Aghchignere," *Hay Gin* 5, no. 5 (March 1, 1924).

49. For a detailed discussion, see Carole Woodall, "Sensing the City: Sound, Movement, and the Night in 1920s Istanbul" (PhD dissertation, New York University, 2008).

50. Hayganush Mark, "Khmpakragan: Hasgtsoghin Shad Parev," *Hay Gin* 6, no. 16 (May 16, 1925).

51. Nissim Benezra, *Une Enfance Juive à Istanbul* (1911–1929) (Istanbul: Isis Press, 1996), 107–8. Mentioned in Rıfat Bali, *The Silent Minority in Turkey: Turkish Jews* (Istanbul: Libra, 2013), 89.

52. Kohar Mazlemian, "Ganatsi Karozner Mer Aghchigneren Vomants Hamar," *Hay Gin* 6, no. 5 (March 1, 1925).

53. In the same article, Mazlemian also gives the example of Armenians settled in

other countries, for example in France. She writes that if Armenians (especially women and girls) in their newly established lands behave properly, kindly and nicely, they could charm the people in their host society who would then "think 'poor Armenians, they are such a kind and civilized people' and they will inevitably infer that it was a pity [that they endured such suffering]." Ibid.

54. Reşat Nuri Güntekin, *Çalıkuşu* (Istanbul: İkbal Kütüphanesi, 1919).

55. Kohar Mazlemian, "Tsakhsarige yev Manch-Aghchige," *Hay Gin* 6, no. 8 (April 16, 1925).

56. Hayganush Mark, "Gineru Kordzagtsutiune Azkayin Mekenayin," *Hay Gin* 12, no. 12 (June 16, 1931).

57. Ibid.

58. Hayganush Mark, "Khmpakragan: Arti Turk Gine yev Ir Tere," *Hay Gin* 11, no. 7 (April 1, 1930). The piece was translated and published in the Turkish daily *Cumhuriyet* (Republic) on April 6, 1930. Yaprak Zihnioğlu, *Kadınsız İnkılap: Nezihe Muhiddin, Kadınlar Halk Fırkası, Kadın Birliği* (Istanbul: Metis, 2003), 253. Mark's second editorial on the issue: "Khmpakragan: Azadakrvadz Turk Gine," *Hay Gin* 11, no. 8 (April 16, 1930).

59. Hayganush Mark, "Khmpakragan: Ginere Azkayin Zhoghovi Mech," *Hay Gin* 1, no. 4 (December 16, 1919); Hayganush Mark, "Khmpakragan: Tebi Panaganutiun," *Hay Gin* 2, no. 12 (April 16, 1921); Hayganush Mark, "Khmpakragan: Vomants Irarantsume," *Hay Gin* 2, no. 14 (May 16, 1921).

60. Beginning in the late nineteenth century, Ottoman Turkish women organized to demand their social and political rights. For more on the Ottoman women's movement, see Aynur Demirdirek, *Osmanlı Kadınlarının Hayat Hakkı Arayışının bir Hikayesi* (Ankara: İmge Kitabevi, 1993); Serpil Çakır, *Osmanlı Kadın Hareketi* (Cağaloğlu Istanbul: Metis Yayınları, 1994); Meral Altındal, *Osmanlıda Kadın* (Istanbul: Altın Kitaplar Yayınevi, 1994); Elizabeth Frierson, "Patriarchal Feminism: Gender and the Public Sphere in the Ottoman Empire" (PhD dissertation, Princeton University, 1996).

61. Mark, "Khmpakragan: Arti Turk Gine yev Ir Tere"; Mark, "Khmpakragan: Azadakrvadz Turk Gine." She added that she did not mean to demean Turkish women or imply that they did not deserve their rights. It should be noted that three issues later, Mark devoted an editorial to condemning a Turkish man who was writing against Turkish women's newly acquired rights in municipal elections. Hayganush Mark, "Khmpakragan: Ayrere Ge Khosin," *Hay Gin* 11, no. 10 (May 16, 1930). For the Turkish translations of two *Hay Gin* articles by Kohar Mazlemian in which the author's changing perceptions regarding the Turkish women's involvement in the Armenian genocide can be tracked, see Lerna Ekmekçioğlu, "'Türk Kadını Savaş Yılları Boyunca Ne Yaptı?' ve 'Fokstrot Yarışması,' Kohar Mazlımyan," *Kültür ve Siyasette Feminist Yaklaşımlar* 2 (2007): 169–74.

62. Among her Turkish contemporaries and successors Mark was not the only feminist to remain silent about Turkish women's organized activity for their political rights. Especially Nezihe Muhiddin, the leader of the Turkish women's movement in

the formative years of the republic (1924–1927), seems to have been ignored by many Turkish woman intellectuals of her time. For more on this, see Zihnioğlu, *Kadınsız İnkılap*, 247–61; Hülya Adak, "Suffragettes of the Empire, Daughters of the Republic: Women Auto/biographers Narrate National History (1918–1935)," *New Perspectives on Turkey* 36 (Spring 2007): 27–51. In addition, beginning in its very early years, Turkish official historiography (and the Kemalist version of women's history in Turkey) insistently overlooked Turkish suffragettes and single-mindedly concentrated on glorifying Mustafa Kemal Atatürk, the founder of the republic, as one of the first political leaders to have bestowed political rights on women. For more on different interpretations of this historical and historiographical silence, see Şirin Tekeli, *Kadınlar ve Siyasal-Toplumsal Hayat* (Istanbul: Birikim Yayınları, 1982).

63. The following pieces/news reports directly refer to Nezihe Muhiddin: "Ganants Askharhen/Artsakank," *Hay Gin* 5, no. 3 (January 16, 1923); "Trkuhinere Bedk E Vor Kaghakagan Gyanki Mech Mdnen," *Hay Gin* 7, no. 3 (February 1, 1926); "Gnochagan Miorinag Artuzarti Khntire," *Hay Gin* 8, no. 1 (June 1, 1927); "Ginere Grnan Smokin Haknil?," *Hay Gin* 8, no. 12 (June 16, 1927).

64. Hayganush Mark, "Khmpakragan: Ginere Havasar Yen Ayrerun?," *Hay Gin* 8, no. 7 (April 1, 1927).

65. Mark was most probably referring to the Congress of the Turkish Women's Association (March 26, 1927) in which it was not the mayor of Istanbul but Emin Ali Bey, a member of the General City Council, who participated. I thank Yaprak Zihnioğlu for providing me the relevant information.

66. Mark, "Khmpakragan: Ginere Havasar Yen Ayrerun?"

67. During the discussions, Nezihe Muhiddin constantly challenged Emin Ali Bey by arguing that it was their mothers who gave the sons/soldiers the blood to shed in the fight against the enemy.

68. Zihnioğlu's *Kadınsız İnkılap*, which succinctly details the activities of the Turkish Women's Association, lacks reference to this instance.

69. The phrase "International Feminist Women's Association" comes from a direct translation of Mark's usage of the name in Armenian. The organization referred to was most probably the International Alliance for Suffrage and Equal Citizenship.

70. Hayganush Mark, "Dzpankner Gyankes," in *Hayganush Mark, Gyankn U Kordze* (Istanbul: n.p., 1954), 56–60. Yaprak Zihnioğlu maintains that she was unable to find reference to Hayganush Mark within sources in her reach. However, it should be noted that the archives of the Turkish Women's Association are not available for research (personal email correspondence with Yaprak Zihnioğlu, March 8, 2009). It is probable that officials in the Turkish Women's Association (perhaps its president, Nezihe Muhiddin) communicated orally to Ann Stis their willingness to see Hayganush Mark as a member.

71. "Diezerki Keghetsgutyan Takuhiin Aytselutiune Hay Gin in," *Hay Gin* 13, no. 18 (September 16, 1932). The piece was originally published in *Nor Lur* on September 11, 1932.

72. Law No. 1881, "Matbuat Kanunu," July 21, 1931. There is no information about *Hay Gin* or its closing in Ottoman and Turkish archives or in the archives of the Directorate General of Press and Information (Basın Yayın ve Enformasyon Genel Müdürlüğü).

73. *Hay Gin*'s closing coincided with an abyss in the Turkish women's movement. In 1935, the ruling political party, Atatürk's Republican People's Party, encouraged, if not forced, the Turkish Women's Association to disband. The president of the association, Latife Bekir, joyfully announced that since Turkish women had been emancipated with the vote in 1934, there was no longer a reason for a separate women's association. The members of the association could work for the (Republican) party and engage in charitable activities. Remarkably, the Turkish Women's Association dissolved itself only days after the annual congress of the International Alliance of Women for Suffrage and Equal Citizenship, which was held in Istanbul in 1935. For an assessment of the connections between the Annual Congress in Istanbul in 1935 and the closing of the Turkish Women's Association, see Kathryn Libal, "Staging Turkish Women's Emancipation: Istanbul, 1935," *Journal of Middle East Women's Studies* 4, no. 1 (Winter 2008); Aslı Davaz, *Eşitsiz Kız Kardeşlik, Uluslararası ve Ortadoğu Kadın Hareketleri, 1935 Kongresi ve Türk Kadın Birliği* (Istanbul: İş Bankası Kültür Yayınları, 2014); Serpil Sancar, *Türk Modernleşmesinin Cinsiyeti, Erkekler Devlet, Kadınlar Aile Kurar*, 3. baskı (Istanbul: İletişim, 2012.) Suad Derviş, a leftist journalist and well-known Turkish novelist of the time, observed the congress in order to report on it in the newspapers. Inspired by the example of the annual congress, she penned an essay in the Armenian weekly *Nor Huys* (New Hope) to invite her "Armenian sisters" to collaborate in establishing a new literary society that would translate Turkish and Armenian literature into each other's language. *Nor Huys* published the essay in full on is cover page and in its original Turkish. Suad Derviş, "Türk Ermeni Kızkardeşlerimle Hasbuhal," *Nor Huys* 1, no. 2 (April 20, 1935). Even though Armenian women responded positively to the invitation in the pages of *Nor Huys*, to my knowledge no such society was established.

74. Letter from Hayganush Mark to Zaruhi Kelemkearian dated June 30, 1948. Yeghishe Charents Museum of Literature and Art (Yerevan), Hayganush Mark Fond.

75. This topic, like most others touched upon in this book, has not been studied.

76. Ara Kochunian, *Voghchuyn Amenkin* (Istanbul: Aras Yayıncılık, 2008), 206.

77. While *Marmara* and *Zhamanag* continue to be published to this day. The state closed down *Nor Lur* in 1946 and prohibited its reopening. Interview with Talin Suciyan, "Examining 'The Denialist Habitus in Post-Genocidal Turkey,'" *Armenian Weekly*, November 11, 2013. A number of documents that Rıfat Bali found in the Turkish Republican Archives and published in their entirety involve Vahan Toshigian and *Nor Lur*. See www.rifatbali.com/images/stories/dokumanlar/turk_ermeni_basini.pdf (last accessed December 2013).

78. Mark, "Dzpankner Gyankes," 64.

79. Zaruhi Kalemkearian, *Gyankis Jampen* (Antelias, Lebanon: Dbaran Gatoghigosutian Giligio, 1952), xix; Anayis [Yevpime Avedisian], *Hushers* (Paris: n.p., 1949), 262; Vahram Papazian, "Hayganush Mark," in *Srdis Bardke* (Yerevan: Hay Bedagan Hradaragchutiun, 1959), 141.

80. Oral history interview conducted on May 13, 2013. Mrs. Bagdiken still lives in the Armenian Nursing and Rehabilitation Center in Jamaica Plains, Massachusetts.

81. The celebration took place on May 7, 1955. The other members of the commission, "Hisnamya Hopelyani Dignants Hantsnakhump," were Spruhi Vartanian, Arpine Alchejian, Siranush Shakar, Mari Sarafian, Hermine Sinanian, Vartuhi Celal, and the well-known mathematician Hermine Kalustian, the principal of the Esayan School and a member of the Istanbul University's Department of Astronomy.

82. Interview with Ara Toshigian (b. 1937), May 26, 2013, Montreal, Canada. Mr. Toshigian's narrative is corroborated by Vahan Toshigian's 1954 second-class train ticket and his passport, which Mark saved and are now kept in the Yeghishe Charents Museum of Literature and Art (Yerevan), Hayganush Mark Fond.

83. Hayganush Mark, "Mi Sder, Gin," *Hay Gin* 12, no. 6 (March 16, 1932).

84. Vartan Matiossian, "Gosdan Zariani Namagnere Arshag Chobanianin (1922–1931)," *Haigazian Haiakidagan Hantes* 30 (2010): 446.

85. *Yeridasart Hayuhi* was published in Beirut by Siran Seza from 1932 to 1934, and then again from 1946 to 1967.

Conclusion

1. She also published a volume of poetry in 1921 entitled *Dzulutyan Baheres* (Istanbul: M. Der Sahagian, 1921), wrote two unpublished novels, translated various texts from French to Armenian, and authored several short stories in various periodicals. Kevork B. Bardakjian, *A Reference Guide to Modern Armenian Literature, 1500–1920* (Detroit: Wayne State University Press, 2000), 414.

2. The "Armenian literature" textbooks taught in Armenian schools in Turkey only mention the names of two Armenian women: Zabel Yesayan and Zabel Asadur (Sibil). The latter co-authored, with her husband, the Armenian language and literature book that is used in Armenian schools in Turkey to this day: Zabel Asadur and Hrant Asadur, *Nor Tankaran Hayeren Lezvi: Partsrakuyn Tasentatsk* (Istanbul: "Selamet"Taniel Hovannesian, 1908). Since the publication of *Bir Adalet Feryadı* some schools have incorporated its content into the curriculum. Lerna Ekmekçioğlu and Melissa Bilal, eds., *Bir Adalet Feryadı: Osmanlı'dan Türkiye'ye Beş Ermeni Feminist Yazar, 1862–1933* (Istanbul: Aras Yayıncılık, 2006),

3. In this regard, Armenians in post-1923 Turkey can be likened to Palestinian citizens of Israel. For a recent assessment of this community's history that can provide a fruitful comparative angle for future studies, see Shira Robinson, *Citizen Strangers: Palestinians and the Birth of Israel's Liberal Settler State* (Stanford, CA: Stanford University

Press, 2013). Even though none of them are perfect equivalents of Turkish Armenians, the following communities bear similarities that can make for illuminating comparisons: Jews in post-Holocaust Poland, Copts in Egypt, Muslims in post-Partition India, ethnic Hungarians in Czechoslovakia, Muslims in Greece, and other ethnic minorities in the newly established nation-states following World War I.

4. Among the examples of recent scholarly interest in Turkish Armenians, see Armaveni Miroğlu, "G. Bolso Hay Hamaynki Gatsoutiune Turkio Hanrabedoutian 20–agan Tvagannerun (Mamuli Knahadmamp)" (Master's thesis, Yerevan, Hayasdani Hanrabedutian Kidutiunneri Azkayin Akademiayi Badmutyan Institut, 2007); Rubina Peroomian, *And Those Who Continued Living in Turkey after 1915: The Metamorphosis of the Post-Genocide Armenian Identity as Reflected in Artistic Literature* (Yerevan: Armenian Genocide Museum-Institute, 2008); Ari Şekeryan, "The Aftermath of the Deportation: The Armenian Population after the Great War and the Jamanag Daily," (M.A. thesis, Boğaziçi University, 2014). For recent sociological studies that focus on Armenians in contemporary Turkey, see Günay Göksu Özdoğan et al., eds., *Türkiye'de Ermeniler: Cemaat, Birey, Yurttaş* (Istanbul: İstanbul Bilgi Üniversitesi Yayınları, 2009); Günay Göksu Özdoğan and Ohannes Kılıçdağı, *Türkiye Ermenilerini Duymak: Sorunlar, Talepler ve Çözüm Önerileri* (Istanbul: TESEV Yayınları, 2011). For a criticism of the approach to Armenian history and the present within contemporary Turkish society, especially by intellectuals, see Ayda Erbal and Talin Suciyan, "One Hundred Years of Abandonment," *Armenian Weekly*, special issue, April 2011 Magazine: 41–45.

5. In the now classical first history of the Ottoman women's movement, Armenians (and other non-Muslim, non-Turkish groups for that matter) are absent. Serpil Çakır, *Osmanlı Kadın Hareketi* (Cağaloğlu, Istanbul: Metis Yayınları, 1994). For a critique of this literature, see Lerna Ekmekcioğlu, "Sonsöz: Osmanlı ve Türkiye Kadın Hareketi Hakkındaki Tarihyazımında Türk ve/veya Müslüman Olmayan Kadınlar, Bir Yokluğun Anatomisi," in Ekmekçioğlu and Bilal, eds., *Bir Adalet Feryadı*, 242–64. Recent evaluations of the relevant scholarship pay due attention to the absence of non-Muslim historical subjects. See Başak Tuğ, "Gender and Ottoman Social History," *International Journal of Middle East Studies* 46, no. 2 (2014): 379–81; and Gülhan Balsoy, "Osmanlı Kadın ve Toplumsal Cinsiyet Tarihçiliği Üzerine," *Toplum ve Bilim* 132 (2015): 222–31.

6. For example, the only essay in the four-volume *Cambridge History of Turkey* that encompasses the war years is silent on the Armenian massacres. See Şükrü Hanioğlu, "The Second Constitutional Period, 1908–1918," in Reşat Kasaba, ed., *The Cambridge History of Turkey: Volume 4, Turkey in the Modern World* (Cambridge: Cambridge University Press, 2008). Another recent example is Carter Findley, *Turkey, Islam, Nationalism, and Modernity: A History, 1789–2007* (New Haven, CT: Yale University Press, 2010).

7. I was a founding member of this group, formed in 1998 and made up of Armenian college students, most of them at Boğaziçi University, who were involved in the Turkish feminist movement on campus. We informally named the group *Hayuhiner*

(Young Armenian Women) and organized activities in the Armenian community to raise awareness of gendered inequalities and the history of Armenian feminism. We first learned about Hayganush Mark in 1999, when Yervant Gobelyan (1923–2010), then a columnist in the Turkish Armenian weekly *Agos*, handed us Mark's 1954 book *Gyankn U Kordze*. As many of us left the country for graduate studies in North America, our group dispersed after 2002. The three members of this group, all students in Boğaziçi University's Department of Sociology, participated in a history writing contest with an essay that they wrote about Hayganush Mark. They won the third prize after which the article was published: Melissa Bilal, Lerna Ekmekçioğlu, and Belinda Mumcu, "Feminizm, Bir Adalet Feryadı, Hayganuş Mark'ın Hayatı, Düşünceleri ve Etkinlikleri," *Toplumsal Tarih* 87 (2001): 48–57.

8. Joan Wallach Scott, *Only Paradoxes to Offer: French Feminists and the Rights of Man* (Cambridge, MA: Harvard University Press, 1996).

INDEX

abduction of women and children into Muslim households: Armenianization of retrieved Turkish/Muslim children, 35, 86, 175n39; as aspect of Armenian genocide, 4, 11–12; demographic significance of, 33; exodus of Armenians after 1922 and, 84–85; feminist involvement with retrieval of, 38–45, 176n48; marriage of retrieved women, 35–38, *37*, 43–45, *44*, 176n44; numbers of, 167n9; paternity/ethnicity of children born in captivity, 35.40; rape, children conceived by, 23, 40, 42, 175n44, 177n56, 178n59; reluctance to accept return of, 36, 44, 175n44, 177n55; reluctant motherhood of women, 40–42, 177n56, 178n59; remaining with abductors, 177n55, 177n57; retrieval of, 23, 33, 34–38, *36*, *37*, 175n36; use as laborers, servants, and concubines, 175n35

Abdülhamid II (sultan), 56

abortion, 32, 40–41

Adana pogrom (1909), 24

adaptation of Armenian minority after 1923, 101–29; children and schools, 123–26; diaspora community, relationship with, 114; domestic/private survival of Armenianness, *100*, 121–29; gendered aspects of, *100*, 102, 122–23; imagining continued presence of community, 102–3; language, importance of, 101–2, 116–17, 128; nationalization, standardization, and secularization goals of Kemalist Turkey and, 106–8, 117–21, *119*, 194n43; Patriarch Naroyan encapsulating, 125–28; press, Armenian, 112–16; religion, importance of, 101–2; secular dhimmitude, 18, 108–9, 117, 121, 128, 160; SETA, 109–12, 192–93n26; silence over expression, choosing, 116–17, 127; as state functionaries, 120–21; surname change requirements, 108, 191–92nn20–21; Turkish status and, 103–6

Adıvar (Halide Edib), 68

AGBU (Armenian General Benevolent Union), 85, 170n32, 175n36

Aghababian, Adrine Indjian, 175n44

Aguni, Sevag, *Milion Me Hayeru Charti*

Badmutiune (The Whole History of the Massacre of One Million Armenians), 50, 180n83
Aharonian, Avedis, 168n17, 188n34
Alchejian, Arpine, 203n81
Alexandropol, Treaty of (1920), 59
Ali, Kılıç, 96
All-Armenian Assembly, 27
Allied occupation of Constantinople, 5, 168–69n18; evacuation of Constantinople (1923), 5–9, 83–84; feminism and feminist Armenians, zenith of, 50, 54; Greeks in Turkey welcoming, 169n18; patriarchate's cooperation with, 27; Turkish women and Allied officers, 55; women working with Allies, 55–56. *See also* rebirth of Armenian nation after WWI
Allies/Great Powers: defined, 188n32; language of Christianity used by, 107; Lausanne treaty with Kemalists (1923), 12–13, 50, 78, 83–84, 90–98, 104–5, 188n32; minority rights as envisioned by, 92–93, 94–95; statements regarding Armenian genocide, 5–6, 169n19
Amenun Daretsuytse (Everyone's Almanac), 28
American Committee for Relief in the Near East. *See* Near East Relief
Anayis (Yevpime Avedisian): archives of, 187n18; on celebration of establishment of Republic of Armenia, 168n17; on closure of *Hay Gin*, 154; commemoration of Armenian genocide and, 179n78; emigration after Kemalist takeover, 82–83, 85, 86, 96; *Hay Gin* and AWA, 60, 61, 72, 184n70, 185n71; memoirs, 86; Tumanian's visit to *Hay Gin* offices with, 59, 181n33; on wedding of retrieved woman to Armenian man, 43–44

Ankara: confiscation of Armenian property in, 120; Kemalist establishment of capital in, 6, 12, 33, 83, 90, 103, 120
Apostolic Church, 24–25, 27, 124, 171n1, 172n10
Aras, Tevfik Rüştü, 95–96
ARF (Armenian Revolutionary Federation; *Tashnagtsutiun*), 67, 176n47, 178n69, 185n77
Armen, Yenovk, 71
Armenia, 2–3; Greater Armenia, dream of, 5–6, 7, 45–50, 110–11; historical homeland, construction of, 166n7; map, *3*; National Home inside Turkey, at Lausanne conference, 91–92; piece of Anatolia sought for independent/autonomous Armenian territory, 59; Soviet Armenia, 50, 59, 81, 90, 91, 153, 155, 188n38, 197n15. *See also* rebirth of Armenian nation after WWI; Republic of Armenia
Armenian Aid Society, 59
Armenian church. *See* patriarchate, Armenian; patriarchs, Armenian; religion
Armenian delegation to Lausanne conference, 90–91, 97, 110
Armenian Doctors Association, 47
Armenian feminists. *See* feminism and feminist Armenians
Armenian General Benevolent Union (AGBU), 85, 170n32, 175n36
Armenian genocide: Allied statements regarding, 5–6, 169n19; amnesties and failures to prosecute perpetrators, 50, 95–96, 172n14, 178n69; assassinations of perpetrators by Armenians, 96; bearing witness to, 49–50; Bolsahay experience of, 4–5; "collaboration with the enemy," Armenians accused of, 7–8; commemoration of, xi, xii, 49–50, 179n78; defined, 3–4, 166n6; as gendered and age-conscious event,

11–12; group survival of, 159–63; number of Armenians perishing in, 3–4; Ottoman empire in WWI and, 3, 45; parliamentary members murdered in, 167n12; SETA on, 111; Turkish views on, xi, 7–8, 166n6; Turkish women's involvement in, 200n61; vengeance, living associated with, 29–30; Werfel's *The Forty Days of Musa Dagh*, 117
Armenian Intellectuals' Foundation, 179n78
Armenian National Assembly. *See* National Assembly
Armenian National Constitution, 26, 70, 149
Armenian National Delegation to Paris Peace Conference, 6, 14, 32, 33, 46, 67, 83, 85, 90, 183n56
Armenian National Hospital, Yedikule, 38, 89, *100*, 126, 128
Armenian National Relief Organization, 27
Armenian patriarchate. *See* patriarchate, Armenian
Armenian press, 15–18, 26, 82, 112–16, *115*, 153, 170–71n33. *See also specific publications*
Armenian Red Cross. *See* Red Cross, Armenian
Armenian Revolutionary Federation (ARF; *Tashnagtsutiun*), 67, 176n47, 178n69, 185n77
Armenian Surp Prgich National Hospital, women's auxiliary for, 76–77, 185n82
Armenian Women's Association (AWA), 16–17; banner in Hayganush Mark caricature, *52*; financial aid for Republic of Armenia collected by, 57–58; *Hay Gin* and, 16–17, 60, *61*; Kalantar, Takuhi and Vartuhi, as members of, 75; lifespan of, 54–55;

political purpose of, 55–57; retrieved women and children, involvement with, 38, 41, 43
Armenian women's charitable associations, 54, 180n7
Armenian Women's Patriotic Association, 56–57, 180n7
Armenians in post-genocide Turkey, xi–xiii, 1–18; adaptation after 1923, 101–29 (*See also* adaptation of Armenian minority after 1923); Allied evacuation of Constantinople post-WWI and, 5–9, 83–84; bearing witness by, 49–50; compared to other minority groups, 203–4n3; definition of post-genocide, 166n6; exodus of 1922, 81–98 (*See also* exodus of 1922 and aftermath); feminism in, 1, 53–78, 131–58 (*See also* feminism and feminist Armenians, after 1923; feminism and feminist Armenians, before 1923); gender and Armenianness, 8, 9–14, 161; group survival of genocide, 159–63; historical background, 1–5; minority status, creation of, 90–98; numbers in 1920s and 1930s, 98, 190n61; power relationship between Turkish state and, 77–78, 163; rebirth of nation, 21–50 (*See also* rebirth of Armenian nation after WWI); self-contrasted with Turks and self-compared to West, 46–47, 67–68; source materials, 14–18; viewed as fifth columnists in Turkey, 7–8, 92, 94
Asadur, Zabel. *See* Sibil
Asbed, Hovannes (Onnik Chifte-Saraf), 186n88
Aslan, Senem, 194n43
Aslanian, Dikran, 186n88
Aslanian, Kevork (patriarchal *locum tenens*), 80, 88–89, 91, 143
Aslanian, Nazeni, 89
Astor, Lady Nancy, 67–68

Atatürk. *See* Kemal, Mustafa
Auclert, Hubertine, 135
Avedisian, Yevpime. *See* Anayis
AWA. *See* Armenian Women's Association
Azaduni (woman abducted into Muslim household), 177

Bagdiken, Armine, 154, 197n13, 203n80
Bahri, Jacques, 187n23
Bahri, Zaruhi: as AWA member, *61*; emigration after Kemalist takeover, 85–86, 96; on financial aid for Republic of Armenia, 57; grandchildren, 187n23; as *Hay Gin* contributor, 39, *61*, 64, 74–75; Kalantar, Takuhi, obituary for, 74–75; memoirs, 86–87, 187n22; narratives collected by, 29; on the old woman and the new woman, 53–54; retrieved women and children, involvement with, 39, 84–85, 176n44, 177n57
Balakian, Grigoris, 14, 55, 170n32, 183n56
Bali, Rıfat, 202n77
St. Bartholomew, 172n10
beaches, mixed-sex, 147
Bebel, August, 64
Bekir, Latife, 202n73
Beylerian, Mari, 4, 168n15
Bilal, Melissa, 171n35
Bolis. *See* Constantinople/Bolis/Istanbul
Bolsahays: Armenian press, post-War revitalization of, 15; bearing witness to Armenian genocide, 49; choosing to remain after Kemalist takeover, 88; defined, 1–2, 165n4; experience of genocide and WWI, 4–5; as feminists (*See* feminism and feminist Armenians); financial aid for Republic of Armenia collected by, 57–58; imagining recovery of Armenia post-WWI, 22, 28 (*See also* rebirth of Armenian nation after WWI); at Lausanne conference, 91; marriage to returned women by, 36, 44; numbers of, 16; on the old woman and the new woman, 53; organization of, 24; in refugee crisis, 24. *See also* adaptation of Armenian minority after 1923; exodus of 1922 and aftermath
books, symbolic meanings of, *142*, 143–45
Boyajian, Hampartsum (Murad), 167n12
Braun, Lily, 64
Bristol, Mark, 56
British Lord Mayor's Fund, 24
Brubaker, Rogers, 166n5

Captanian, Payladzu Aragel, 29–30, 173–74n23
Catholic Armenians, 24–25, 27, 171n1
Celal, Vartuhi, 203n81
Chanak Affair, 187n14
charitable associations for Armenian women, 54, 180n7
Chifte-Saraf, Onnik (Hovannes Asbed), 186n88
children: adaptation of Armenian minority after 1923 and, 123–26; Greeks in Turkey, Armenian children cared for by, 29–30, 173–74n23; Mark's lack of, 85, 136, 153; maternal passage of Armenian identity to, 100, 128–29, 157; pretty baby contests, *31*, 31–32; rebirth of Armenian nation after WWI, significance for, 20, 21–23, 28–33, 47–49, 160–61, 174n25; *Sargavakin Daretsuytse*, children defending Mother Armenia depicted in, *20*, 21–22, 46, 47, 60, 88, 129. *See also* abduction of women and children into Muslim households
Chirajian, Stepan, 167n12
church, Armenian. *See* patriarchate, Armenian; patriarchs, Armenian; religion

INDEX

Cilicia: massacre of Armenians by Kemalists in (1920), 56, 180n17; post-WWI refugees in, 23
commemoration of Armenian genocide, xi, xii, 49–50, 179n78
Committee of Union and Progress (CUP; Young Turks), 2–5, 7, 11–12, 34
Constantinople/Bolis/Istanbul: actual Kemalist takeover of, 83, 84; Armenian press in, 15; Armenian Red Cross in, 38; financial aid for Republic of Armenia collected in, 57–58; names for, 165n2; national government of Armenians in, 24–27, 172–73n14; population in 1919, 168n14; reduction in status, 1; refugee crisis after WWI, 23–24, 25, 27; threat of Kemalist capture and Armenian flight from, 6–7, 50, 78, 81–83. *See also* Allied occupation of Constantinople; Bolsahays
Constitutions: Armenian, 26, 70, 149; Ottoman, 103, 190n3; Turkish, 103, 105, 106, 190n2
Cooper, Frederick, 166n5
Cuence, Ms., 147
CUP (Committee of Union and Progress; Young Turks), 2–5, 7, 11–12, 34
Curzon, Lord, 33

Daghavarian, Nazaret, 167n12
Darekirk, Dzablvar, 52
Declaration of the Rights of Woman and the Female Citizen, 136
deportees: aid for, 23–24, 25, 27; feminist involvement with, 38–45; return after WWI, 23–24, 171n3; terms for, 23, 171n6; unmarried Armenian men living in Istanbul but born outside, 167n10; urged to return to populate Armenia, 33
Derviş, Suad, 202n73

D'Esperey, Louis Franchet, 84
dhimma and dhimmitude: Armenian experience under Ottomans as, 8; gender and, 9–10; internalization of, 112; minority rights in Republic of Turkey and, 13, 18, 93, 104; origins of, 169n23, 192n23; as permanent resident aliens, 191n19; secular dhimmitude after 1923, 18, 108–9, 117, 121, 128, 160
diaspora community, relationship of Turkish Armenians after 1923 with, 114
"diasporic moment," 102, 190n2
Dilaçar, Hagop Martayan, 120–21, 195n55
divorce, 68–69
domestic violence, 42, 68–69
Durand, Marguerite, 62, 64
Dussape, Srpuhi, 133–34, 197n10
Dzaghig (Flower), 62, 155, 182n43

Eblightatian, Madteos, 175n39
Ece, Keriman Halis, *130*, 152
Edib, Halide (Adıvar), 68
education: adaptation of Armenian minority after 1923 and, 123–26; Armenian patriarchate, on education of women, 162–63; books, symbolic meanings of, *142*, 143–45; girls' schooling, Armenian prioritization of, 143; of Mark, 62; Unification of Education Act (Turkey, 1924), 78, 124
Education Commission of (Armenian) National Assembly, 75–77, 186n85
elites, concept of, 166n5
Elliott, Mabel Evelyn, 176n45
Elmayan, Aline, 187n23
Elmayan, Noyemi, 86
Emin, Ahmed (Yalman), 82
Emin Ali Bey, 201n65, 201n67
Emon, Anver, 191n19
Eve, 198n30

exodus of 1922 and aftermath, 81–98; church and patriarchate during, 87–89; denial of reentry and confiscation of property, 86, 96–97, 120; departures after Turkish takeover, 84–87; Kemalist takeover and Allied departure, 83–84; Mark's decision to remain, 84, 86, 89–90; memoirs of exiles, 86–87; numbers of Armenians in Turkey following, 98; threat of Kemalist capture of Constantinople, starting with, 6–7, 50, 78, 81–83; Treaty of Lausanne and creation of Armenian minority within Turkey, 90–98; Turkish encouragement of, 83, 97–98

fatherhood and feminism, 132, 138–39, 157
Fatherland Tax, 27, 28, 70, 173n17
feminism and feminist Armenians, after 1923, 131–58; cultural critiques of women's dress and behavior, 147–48; "dolls" versus individuals, 134–36, 140, 157; on domesticity, 133–39; domestic/private survival of Armenianness and, 122–23; fatherhood and, 132, 138–39, 157; gender, beliefs about, 136–38; manch-aghchig (boy-girl; flapper) stereotype and, 139–48, *141*, *142*, *144*, 152, 157; on marriage, 131–32, 133; the old woman and the new woman, 131–32, 140, 143, 146, 155; on political equality for women, 148–52; tensions between Armenian community and, 131–32, 161; Turkish women's movement and, 149–52, 162, 200–201nn61–62, 202n73, 204n5. *See also Hay Gin*; Mark, Haygunush; *other specific feminists*
feminism and feminist Armenians, before 1923, 53–78; abducted Armenian women, reporting on, 23; Allies, women working with, 55–56;

antifeminist arguments, grappling with, 70–72; auxiliary roles, Mark on, 76–77; charitable associations for women and, 54, 180n7; compatibility with traditional feminine roles, 70–75, *73*; defined by Mark, 63–64; demands of, 9; divorce, 68–69; domestic violence and, 42, 68–69; exodus following Kemalist takeover and, 88, 89–90; marriage critiques, 42; memoirs of, 177–78n57; nationalism, gendered character of, 11; the old woman and the new woman, 52–53, 64–67, *65*; peacefulness of women, arguments regarding, 75–76; political equality for women, arguments for, 67–70, 75–77, 184n67; political roles in Armenian rebirth, 54–59; power relationship between Armenians and Turkish state affecting, 77–78; pro-church stance taken by Mark and, 88; reciprocity and women's rights, 69–70, 72–73, 183n51; retrieval of abducted women and children and care of refugees, involvement with, 38–45; traditionalism of Armenianness in Turkey and, 14; universities, admission of women to, 184n64; zenith in post-genocide Istanbul, 50, 54. *See also Hay Gin*; Mark, Haygunush; *other specific feminists*
fez, 81, 84, 106
First World War. *See* World War I
forced conversion to Islam, 4, 34
Fortier, Anne-Marie, 190n2
France, Anatole, 146
French Legion d'Orient, Armenians in, 178n67
French Republicanism: feminism of, 62–64, 69, 135–36, 182n45; Turkish emulation of citizenship standards, 105

La Fronde, 62
Fuad Bey, Köprülüzade (Mehmet Fuad Köprülü), 116, 193–94n41
Fuzûlî, 114

Garabedian, Kegham Der, 176n47
Garougian, Varteres, 178n67
gender: adaptation of Armenian minority after 1923 and, *100*, 102, 122–23; Armenian feminism and, 136–38; Armenian genocide and, 11–12; Armenianness and, 8, 9–14, 161; dhimmitude and, 9–10; nationalism and, 10–11, 161
genocide, Armenian. See Armenian genocide
Ghazarosian, Koharig, 155
Gobelyan, Yervant, 206n7
Gochnag (Rattle), 71, 184n67
"Gold Fund" day for Republic of Armenia, 57–58
Gordon, Yehuda Leib, "Awake! My People," 170n31
Gouges, Olympe de, 69, 135–36
Grand National Assembly, Turkish, 33, 59, 103, 110
Great Crime. See Armenian genocide
Great Powers. See Allies/Great Powers
Greek patriarchate, 87, 97, 174n23
Greeks in Turkey: Allies welcomed by, 169n18; Armenian children cared for by, 29–30, 173–74n23; Armenians assisted by, 174n23; minority rights of, 92, 94, 95; population in 1927, 190n61; Smyrna/Izmir captured from, 81–82; Turkish suspicion of, 94
St. Gregory the Illuminator, 172n10
Grigorian, Kegham, 186n88
Grossman, Atina, 30
Guitar (journal), 62
Güler, Ara, 155, *156*
Güntekin, Reşat Nuri, *Çalıkuşu* (The Wren), 148

Hacikyan, Agop, 116, 194n46, 194n50, 195n51
Hagopian, Abraham Der, 183n56
Hairenik (Fatherland), 35–36
Halis (Ece), Keriman, *130*, 152
Hamidian massacres (1894–1896), 24, 88
Harington, Charles, 82, 83–84
Hashashian, Mrs. Hripsime, 53
Hay Gin (Armenian Woman), 1, 16–17; adaptation of Armenian community after 1923 and, 101, 122–23, 124; antifeminist arguments, grappling with, 70–72; on Armenian female university students, 184n64; Armenian symbols used by, 64–66, *65*; AWA and, 16–17, 60, *61*; banner in Hayganush Mark caricature, *52*; on bearing witness to Armenian genocide, 50, 179–80n82; church, articles about, 87–89, 101–2; closure of, 153–54, 157–58; on compatibility of feminism with traditional feminine roles, 70–75, *73*; contributors to, 64, 84–85, 86, 186n88, 195n55 (*See also specific contributors*); on domesticity, 133–39; establishment of, 16–17, 62–63; exodus after Kemalist takeover and, 84, 87–88, 89; feminist purpose of, 60, 64, 132, 156–57; funding for, 63; on Mustafa Kemal, 112–13; legacy of, 154, 157–58, 161–62; manch-aghchig (boy-girl; flapper) stereotype and, 140–48; Mark's identification with, 153–54, 155–57, *156*; masthead, 64–66, *65*; maternalist discourse embraced by, 30–32, *31*, 48–49, 175n25; Miss Turkey/Miss Universe contests, *130*, 152; on nursing training for Armenian girls, 47; offices in Mark's apartments, 60; on the old woman and the new woman, 52–53, 64–67, *65*; "Our Road" (first editorial, 1919), 66–67; on political equality for women, 67–70,

75–77, 148–52, 184n67; on political role of women in Armenian rebirth, 57–59; retrieval of abducted women and children and, 38, 39, 40–43, *44*; tensions between Armenian community after 1923 and, 131–32; on Turkish women's movement, 151

Hay Gin tombstone, Şişli Armenian Cemetery, 1, 155, *158*, 165n3

Hay Khosnag (Armenian Spokesperson), 124

Hay Puzhag (Armenian Healer), 32

Hay Tad (Armenian cause), 5–6

Haydar Pasha Refugee Station, *25*, 42

Haygaz, Aram, 35

Hayuhiner (Young Armenian Women), 205–6n7

Hisarlian, Madame, 29, 30

Holquist, Peter, 169n19

Ibsen, Henrik, *A Doll's House*, 134, 197n15

identity: concept of, 166n5; domestic/private survival of Armenianness, *100*, 121–29; Mark and Turkishness, 150; Mark's identification with *Hay Gin*, 153–54, 155–57, *156*; maternal passage of Armenian identity to children, *100*, 128–29, 157; Republic of Turkey, Turkish status in, 103–6

İleri, Celal Nuri, 103, 105–6, 116

"Infant Armenia," concept of, 47

infanticide, 32, 41, 177n56

İnönü, İsmet (İsmet Pasha; Milli Şef), 14, 92, 94, 96, 110, 189n45, 189n48, 195n51

International Feminist Women's Association (probably International Alliance for Suffrage and Equal Citizenship), 152, 201n69, 202n73

Islam: forced conversion to, 4, 34; in secular Republic of Turkey, 106–8, 118; unveiling of Muslim women in Turkey, 118. *See also* abduction of women and children into Muslim households

Islamic (sharia) law, 10, 12, 35, 78, 106–9, 169n23, 191n19

İsmet Pasha (İsmet İnönü; Milli Şef), 14, 92, 94, 96, 110, 189n45, 189n48, 195n51

Istanbul. *See* Constantinople/Bolis/Istanbul

Izmir/Smyrna, Kemalist capture of, 14, 81–82

Jagadamard (Battle), 57

Jelal, Matilda, 123–24

Jews: Armenian genocide compared to Holocaust, 8; Armenians compared, 8, 14, 116, 204n3; baby boom following Holocaust, 30; in France compared to Turkey, 104, 105; at Lausanne conference, 189n48; mixed-sex beaches, use of, 147; normalcy, maintenance of, 116, 194n42; origins of dhimmitude and, 192n23; reception of Allied forces by, 169n18, 189n48; treatment as minorities in Bulgaria and Romania, 97; in Turkey, 94, 104, 169n18, 190n61; Werfel's *The Forty Days of Musa Dagh*, 117

Judicial Commission of (Armenian) National Assembly, 68–69, 72–73, 76, 78

Kadıköy Davros women's society, 180n17

Kalantar, Takuhi Tavit, *73*, 73–75, 145

Kalantar, Vartuhi, 53–54, 74–75, 185n77

Kalemkearian, Zaruhi: archives of, 187n19; closure of *Hay Gin* and, 153, 154; commemoration of Armenian genocide and, 179n78; emigration after Kemalist takeover, 85, 96; Mark and, 85; as member of AWA and contributor to *Hay Gin*, *61*, 85; memoirs, 86; retrieval of abducted women and children, involvement in, 39, 40, 177n56

Kalpakjian, Ardashes, 184n68
Kalustian, Hermine, 203n81
Kaplan, Marion, 194n42
Kaprielian-Churchill, Isabel, 43
Karabekir, Kâzım, 58–59
Kasapian family, 120
Kaya, Şükrü, 96
Kemal, Mustafa (Atatürk): adaptation of Armenian community after 1923 and, 103, 110, 112–14, *115*; Armenian assassination plots, 114; Armenian fondness for, 17, 117, 195n51; image of, *115*; as leader of Kemalists, 6, 33, 58; perpetrators of Armenian genocide supported by, 189n52; Princess Mevhibe and, 56; as Westernizer and modernizer, 118–19, *119*; women's suffrage in Turkey and, 150, 201n62
Kemalists: actual takeover of Constantinople, 83, 84; Ankara, establishment of capital in, 6, 12, 33, 83, 90, 103, 120; AWA archives burned during taking of Constantinople by, 54–55; emergence as resistance movement opposed to partitioning of Anatolia, 33; Lausanne treaty with Allies (1923), 12–13, 50, 78, 83–84, 90–98, 104–5, 188n32; massacre of Armenians in Cilicia, 1920, 56, 180n17; positive aspects for Armenians, 17, 117; Smyrna/Izmir captured by, 14, 81–82; threatened capture of Constantinople and Armenian flight from city, 6–7, 50, 78, 81–83; Turkish-Armenian War, 58–59
Keresteciyan, Berch (Türker), 110
Kevork VI (Catholicos of All Armenians), 155
Khachadurian, Karekin (Armenian patriarch), 154
Khachadurian, Reverend, 45–46
Khachadurian, Sarkis, 64, 183n49

Khadisian, Alexander, 57–59, 168n17, 188n34
Khosrovian, Takuhi, 181n26
kidnapping of Armenian women and children. *See* abduction of women and children into Muslim households
Kipritjian, Nargiz, 48–49
Kınalıada (Hay Ghghzi or Armenian Island), 74, 168n17
Knar, Digin, 133, 196–97n8
Kochunian, Ara, 153
Koçoğlu, Mehmed Şükrü, 92
Köprülü, Mehmet Fuad (Köprülüzade Fuad Bey), 116, 193–94n41
Kör (blind) Hüseyin, 42
Krikorian, Kegham, 71–72
Kulin, Ayşe, 8
Kurdish Sheikh Said Rebellion, 112
Kurds, minority protection not granted to, 94

Lacour, Leopold, 64
Laguerre, Odette, 63, 64, 182n45
language: in Armenian schools, 125; cleansing Persian and Arabic influences from modern Turkish, 121; embarrassment at Armenian accented Turkish, 116–17, 194n46; importance to Armenian minority after 1923, 101–2, 116–17, 128; Speak Turkish campaigns, 116, 117; surname change requirements, 108, 191–92nn20–21; Turkish status and, 104–6
Lausanne conference and Treaty (1923), 12–13, 50, 78, 83–84, 90–98, 104–5, 188n32
League of Nations, 55, 95, 97, 114
Lloyd George, David, 187n14
Lombroso, Gina, 64

Makkasian, Knar, 17
Manavian, Harutyun, 171n1

manch-aghchig (boy-girl; flapper) stereotype, 139–48, *141*, *142*, *144*, 152, 157
Manugian, Katarine, 183n54
Margueritte, Victor, *La Garçonne*, 139, 140, 143, 146, 148, 198n38
Mark, Hayganush: adaptations by Armenian community after 1923 and, 101–3, 123; antifeminist arguments, grappling with, 70–72; Armenianness as crucial aspect of feminism of, 60; autobiography, 31, 60, 69.70, 84, 152, 155, 182n43, 198n23; on auxiliary roles for women, 76–77; birth and early life, 62, 165n1; caricature as editor, *144*, 145–46; caricature as suffragette, *52*, 60; children, lack of, 85, 136, 153; on compatibility of feminism with traditional feminine roles, 70–75, *73*; decision to remain in Istanbul during exodus after 1922, 84, 86, 89–90; on "dolls" versus individuals, 134–36, 140, 157; on domesticity, 133–39; escape from Armenian genocide, 4; experience of WWI, 4–5; on fatherhood, 132, 138–39; feminist definition and ideology of, 63–64, 156–57; Greater Armenia, involvement in lobbying for, 6; *Gyankn U Kordze*, 155, 206n7; hearing loss of, 185n81; identification with *Hay Gin*, 153–54, 155–57, *156*; as journalist, 62–63; jubilee celebration of, 154–55, 203n81; Kalemkearian and, 85; as leader of Armenian feminism, 54, 60; legacy of, 155–58, 161–63; manch-aghchig (boy-girl; flapper) stereotype and, 139–48, *141*, *142*, *144*, 152, 157; on marriage, 42, 131–32; Miss Turkey/Miss Universe contests, *130*, 152; as *Nor Lur* contributor, 148, 154; photos, *xviii*, *63*, *130*, *145*, 145–46, *155*, *156*; poetry, novels, and short stories of, 203n1; on political equality for women, 67–70, 75–77, 148–52, 184n67; political role of women in Armenian rebirth and, 59; pro-church stance after Kemalist takeover, 87–89, 101–2; on reciprocity and women's rights, 69–70, 72–73, 183n51; relationship with Vahan Toshigian, *xviii*, 62, 63; Sibil as teacher of, 133, 185–86n83; surname(s) of, 62, 182n44; tensions between feminism and Armenian community, 131–32; tombstone, 1, 155, *158*, 165n3; trajectory of life of, 1; Turkish women's movement and, 149–52, 200n61; Turkishness and, 150; Western influences on, 60, 64, 88. See also *Hay Gin*

Marmara, 148, 153, 202n77
marriage: of Armenian women retrieved from Islamic abduction, 35–38, *37*, 43–45, *44*, 176n44; feminism and, 42, 72, 131–32, 133; interfaith/exogamous, 9–10, 163; Judicial Commission of (Armenian) National Assembly, 68–69; as slavery, 42, 133; vows of obedience in Armenian liturgy, 138, 198n31
Martayan, Hagop (Dilaçar), 120–21, 195n55
Mayr Hayrenik (Mother Fatherland), 47, 56, 180n14
Mazlemian, Kohar: as *Hay Gin* contributor, 64, 131, 133, 147–48, 185n82; *khavidz* recipe, 133; retrieval of abducted women and children, involvement in, 40, 42; on Turkish women, 55, 200n61; on women's dress and behavior, 147–48, 199–200n53
Medz Yeghern. See Armenian genocide
Mehmed II (sultan), 24
Metaxakis, Meletios (Greek patriarch), 87
Mevhibe Celalettin (niece of Sultan Abdülhamid II), 56
Mikaelian, Mr. (of Izmir), 53

Mill, John Stuart, 64
millet system, 1, 8, 24–27, 92, 93, 104, 121
Minassian, Dikranuhi Der, 58
minorities and minority rights: dhimmitude compared, 13, 18, 93, 104; at Lausanne conference, 92–98, 104–5; nationalization, standardization, and secularization goals in Turkey and, 106–8; in Republic of Turkey, 13–14, 92–98, 104–5; Western concepts of, 92–93, 94–95
Miss Turkey/Miss Universe contests, *130*, 152
modernizing campaign: of Kemalists, 118–21, *119*, 152; of Ottoman Empire, 26
Morgenthau, Henry, 49–50, 117, 183n55
Mosdichian, Harutiun, 112, 193nn29–30
Mosdichian, Varteni, 175n44
mothers. *See* women and mothers
Mount Ararat, 45, 81, 112
Movsesian, Alexander (Shirvanzade), 184–85n71
Mudros Armistice, 5, 23, 34, 172n14
Muhiddin, Nezihe, 151, 200–201n62, 201n67, 201n70
Murad (Hampartsum Boyajian), 167n12
Musa Bey, 176n47
Mutafian, Mesrob (Armenian patriarch), 162–63

Nâbi (Ottoman poet), 111
Nahum, Haim, 189n48
Nalbandian, Zaven, 185n77
Naroyan, Mesrob (Armenian patriarch), 89, 125–28, 157, 196n66, 196n71
National Assembly (Armenian): AWA and, 56; Board of Directors of Armenian National Hospital and National Trusteeship, 148; Education Commission, 75–77, 186n85; institution of, 26–27; Judicial Commission, 68–69, 72–73, 76, 78; lay membership, 172n12; minutes of, 14; removal of patriarch from office and, 87, 90–91, 112; SETA members and, 110, 112; Surp Prgich National Hospital, women's auxiliary for, 76–77, 185n82; women's representation in, 67–68, 70
National Assembly (Turkish Grand National Assembly), 33, 59, 103, 110
National (Armenian) Constitution, 26, 70
national government of Armenians in Constantinople, 24–27, 172–73n14
National Hospital (Armenian), Yedikule, 38, 89, *100*, 126, 128
nationalism and gender, 10–11, 161
Nazeni (woman abducted into Muslim household), 40, 42
Near East, 24, 47
Near East Relief (NER; American Committee for Relief in the Near East), 24, 47, 56, 123, 176n45
"Nemesis" operation, 96
NER (Near East Relief or American Committee for Relief in the Near East), 24, 47, 56, 123, 176n45
the new woman and the old woman, 52–53, 64–67, *65*, 131–32, 140, 143, 146, 155
Nor Huys (New Hope), 113–14, *115*, 202n73
Nor Lur, 148, 153, 154, 155, 202n77
Nor Or, 1
Noradungian, Gabriel, 85, 188n34
Nubar, Boghos Pasha, 183n56
Nur, Riza, 97–98
Nuri, Celal (İleri), 103, 105–6, 116
Nurian, Garabed, 55, 56
nursing, training of Armenian girls in, 47–48, *48*

Odian, Yervant, 60, 185n71
the old woman and the new woman, 52–53, 64–67, *65*, 131–32, 140, 143, 146, 155

Omar (second caliph), 192n23
oral history interviews, 17
orphans, concept of, 28–29
Ottoman empire: Constitution, 103, 190n3; dhimmi women in, 9–10; map, *3*; *millet* system, 1, 8, 24–27, 92, 93, 104, 121; Mudros Armistice and defeat of, 5; revolution of 1908, 7; sultanate, abolition of, 6; Tanzimat (Reorganization) modernization program, 26; WWI, entry into, 2
Ottoman parliament, 133, 167n12, 172–73n14
Özalp, Kazım, 96

Pact of Omar, 192n23
Papajanian, Mikael, 168n17
Papazian, Vahram, 154, 186n83, 197n15
Paris Peace Conference, 6, 14, 32, 33, 46, 67, 83, 85, 90, 183n56
parliaments: British, 67; Ottoman, 133, 167n12, 172–73n14; Republic of Armenia, 67; Turkish, 33, 97, 110, 112
Parseghian, Armenag, 67–68, 183n55
Parseghian, Berjouhi, 183n54
Parunagian, Vartan, 123
Pashaian, Garabed, 167n12
patriarchate, Armenian: as administrative and spiritual center for Ottoman Armenians, 24–27; archives of, 14–15, 170n32; closure during WWI, 26; cooperation with Allies, 27; on education of women, 162–63; founding of, 24; information bureau, 55; in Jerusalem, 170n32; after Lausanne treaty, 97; power relationship between Turkish state and, 163; removal of patriarch from office after Kemalist takeover, 87, 90–91; SETA and, 110; statistics on abducted Armenian women and children, 167n9
patriarchate, Greek, 87, 97, 174n23

patriarchs, Armenian: Aslanian, Kevork (patriarchal *locum tenens*), 80, 88–89, 91, 143; Kevork VI (Catholicos of All Armenians), 155; Khachadurian, Karekin, 154; Mutafian, Mesrob, 162–63; Naroyan, Mesrob, 89, 125–28, 157, 196n66, 196n71; Surenian, Kevork V (Catholicos of All Armenians), 196n71; T[o]urian, Yeghishe, 183n56, 196n71. *See also* Yeghiayan, Zaven Der
Patrick, Andre, 166n5
patrilineal societies, 9–10, 12, 35
Poland, Allied treaty with (1919), 92
press, Armenian, 15–18, 26, 82, 112–16, *115*, 153, 170–71n33. *See also specific publications*
pretty baby contests, *31*, 31–32
privatization of Armenianness, 14
prostitution, 36, 38, 42, 140
Protestant Armenians, 24–25, 27, 171n1

rape, 12, 23, 29, 35, 40, 42, 175n44, 177n56, 178n59
rebirth of Armenian nation after WWI, 21–50; bearing witness to Armenian genocide and, 49–50; children, mothers, and family, significance of, *20*, 21–23, 28–33, 47–49, 160–61, 174n25; cooperation with Allied occupation, 27; demography and self-determination principles, 32–33; deportees, return of, 23–24, *25*, 27, 33; feminist involvement with refugees and retrieved women, 38–45, 176n48; national government of Armenians in Constantinople, 24–27, 172–73n14; nursing, training of Armenian girls in, 47–48, *48*; retrieval of abducted women and children, 23, 33, 34–38, *36*, *37*, *39*, *44*; revenge, as form of, 45–50; terms for, 22; women's interests conflicting with, 40–41, 69

Recep Zühtü Bey (Soyak), 96
reciprocity and women's rights, 69–70, 72–73, 183n51
Red Cross, Armenian: Kalantar, Takuhi, and, 74; nursing training for girls, 47; retrieval and care of abducted women and children by, 27, 36, 38–39, 39, 40–41; *Sargavakin Daretsuytse*, girl in Red Cross uniform in, 20, 21, 47, 60, 88, 129; Şişli branch hospital and maternity ward, 39, 40; Stambulian, Mari, and, 61, 179n78
Refet Pasha, 86, 87, 90–91
refugees. *See* deportees; exodus of 1922 and aftermath
religion: Apostolic Church, 24–25, 27, 124, 171n1, 172n10; Catholic Armenians, 24–25, 27, 171n1; Greek patriarchate, 87, 97, 174n23; importance to Armenian minority after 1923, 101–2; marriage liturgy, vows of obedience in, 138, 198n31; pro-church stance taken by Mark and *Hay Gin* after Kemalist takeover, 87–89, 101–2; Protestant Armenians, 24–25, 27, 171n1; in secular Republic of Turkey, 106–8, 118. *See also* Islam; patriarchate, Armenian; patriarchs, Armenian
reluctant motherhood of abducted women, 40–42
Republic of Armenia, 150, 183n54, 188n34; absorption by Soviet Union (1920), 50, 59, 90 (*See also* Soviet Armenia); celebration of establishment of (1918), 45–46, 168n17; collection of financial aid for, 57–58; flag of, 20, 21; Greater Armenia, dream of, 5; as infant or newborn, 47; political relationship of Ottoman Armenians to, 179n72; suffrage given to women in, 54; Turkish-Armenian War (1920), 58–59; women in National Parliament, 67, 183n54

Republic of Turkey. *See* Turkey, Republic of
Reshad Bay, 196n71
revenge: bearing witness to Armenian genocide and, 49–50; living associated with, 29–30; marriage ceremony of retrieved woman as form of, 45; rebirth of Armenian nation as form of, 45–50; as violent reprisal, 46
Russia, Ottoman concerns about Armenians in, 3

Sahagian, Varvara, 183n54
Sarafian, Mari, 203n81
Sargavakin Daretsuytse: children defending Mother Armenia depicted in, 20, 21–22, 46, 47, 60, 88, 129; publication and readership, 171n1
Schick, Irvin C., 182n45
Scutari Women's Shelter, 36–37, 37
Sebuhian, Nevrig, 64, 186n85
secular dhimmitude, 18, 108–9, 117, 121, 128, 160
secularism in Republic of Turkey, 106–8, 118
Şef, Milli (İsmet Pasha; İsmet İnönü), 14, 92, 94, 96, 110, 189n45, 189n48, 195n51
self-determination, concept of, 5–6, 32, 93, 124, 188n43
Serengiulian, Hovhannes (Vartkes), 167n12
SETA (Society for the Elevation of Turks and Armenians), 109–12, 192–93n26
Sèvres, Treaty of (1920), 33, 58, 59, 90
Seza, Siran, 157–58
Shahbaz, Parsegh, 85
Shahbaz, Stepan, 186n88, 198n23
Shakar, Siranush, 203n81
Shamlian, Suren, 153, 154
sharia (Islamic) law, 10, 12, 35, 78, 106–9, 169n23, 191n19
Sharzhum (Movement), 114–16

Shelemian, Ardashes, 194–95n51
Shelemian, Shakhe, 117
Shirvanzade (Alexander Movsesian), 184–85n71
Sibil (Zabel Asadur): academic study of, 162, 203n2; on Dussape, 134; Education Commission and, 75–77; Mark and, 75–77, 185–86n83; Zorab, relationship with, 134, 197n13
Sinanian, Hermine, 203n81
Şişli: Armenian Cemetery, Mark and Toshigian buried at, 1, 155, *158*, 165n3; Armenian Red Cross branch hospital and maternity ward, *39*, 40; neutral house in, 39, 85, 176n44
slavery: Armenians living in, 29, 42, 167n9; emancipation of women and, 54; marriage as form of, 42, 133
Smyrna/Izmir, Kemalist capture of, 14, 81–82
Society for the Elevation of Turks and Armenians (SETA), 109–12, 192–93n26
Soviet Armenia, 50, 59, 81, 90, 91, 153, 155, 188n38, 197n15
Soyak, Recep Zühtü Bey, 96
Stambulian, Mari, *61*, 179n78
Stis, Ann, 152, 201n70
Stowe, Harriet Beecher, *Uncle Tom's Cabin*, 72–73, 134
Student's Pledge, 108
Şükrü, Mehmed (Koçoğlu), 92
Suphi, Hamdullah (Tanrıöver), 103–4, 105, 112, 126
Surenian, Kevork V (Catholicos of All Armenians), 196n71
Surmelian, Zaven, 83
surnames: of Hayganush Mark, 62, 182n44; Turkish law on, 108, 191–92nn20–21; women's feelings about, 62, 131
Surp Prgich National Hospital, women's auxiliary for, 76–77, 185n82

Swiss-Armenian Society, 24

Talat Pasha, 96, 168n17
Tanrıöver, Hamdullah Suphi, 103–4, 105, 112, 126
Tanzimat (Reorganization) campaign, 26
Tashnagtsutiun (Armenian Revolutionary Federation or ARF), 67, 176n47, 178n69, 185n77
Tavitian, Anahid, 168n17, 187n22
Tekeyan, Vahan, 83
Teotig, 28, 173n19, 179n78
Teotig, Arsaguhi, *61*
Tertsagian, Onnik (Vramian), 167n12
Terzibashian, Kevork, 114, 193n40
St. Thaddeus, 172n10
Theatrical Union of Constantinople., 197n15
Theotokas, Yorgos, *Leonis*, 169n18
Toshigian, Ara, 155, 185n81, 203n82
Toshigian, Hayganush Mark. *See* Mark, Hayganush
Toshigian, Vahan: death of, 155, 203n82; decision to remain in Istanbul, 84; escape from Armenian genocide, 4; experience of WWI, 4–5; Greater Armenia, involvement in lobbying for, 6; *Hay Gin* initially funded by, 63; photos, *xviii*; as publisher and editor, 1, 148, 153, 202n77; relationship with Hayganush Mark, *xviii*, 62, 63; tombstone, 1, *158*
T[o]urian, Yeghishe (Armenian patriarch), 183n56, 196n71
Tumanian, Hovhannes, 59
Türker, Berch Keresteciyan, 110
Turkey, Republic of: Armenian genocide, views on, xi, 7–8, 166n6; Constitution, 103, 105, 106, 190n2; declaration of (1923), 103; exchange of populations, 91–92; feminist Armenians and Turkish women, 149–52; fifth columnists, view of

Armenians as, 7–8, 92, 94; French Republican citizenship emulated by, 105; Lausanne conference, hope for Armenian National Home inside Turkey at, 91–92; Law on Civil Servants (1926), 121, 195n56; map, *3*; minorities and minority rights in, 13–14, 92–98, 104–5; mixed-sex beaches in, 147; modernization project, 13–14; nationalization, standardization, and secularization goals, 78, 92, 106–8, 117–21, *119*, 194n43; parliament, 33, 97, 110, 112; population distribution in 1927, 190n61; power relationship between Armenians and, 77–78, 163; sharia outlawed by, 10; surname change requirements, 108, 191–92nn20–21; Turkish status in, 103–6; Unification of Education Act (1924), 78, 124; women's dress and behavior, cultural critiques of, 147–48; women's rights movement in, 149–52, 162, 200–201nn61–62, 202n73, 204n5; women's suffrage in, 150, 151, 202n73. *See also* Armenians in post-genocide Turkey; Kemalists

Turkish Civil Code, 10, 78, 108

Turkish empire. *See* Ottoman empire

Turkish Grand National Assembly, 33, 59, 103, 110

Turkish Language Association, 121

Turkish women and Allied officers, 55–56

Turkish Women's Association, 151–52, 201n65, 201n70, 202n73

Turkish Writers' Union, 114

Turkish-Armenian War, 58–59

Turkish/Muslim children retrieved as Armenians, 35, 86, 175n39

typhus, 29, 57

Unification of Education Act (Turkey, 1924), 78, 124

universities, admission of women to, 184n64

Vahdettin (sultan), 87

Vakit (Times), 82

Vankaya, M., 113

Vartanian, Spruhi, 203n81

Vartkes (Hovhannes Serengiulian), 167n12

vengeance. *See* revenge

Verchin Lur (Latest News), 63

vorpahavak (retrieval of abducted women and children). *See* abduction of women and children into Muslim households

Vramian (Onnik Tertsagian), 167n12

Vratsian, Simon, 59

Werfel, Franz, *The Forty Days of Musa Dagh*, 117, 194n50

West and Westernization: Armenians self-contrasted with Turks and self-compared to, 46–47, 67–68; Mark influenced by, 60, 64, 88; on minorities and minority rights, 92–93, 94–95; Miss Turkey/Miss Universe contests, *130*, 152; modernizing and Westernizing campaign under Kemalists, 118–21, *119*. *See also* Allies/Great Powers

Wilson, Woodrow, and Wilsonianism, 5–6, 32, 33, 59, 93, 105

women and mothers: cultural critiques of dress and behavior, 147–48; *Hay Gin*, maternalist discourse embraced by, 30–32, *31*, 48–49, 175n25; maternal passage of Armenian identity to children, *100*, 128–29, 157; rebirth of Armenian nation after WWI, significance for, 20, 21–23, 28–33, 47–49, 160–61, 174n25; *Sargavakin Daretsuytse*, children defending Mother Armenia depicted in, 20,

21–22, 46, 47, 60, 88, 129; secular modernism and female body, 152; Turkish cultural critiques of dress and behavior of, 147–48; unveiling of Muslim women, 118. *See also* abduction of women and children into Muslim households; feminism and feminist Armenians; gender; marriage

World War I: Allied evacuation of Constantinople following, 5–9, 83–84; Armenian genocide and, 3, 45; Bolsahay experience of, 4–5; French Legion d'Orient, Armenians in, 178n67; Ottoman Empire's entry into, 2; patriarchate closed during, 26. *See also* Allied occupation of Constantinople; Paris Peace Conference; *specific treaties*

Yaghubian, Dr., 40–41
Yalman (Ahmed Emin), 82
Yeghiayan, Zaven Der (Armenian patriarch): Aslanian's continuity with, 88; AWA, formation of, 55, 56; cooperation with Allies, 27; departure from Constantinople, 14; European tour in support of Armenian National Delegation at Paris Peace Conference, 33; in exile during WWI, 26; exodus of Armenians after 1922 and, 83, 85; on Greek assistance, 174n23; Naroyan and, 127, 196n71; patriarchal archive and, 14, 170n32; removal from office and exile after Kemalist takeover, 87, 90–91, 112; retrieval of abducted Armenians and, 34, 36, 38–39, 43, 175n42, 177n57; SETA and, 109, 110, 112

Yeridasart Hayuhi (Young Armenian Woman), 157–58

Yesayan, Zabel, 4, 168n15, 203n2

Young Turks (Committee of Union and Progress or CUP), 2–5, 7, 11–12, 34

Young Women's Christian Association (YWCA), 56

Zarevand, *United and Independent Turania*, 185n77
Zarian, Gosdan, 81, 157
Zaven (patriarch). *See* Yeghiayan, Zaven Der
Zhamanag, 153, 202n77
Zhoghovurti Tsayne (Voice of the People), 57
Zihnioğlu, Yaprak, 201n70
Zohrab, Krikor, 133–34, 167n12, 197n13
Zürcher, Erik, 96

The authorized representative in the EU for product safety and compliance is:
Mare Nostrum Group
B.V Doelen 72
4831 GR Breda
The Netherlands

www.ingramcontent.com/pod-product-compliance
Lightning Source LLC
Chambersburg PA
CBHW032058230426
43662CB00035B/594